The Secret Listeners

The Secret Listeners

How the Y Service Intercepted German Codes for Bletchley Park

SINCLAIR McKAY

history

A catalogue record for this book is available from the British Library.

ISBN 978 1 84513 763 2

1 3 5 7 9 10 8 6 4 2
2012 2014 2016 2015 2013

Typeset in ITC New Baskerville by SX Composing DTP, Rayleigh Essex
Printed and bound in Great Britain by Clays Ltd, St Ives plc

Contents

THE Y SERVICE
Principal Listening Stations

MURMANSK

EUROPE

BELGRADE

LISBON

MADRID

SARDINIA

ATHENS

GIBRALTAR

ALGIERS

MALTA

ALEXANDRIA

CASABLANCA

HELIOPOLIS

BENGHAZI

CAIRO

ATLANTIC

OCEAN

AFRICA

KHARTOUM

MOMBASA

ISLE OF MAN

SCARBOROUGH

SHERINGHAM

BEAUMANOR HOUSE

SOUTHWOLD

HANSLOPE PARK

CHICKSANDS PRIORY

WHADDON HALL

BLETCHLEY PARK

FORT OF CHATHAM

HARTLAND POINT

FLOWERDOWN

KINGSDOWN

PLYMOUTH

ISLE OF WIGHT

PORTLAND
DORSET

(on larger scale)

As an approximate guide to distance each segment of the border represents 500 mile

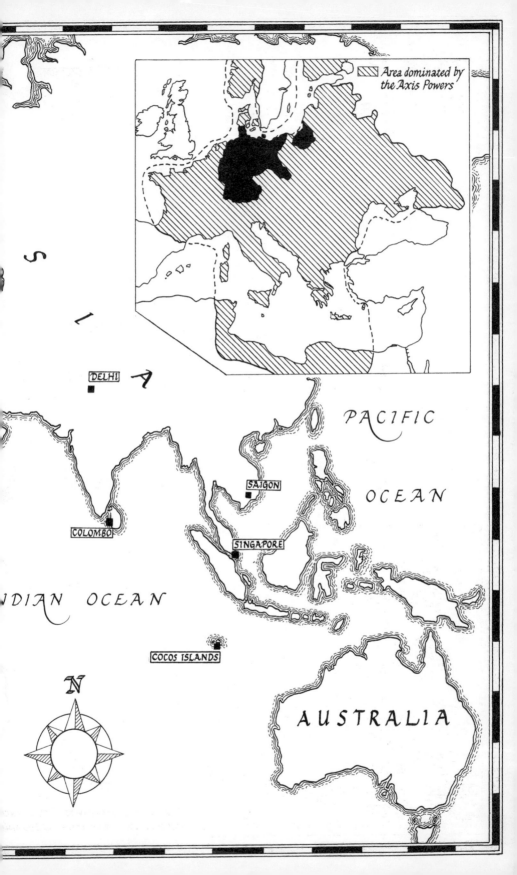

1 Tuning in to the Enemy

Through the silence of the night, they were listening to the heart of the conflict. In stark rooms with green-shaded lights, furnished with plain desks and chairs and tables upon which rested the sleekest new wireless equipment – smooth grey bakelite, black metal, the vanilla glow of illuminated dials – dedicated women and men would sit, their ears clamped in warm headphones, in a strange half-world. The signals they were receiving might occasionally have been actual voices, although more often they were the abstract, monotone dots and dashes of Morse: but these coded messages represented chillingly implacable determination, explosive anger and frustration, intrigue and intelligence, and sometimes even the poignant laughter of fear.

Wherever in the world the operative was working – from England's south coast to the Orkneys, from Murmansk to Cairo, from Mombasa to Delhi to Hong Kong – the 2 a.m. watches were the worst. For Victor Newman in Colombo, nocturnal watches might be disrupted by mighty storms, violent rain smashing down on woven palm leaf roofs. In Alexandria, apart from the perpetual banes of dust and sand and flies, night shifts for Special Wireless Operator Bob Hughes would sometimes be made impossible by distant thunder, which would create agonising feedback – 'this terrible crackling' – in the headphones. In Singapore, Joan Dinwoodie suffered from the relentless suffocating heat, 'the perspiration running into [her] shoes'. Meanwhile, in the middle of the Indian Ocean, on the tiny, barely inhabited Cocos Islands, nineteen-year-old Peter Budd would start a night shift by walking to his listening station through the profound and 'eerie' darkness of the palm trees, taking great care to avoid the lethal insect life whose venom had completely paralysed one of his predecessors.

In every station, the listeners had one thing in common: they worked punishing round-the-clock rotas, with after-effects that some would continue to suffer years after the war. This was as true for those working deep in the familiar English countryside as those in far-off lands. But their work was more than crucial. These young people were intercepting coded messages sent by the Germans, seeking out and faithfully transcribing the chaos of communications first scrambled by the Enigma encryption machines – with their almost countless permutations – and then sent via radio on ever-elusive frequencies. The listeners would pluck apparently random letters from the air and, having instantly translated them from Morse, send them on to the British codebreakers based at Station X, otherwise known as the requisitioned country house of Bletchley Park in Buckinghamshire. Some listeners – particularly those in the field in Bletchley out-stations – would both intercept and decode the signals they received. The work was fantastically demanding, at every level.

It is sometimes said that the life of a soldier in a theatre of war is 90 per cent boredom and 10 per cent terror and exhilaration. For all those women and men listening and recording the course of war, the proportions were not so very different. But a soldier's attention could at least wander; there was no such luxury for those crammed over wireless equipment, trying to pluck order from an ocean of fuzzy noise. More than this: accuracy was paramount. A misheard signal concerning manoeuvres or forthcoming air raids could cost lives. 'Boredom – a word not allowed,' noted Wren and Y Service veteran Joan Nicholls.

For Maurice de la Bertauche, a precocious seventeen-year-old wireless operator based at one of the larger listening stations in the Midlands, such disorientating days would start loweringly. 'One entered the bus to be met by a fug of cigarette and pipe smoke and a prevailing atmosphere of depression,' he wrote. The bus drove operators from their Northamptonshire billets to the country house of Beaumanor Hall. 'One came to a brick building disguised as a country cottage. Beyond the entrance vestibule, containing coat hooks and smelling of damp clothes, one could detect the smell of ozone from the thermionic valves used in the short wave receivers.'

The handover from the previous watch was brisk; on nights and days when the airwaves were filled with noise, when battles were being fought and won and lost, time could not be wasted. 'If you relieved an operator who was recording a message,' wrote de la Bertauche, 'the person being relieved would turn up the volume control, slip off his headphones, while still recording the message, hand the headphones to his relief, who at an appropriate moment would continue writing down the message.'[1]

This young man at least had the consolation of working in a busy room with several dozen other wireless operators. For many young women around the country, in smaller listening posts on the coast – and for the young women posted overseas to countries stranger and more exotic than they could have imagined – these small-hours shifts were not so much depressing as unsettling. 'Oh, the night shifts,' says Jean Valentine, who – having been posted to Colombo in what was then Ceylon – was breaking Japanese codes for Bletchley Park out of a low building fretted with palms, and assailed by a rich variety of tropical flying insects. 'Of course night shifts were lonely. You were there all by yourself, for those eight hours, and the only person you saw was the sailor who came in every hour, or every couple of hours, with a batch of new signals for you to sort out.'

And for those listeners in exposed positions on the British coast, or in far-off places such as Tangier or the Western Desert, Malta or Colombo, the threat of being shelled or bombed was ever present. On one night watch in the listening station at Scarborough, a Wren was upbraided by her superiors for having failed to keep a constant record of a stream of messages exchanged that night. Her matter-of-fact excuse was that she kept on having to run outside to 'swat away incendiaries' with a bat; her post had been targeted by bombers and just one incendiary bomb could have set the place alight. Twenty-three-year-old Women's Air Force volunteer and wireless interceptor Aileen Clayton – posted around the Mediterranean throughout the conflict – was strafed by a German fighter on Malta while on her way to her shift. She took it with remarkable good humour.

The work carried out by these thousands of women and men was intensely skilled; it was also extremely pressurised. Accuracy in relaying these coded enemy messages could mean the difference between life and death. The efforts of those men and women are sadly and curiously uncelebrated today. While the codebreakers of Bletchley Park – who fought so long to achieve recognition – are now properly honoured, the many people who made their work possible remain in the shadows. So much so that the very term 'Y Service' is still unfamiliar to many.

Yet it was the Y Service that kept the mighty machinery of Bletchley Park fed with information; it was Y Service operatives who listened in on the entire German war apparatus, every hour, every minute of every day; it was these young people who were the first to hear of any tactical shift, any manoeuvre, any soaring victory, any crushing defeat. The fruits of their labours, dispatched to Bletchley Park at top speed, enabled codes to be cracked quickly and German strategies unravelled.

Some months before war broke out, the Government Code and Cypher School (GC&CS) – in essence, the codebreaking arm of the Foreign Office – had established itself in a faintly ugly country house on the edge of an unremarkable provincial town. And it was within the bounds of this plain house and its estate – Bletchley Park – that an extraordinary line-up of the country's finest minds was assembled. All of them, from the irascible veteran cryptographer Alfred Dillwyn 'Dilly' Knox to the visionary young mathematician Alan Turing, faced an apparently insoluble and frightening problem: a means of breaking the German Enigma codes. The Germans themselves considered their Enigma coding machines – simple to use, very portable, yet capable of producing millions upon millions of potential letter combinations – completely invincible. Looking deceptively like typewriters with lights, these machines of bakelite and wood, with letter rotors of gleaming brass and discreet mazes of electric wiring, were brilliantly, lethally complex. First the machines would make implacable letter substitutions, and then the operator's colleague would transmit the letters, by Morse, in blocks of four or five. With code settings changed every midnight, and the letter substitutions produced electrically, how could any human mind begin to find patterns or order in that storm of random letters?

While the pressure upon the codebreakers was obvious, it was no less intense upon the young women and men who had to supply Bletchley Park with its raw material. The art of transcribing Morse code at very high speeds under stressful circumstances was already quite specialised; the ability to spend hours receiving such encoded messages was something else again. Yet the listeners also found ways to assist the Bletchley Park codebreakers to break certain ciphers. Their work was inextricably linked.

'Listen to all the noises in the air,' intoned the narrator at the start of the 1946 film *A Matter of Life and Death,* as the camera swept down over a fogbound wartime English Channel and the soundtrack was filled with the pleading electronic beeps of different Morse signals. 'Even the big ships sound frightened.'

The term 'Y Service' derives quite simply from the words 'Wireless Interception' – or 'WI'. As a technical proposition, the idea of clandestine world-wide interception was a daunting one; when the war started, the technology of radio was still relatively young. In some ways, the fledgling Y Service was to be asked to perform technological and organisational miracles.

All those German fighter pilots in the skies above; how would we record their conversations and their movements? All those aerodromes and rocket bases, all those divisions and battalions; who would be there to intercept the radio messages that they transmitted back to their superiors? What sort of infrastructure would be needed for an operation of such complexity?

Anyone on a train approaching Rugby station these days will notice, in a field just outside the town, an array of tall radio masts, like a steel Stonehenge. During wartime, the countryside was dotted with such elaborate structures, through which would pour the voices and the encrypted communications of the enemy, monitored continuously.

The Y Service in some ways provided a pleasing balance to Bletchley Park. Whereas the latter had an atmosphere of genteel chaos and anarchy – an ethos deliberately fostered to facilitate lateral thinking – the Y Service had a make-do-and-mend efficiency and organisational brilliance Baden-Powell might have been proud of. It encompassed accomplished linguists and highly intelligent Wrens; but it also reached out to schoolboys who knew how to build their own wireless sets and were thrilled to have the chance to participate in espionage against the enemy.

'All sections of the Y Service – Army, Navy, Air-Force and civilian, had special selection procedures when recruiting their operators,' wrote veteran Geoffrey Pidgeon. 'They had to pass the IQ test above a certain score, they had to be assessed as being capable of working under pressure, have the patience to sit waiting for hours for [an enemy] station to come to life and remain alert, to be mature enough not to gossip about what they did and not least maintain a very difficult work pattern with meals and sleep patterns disrupted . . . for the forces special operators . . . [training] was 19 weeks. In that time they were taught Morse Code, wireless procedures and electromagnetism all alongside the military training of marching, cleaning billets.'

And so, swiftly, this shadowy organisation started spreading across the country, as well as around the world. There were the larger bases, at requisitioned country houses such as Beaumanor Hall in Leicestershire or Whaddon Hall in Bedfordshire, at the old fort of Chatham and at Kingsdown, both in Kent. There were smaller, more discreet listening posts – often little more than huts, caravans and small bunkers – in locations such as Hartland Point in Devon, Southwold in Suffolk, or along the coast of Kent – the latter becoming known as 'Hellfire Corner' on account of the fact that the Germans seemed to find them remarkably tempting targets.

So, while the Y Service operatives seem at first glance to be in the background, their experiences of the war are paradoxically much more central than most would assume. 'In France, 1940,' stated a top secret War Office memo from 1941, when members of the Y Service were being deployed in all parts of the world, 'warning of dive-bomber attacks on the Corps and adjoining fronts was given by the interception of plain language messages.' Those were the immediate cases; most other messages would have been encrypted as a matter of course via the Enigma machines. Yet, as listeners, it was almost as though they were in a prime position to observe the world being torn apart around them.

'Freelance or haphazard interception lead nowhere,' stated a War Office memo. In other words, the listeners had to be carefully directed; their antennae were fixed on very particular targets – whether it was young Peter Budd in the middle of the Indian Ocean, tracking and eavesdropping on Japanese submarines, or the dance-loving Wrens of HMS *Flowerdown* in Hampshire – a land-based naval station – picking up the frequencies used by German naval command posts in Europe, and of those used by the lethal U-boats in the waters of the English Channel.

But the task of the Y Service was not merely to take down these complex messages with complete accuracy, but also, in the case of the out-stations far from Britain, to engage in decryption work. Codebreaking personnel from Bletchley Park were sent on voyages around the world – to the Middle East, Africa, Asia – in order to capture and decipher the encrypted messages buzzing through the tropical air. Out in the desert, or in the asphyxiating jungles of the Far East, mobile Y Service teams, men and women working with single-minded zeal, would provide instant decrypts which could turn the course of events. Field Marshal Rommel would later have reason to curse the Y Service operatives with particular vehemence – for it was the listeners who played a decisive role in the turning of the desert war.

For many recruits, earlier experience of Germany – being sent to live there as young women in the 1930s, and learning the language – ensured that they were ushered straight into positions of importance within the Y Service. Their experience enabled them not merely to know the language grammatically, but also to read its nuances and cadences, to analyse and interpret the motivations of the men speaking it. If half the battle of intelligence is learning to think the way the enemy thinks, then many of the young women recruited into this darkened world would prove to have a substantial advantage over their commanding officers.

For all the plucky spirit of the recruits, there were those for whom the work would get too much. The intense concentration required could have serious side-effects. Occasionally, even officers would have minor nervous breakdowns. It is not difficult to understand why: the job was not merely about interception, but also about using the knowledge gained to stay one step ahead of the enemy. The pressure was unfathomable: and what exacerbated it was the sense of proximity to each and every battle.

For the secret listeners, these voices in the air were much more than merely abstract dots and dashes of Morse; they were live commentaries on events. Unlike other combatants, who would receive news second hand after a time lag, the men and women of the Y Service were at the very front of the information line, and it was through them that the fortunes of war were transmitted to high command. The messages may have been encoded, but in times of crisis, their essential weight and import would have been none-theless easily understood by those who were listening in on them.

These men and women found ways to compensate for the intensity. On long shifts, when the airwaves were sullen in their hissing silence, unexpected and unlikely friendships would form. And although they might have worked in the shadows, the secret listeners always made the most of their time off, away from the mind-boggling intensity of work. From Alexandria to Algiers, Bombay to Plymouth, their stories now are of romance, and youthful laughter, and quite often a certain glamour. On top of this, even the privations of rural Devon, for instance, have been recalled with immense fondness.

Many of those packed off abroad were young women. Cherrie Ballantine had originally been recruited to Bletchley Park at the age of nineteen; in 1941, she was told that she would be sent across the Mediterranean to Cairo. The life that she – and many others – found there was beguiling. She and others like her were doing what very few other women had ever been able to do before: take an active role in a conflict that stretched across the globe.

Those others included eighteen-year-old Jean Valentine, whose six-week voyage to Ceylon was marked with the constant peril of U-boats, and Aileen Clayton, who as well as dodging Stukas on Malta, spent time in the desert alongside Montgomery and Eisenhower's men. The women would sometimes meet resistance from officers and commanders, appalled that females should have been allowed anywhere near the front; but they were very much in the forefront of a new age – precursors of a more assertive generation to come.

But alongside this went an abiding sense – especially among the young women posted around the world – that they were growing up tremendously fast. Several such women recall that by their mid-twenties, a certain carefree element of youth had passed them by. The sights they saw, their intense experiences, forced them to swiftly adjust their perspectives on life; from the old expectations of quiet domesticity to the sophistication and confidence that their new, exciting, cosmopolitan lives bestowed. War is of course always transformative; for the women and the men of the Y Service, that metamorphosis was deep and fast.

Like their colleagues at Bletchley Park, those enlisted into the Y Services were compelled to sign the Official Secrets Act. Security was paramount – not merely throughout the years of conflict, but during the years afterwards. Like their Bletchley Park colleagues, the secret listeners of the Y Service had to keep quiet about their achievements, and even about the equipment that they had used. 'I would have loved to have been able to tell my dad,' says veteran Y Service operative Betty White with some feeling. 'I would have loved to have told him about the work I did in the war. But I couldn't. You couldn't tell anyone for over thirty years.'

'It was dinned into us right from the start,' says Jay McDonald, who had also been recruited as a wireless operator. 'Not only were we not to say anything. But we also knew just how vital the work was.'

Even if they have not had the full recognition that their colleagues at Bletchley Park have won, the secret listeners have at least their own private satisfactions: that they played a constant role in the war, and that without their quick-wittedness, focus, and good humour in the face of sometimes unimaginable pressure, that war would have been very much more difficult to win.

2 Reporting for Special Duties

Not everyone had an aptitude for the work of the Y Service. At the most fundamental level, it required, as one veteran says, 'a sort of flexibility of the brain'. For some Y Service operatives, the various skills required of them seemed mysteriously innate. For others, it was a matter of months of very hard training. The training itself partly resembled a linguistic crash course, with high-speed Morse as the language; and partly a futuristic introduction to a mysterious new world of radio waves, and the physics of atmospheres and ionospheres. For many young women, the latter was one of the most appealing aspects of the role. There was something immediately liberating about the chance to demonstrate proficiency in what had previously been a male arena.

Many young women, such as Pat Sinclair and Betty White, who joined the Wrens – the Women's Royal Naval Service – as fast as they could, almost flaunted this skill. First, there was the patience required as they sat down at short-wave receivers and went through the process of trying to find the correct German frequency, transmissions being made from Europe in this case; then there was the laser-beam focus required as the German operator began tapping out Morse and the young women, armed only with pencils and specially lined pads, swiftly wrote out the letters as they heard them, simultaneously translating from Morse to the ordinary alphabet.

Not everyone had this skill. One veteran recalled in the early stages of the war a young officer in France frantically taking down an enemy transmission and having to note down the actual dots and dashes as he heard them; not a great deal of use as they could so easily merge and be misread.

The other crucial qualification was an almost boundless enthusiasm. 'Civilian wireless operators were called Experimental Wireless Assistants,' noted Maurice de la Bertauche. 'Many of the younger members had been recruited from grammar schools and trained by the War Office.'[1]

But for others, it was not even half so formal. On the Sunday morning of 3 September 1939, as Prime Minister Neville Chamberlain broadcast to the nation that it was at war, there were those who knew instantly how they wanted to do their bit.

'I had left school in August 1939, just before war broke out,' says former Wren Marjorie Gerken. At the time, she was living in Richmond, Surrey, with her family. Very quickly, she had got an administrative job in the civil service. 'On that September 3, we really thought that the German bombers would be coming immediately. Not that there was any panic. My family already had an air-raid shelter. And it happened that shortly after Chamberlain gave his speech, the sirens actually did go off. But we didn't actually go into the shelter at that point – we all stood in the garden, listening for aeroplanes.' Marjorie knew absolutely that she wanted to go into the Wrens, and she also knew what she wanted to do. For as it happened, when she had been in the Girl Guides, she had learned rudimentary Morse code. She had to wait a while before she got her wish. But when she did, she was thrown right into the heart of the Y Service operation.

Elsewhere, all sorts of different skills were being sought. In her memoirs of the war, Miggs Ackroyd recalled: 'My father heard they wanted German speakers at the Admiralty. So I went along and was briefly interviewed by a man, not even in uniform, who said I would do and gave me a ticket to Dover a few days hence.' At this stage, Miggs did not actually realise she had enlisted in the Wrens. It was only when she met up with her colleagues on the south coast that the urgency and secrecy of the role became fully apparent.

Elsewhere, Jay McDonald lived with her family in Tobermory on the Hebridean Isle of Mull. She joined up at the age of nineteen with a vague idea of being a physical education instructor. But after some interviews, she was funnelled into quite a different line. 'We were sent to a basic training camp at Dalkeith,' she says. 'They were sorting out who could be drivers, and so on. Well – I was never going to be a driver. I was just so unmechanical. As part of the process, they gave us bits of Meccano to assemble. I couldn't even put two bits together.' The testing went on, this time angled more towards intelligence. Jay McDonald had found something rather more suitable to contribute to the war effort. 'I was picked out as a wireless operator, which was a good thing,' says Miss McDonald with a dry chuckle now. 'After all, it was better than being a cleaner – or orderly, as they were called – and better than being a cook. On the scale of things, wireless operator was a very good thing to be.' A skilled thing, too: one which would require months of training. She was dispatched at once, with about twenty-five others, to a remarkably agreeable set-up on the Isle of Man.

Meanwhile, joining up for the Women's Auxiliary Air Force, the WAAFs, German-speaking Peggy West was swiftly inducted into the hermetic world of RAF Kingsdown in Kent; there she discovered she was to be working alongside an extraordinary team of people from across Europe. 'Volunteers who had moved to the United Kingdom from the occupied countries wore their Austrian, Czechoslovakian, Polish, Dutch, Belgian, Norwegian, Greek, and French "flashes" proudly on their shoulders,' she recalled.

We were trained in wireless telegraphy to use Morse code and become known as W/T operators. We were also introduced to radio telegraphy with its use of plain-language intercepts, to become R/T operators, and then shown the intricacies of obtaining line bearings for use in Direction Finding Units . . . After all that, we found to our surprise that we had become 'Instant Sergeants'.

The work was, of course, absolutely top secret, and conducted with pleasing incongruity from one of the very many country houses that had been requisitioned for the war:

Arriving at Hollywood Manor in Kent, the RAF 'Y' Service Headquarters, we learned of a network of highly secret radio stations and small direction finding units whose frequencies were tuned to the German Luftwaffe. These stations stretched from Montrose in Scotland down the east coast and round southern England to Strete in Devon.

Moreover, the work they were to do required an unusual level of immersion: 'Inside the tightly secured radio intelligence sections,' she said, 'primarily German was spoken, thought, and written. Our reactions had to be those of the enemy.'[2]

For Vivienne Alford, the recruitment procedure had a similarly linguistic slant. 'I went up Whitehall to the Admiralty,' she wrote, 'to be interviewed by a young man who actually conversed in German. I'd given up trying to find out about the work and was prepared to settle on the basis of living conditions. "Did I mind being in remote places with only a few people?" Just the thing for me.'[3]

For some, Y Service work entailed rather more physical jeopardy than simple 'squad drill'. There was an affable young radio buff called Bill Miller, whose wireless war was swiftly to develop into an extraordinary and quite unexpected series of espionage skirmishes in the Mediterranean. Yet it all began quietly enough. 'As a boy, [Miller] was fascinated by short wave wireless, then in its infancy,' wrote his friend and colleague Geoffrey Pidgeon, who collected Miller's story. 'He learned Morse code, and spent hours copying ships' wireless messages and constructing simple short wave radio receivers. It was his hope some day that he would become an amateur wireless operator and eventually open his own amateur wireless station.'

And so it was that Miller's enthusiasm was brought to the attention of the authorities. 'When he registered for military service in 1938, aged 19, his wireless and Morse code qualifications were noted . . . he was enrolled into the 1st London Divisional Signals of the Royal Corps of Signals.'[4] The young recruits were taken to Eastbourne. The next three months were taken up with military training and also, as Pidgeon notes, learning Morse by flag and by Aldis lamp. What was to follow was rather more involved and colourful.

A few recruits, such as Joy Hale, specifically wanted to work in the field of cryptography. 'When I applied to join the Wrens, I stated that I would like to be a coder,' she wrote. 'I had been good at Algebra at school and had plenty of patience.' But her straightforward wishes did not apparently seem to coincide with those of the Navy. The authorities were altogether more interested in Hale's proficiency in German, acquired both at school and following an extended stay with a German family. 'Consequently, when my call-up papers eventually came through stating that my category was to be "Special Duties",' she wrote, 'it meant nothing to me. I just assumed that I was being assigned to some special form of coding.'

Hale's determination was shared by Londoner Pat Sinclair, who as a young woman was working for the electricity board – a reserved occupation – when the war broke out. 'My one ambition was to join the Wrens,' she says now. 'It was very glamorous. And I decided I wanted to be a wireless telegraphist even though I knew nothing at that time about Morse code.' Mrs Sinclair did not waste her time, though; before joining up, she ensured that she taught herself the rudiments of the code so that she wouldn't be diverted into other war duties. Her heart was set on it. And this single-mindedness was to fix the course of her life.

Other, less immediately obvious candidates were spotted. Elizabeth Mashall remembered with terrible clarity the embarrassment of her own bid to join:

> I attended an Officers Selection Board in London. I only just made it at the appointed time. I was the last to be interviewed and had watched Wrens emerging from interviews lasting about 15 minutes. 'Five queen bees,' they gasped, 'all firing questions.' I went in and was asked the usual short preliminary questions. Then, 'Why did you join the Wrens?' I sought wildly and unsuccessfully for a suitable answer and then, to my horror, blurted out the truth. 'Because I was told I would never get in, ma'am.'

The response to this, apparently, was a combination of shock and suppressed laughter.

But Mrs Mashall's abilities were being noted elsewhere. She had also written a letter to the Admiralty, stressing her expertise in German and pointing up 'carefully chosen' personal references. Days later, she received a telephone call, and instructions to report to the Admiralty for a chat. Outside the building, a naval officer quietly took her to one side and said '*Können Sie Deutsch sprechen?*' To which she replied '*Ja, ich kann ganz gut Deutsch sprechen.*' The naval officer had heard quite enough. 'You'll do,' he said.[5]

Just as the cryptanalysts of the Government Code and Cypher School had, from the mid-1930s onwards, tasted the air and made preparations for the coming war, so too did the section of MI6 concerned with wireless interception. Thanks to firms such as Marconi, wireless technology had advanced a great deal since the 1920s. But this new science had a more homely element too: radio was a hobby pursued with almost holy zeal by boys and men across the country, many of whom learned how to rig up their own receivers.

For military intelligence, the coming conflict would place a great deal of emphasis on pioneering technology. The science of communications had, in the space of fifty years, changed beyond recognition. The nineteenth-century innovation of telegraphy – and the subsequent submarine cable network – had opened the way to the transmission of messages and intelligence at previously unthinkable speeds. Marconi's ingenious development of wireless technology – in part an act of spirited piracy, yanking the idea from under the nose of several more eminent scientists who were working on the same lines – was recognised as having revolutionary potential.

The British Army had adopted early wireless apparatus for use during the Boer War. This, though, was not a success. There was the suggestion that its failure was due to inexpert operators' inability to understand exactly what they were doing, or the finer points of tuning.

But the technology grew easier to use, with more focused, delicate tuning, better calibrated transmission and reception, and even a limited capacity for portable use; understanding the vast potential of such developments, the military commands in Britain and Europe were scrabbling to stay ahead of one another, especially in the period leading up to the Great War. The British established radio stations across the country; so too did the Germans.

For some young civilians, the science of the wireless was hypnotically fascinating. And for William Le Queux, one of the period's most popular novelists, the technology was irresistible as a futuristic plot device in his many spy thrillers. In 1909's *Spies of the Kaiser* (now a hilarious as well as politically incorrect read), our heroes are following the activities of agents in Hull, and in the south London district of Sydenham. What can be the connection between the northern docks and the leafy southern suburban hills? It is, as our heroes discover, the cutting-edge art of wireless telegraphy; the enemy agents in Hull are relaying the movements of ships in the North Sea back to their colleagues down south. The installation of their secret equipment – half given away by the discovery of yards of cabling in an old Clerkenwell warehouse – is a diabolical technical triumph.

The notion, in the early years of the century, of treacherous spies using secret transmitters to send intelligence back to Germany was indeed so powerful that le Queux – along with countless others – seemingly came to believe it in real life. There was, in the Edwardian era, a widespread fear that the Germans were plotting an invasion of Britain, and le Queux took to the popular press elaborating his conviction that undercover agents were establishing radio stations right the way along England's coast, the better to purvey stolen secrets.

It was also in 1909 that the Secret Intelligence Service (SIS) (later to become known as MI6, to mark the connection with the homeland security service MI5) was founded, and with it came long and serious investigations not just into lurid spy rumours, but into the potential of the new technology.

The serious question was to do with security. On the eve of the Great War, the government took precautions in case le Queux's fantasies turned out to have some basis in fact; it ordered the immediate closure of amateur wireless stations. The official government communication read: 'Remove at once your aerial wires and dismantle your apparatus.' On top of this came the strict Defence of the Realm Act: 'No person shall, without the written permission of the Postmaster General, buy, sell, or have in his possession or under his control any apparatus for the sending or receiving of messages by wireless telegraphy, or any apparatus intended to be used as a component part of such apparatus.'

The earlier scares had their knock-on effects too. There were some amateur radio enthusiasts whose hobby had been noted by suspicious neighbours who went to the police with their suspicions of German espionage – and after the Defence Act was passed, anyone found even with a long-disused bit of radio kit was liable to face prosecution.

Traffic was, of course, encoded. And as the First World War escalated, the Navy was to prove most innovative in this new field. It set up a special listening post in Hunstanton, on the Norfolk coast near King's Lynn, through which German wireless traffic coming from across the North Sea was received. The coded messages were then relayed with all haste to an establishment termed 'Room 40', whose interception of these German coded messages played a significant part in the Battle of Jutland – although, as Bletchley veteran Ralph Bennett argued, the Navy's use of the intelligence was so hampered by outmoded procedures that the battle ended up at best as a draw. Bennett also noted that this slowness on the part of the Navy was not really to change until the late 1920s, when a young Lord Louis Mountbatten advocated a proper wireless interception service in order to eavesdrop on potential enemies in the Mediterranean.

'Room 40' was the First World War equivalent of Bletchley Park. It was also the immediate forerunner of the Government Code and Cypher School. Here, in dusty and labyrinthine Whitehall corridors, were gathered a blend of naval officers and freshly recruited academics – notably Alastair Denniston and a brilliant classicist down from Cambridge, Alfred 'Dilly' Knox. Once the Room 40 operatives had received the messages, they would set to work unravelling the complex codes; and then would pass the resulting decrypts to intelligence. What is striking now is the low-key, almost improvised nature of this operation.

The Germans, as it happened, had been a trifle slower to set up an organisation of wireless interception, and only caught up when High Command instructed military radio bases to monitor all signals coming from Russia. The idea was that they might be able to jam such signals in case they also found themselves fighting on the eastern front.

According to veteran interceptor Bill Baker: 'By 1916, all three armed services were depending heavily upon wireless. Paratroops were first employed in 1916 when Belgian soldiers, who in civilian life had been marine wireless officers, were asked to volunteer for special duties. After parachute instruction and a period of training by Marconi's, these men were dropped into enemy territory with small sets manufactured by the company strapped to their backs, their task being to transmit intelligence from behind the German lines.' And according to another veteran wireless expert, Pat Hawker, the famous female agent 'Mata Hari . . . was convicted largely on the basis of intercepted wireless messages between Spain and Germany.'

Not long after Armistice Day in 1918, some of these secrets began leaking out. In a 1921 book by two journalists – Hector Bywater and H.C. Ferraby – called *Strange Intelligence: Memoirs of Naval Secret Service*, was a chapter entitled 'The Men Who Heard The U-Boats Talk'. The authors boldly declared that the 'sources of information were many and varied. The most valuable of all were the wireless directional stations around our coast.'

That there were such stations would have come as a surprise to few. Yet there is a perpetual feeling in intelligence circles that such tactical posts should never be discussed, for fear of giving an inadvertent advantage to the enemy. Intriguingly, though, in this instance Bywater and Ferraby's book was given the tacit backing of Admiral Hall, the naval commander behind many of the innovations. He wrote in a foreword that the disclosures 'can now do no harm either to the public service or individuals'.

After the war, Room 40 evolved into the Government Code and Cypher School; and the focus of wireless interception – under its head Alastair Denniston – changed to new subjects for surveillance, such as the fledgling Soviet Union. During the 1920s, British Intelligence made the threat of the spread of Bolshevism a priority. Indeed, it was at this time that the operatives of GC&CS became wary of handing over their information to politicians, largely because blundering politicians were liable to make loud public speeches in the Commons containing intelligence which could only have been gleaned from sensitive sources. As a result of such blunders, the Soviets, now alerted to British interception techniques, switched to the use of unbreakable 'one-time pads' – that is, paper pads featuring encrypted letters and digits in groups of five, with tear-off sheets, meaning they could be used once, then destroyed.

In 1928 came the formation of a new body, the Y Committee: the idea behind this was to try and bring some co-ordination to the various intercepting operations across the Army, Navy and Air Force. Room 40 personnel under Alastair Denniston were joined by figures from the services, such as Major John Tiltman of the King's Own Scottish Borderers. Tiltman's name now lives on in cryptography lore; one of the figures later to achieve so much at Bletchley Park, he was not only a brilliant codebreaker but also inspirational to others.

Around the world, as radio technology spread and improved, with ever more delicate aerial and valve designs, there was a rise in the number of signals deemed urgent enough to listen in on. The Navy, for instance, developed expertise in eavesdropping on Japanese signals; this obviously required specialised, highly trained operatives to navigate the special difficulties of Japanese Morse. The War Office in the meantime had an interception base in Palestine which would listen in on Arab and French signals.

During this period, amateur interest in wireless technology continued to grow. One such enthusiast, a young man called Richard Gambier-Parry, who had attended Eton College, was by 1920 a licensed amateur radio operator. Indeed, anyone wishing to pursue wireless hobbies had to be similarly licensed and for a small but extremely dedicated number of people, getting a licence was a priority.

But Gambier-Parry's enthusiasm was on another level entirely, and it was to have a profound impact upon the course of his life. In 1926, he became press officer for the BBC (and in a modern age where the Corporation now has around 200 such officers, how extraordinary to think back to an era when only one was required). Five years after that, he joined the British offices of American firm Philco, which specialised in the manufacture of radios, becoming general sales manager for the United Kingdom. This unglamorous sounding occupation (though utterly enthralling to Gambier-Parry) was actually a formative prelude to a remarkable war.

Also key to his career – and it is in no way a slight on his abilities to point this out – was the matter of his social position. As well as his grand education, his family owned lands in Oxfordshire; in the socially rigid 1930s, this meant that at some point he was certain to meet smart, well-connected intelligence officers. And indeed, Gambier-Parry used to go fox-hunting with a senior intelligence official called Stewart Menzies, who was later to become head of MI6. It was as a result of this connection – combined with his undoubted flair and expertise with wireless technology – that towards the end of that decade, at around the time of the Munich crisis, Gambier-Parry was invited by Menzies to join a new communications section of the security services. Like a great many of his fellow Old Etonians, Gambier-Parry had a relaxed, charming and confident manner – universal attributes that nevertheless carried perhaps a little extra weight in that era.

Thanks to his contacts from his Philco years, as well as his general enthusiasm, Gambier-Parry was able to begin headhunting some of the liveliest minds in the wireless world. 'Richard Gambier-Parry took the top layer of Philco,' says Geoffrey Pidgeon, himself later to work for Brigadier Gambier-Parry, and who developed a level of admiration and affection for him that is still evident in his voice whenever he talks of his old boss. 'Philco was at that time the world's biggest radio manufacturer, and the biggest in England – he'd taken the top tranche of their top men.

'Lots of top businessmen were recruited from elsewhere as well. Because they had worldwide connections. They knew a lot of information.'

The first idea was for his organisation to strengthen its clandestine links with agents in neutral countries, as well as to forge new bonds with governments in exile. Even more crucially, by the months leading up to the war, the organisation was responsible for ensuring that traffic intended for Bletchley – either by dispatch rider or radio – got through smoothly, as well as looking after the so-called Black Broadcasts (brilliant propaganda tricks, beamed through to the radios of ordinary Germans, with the aim of disorientating and destabilising their listeners).

It is often noted of the institution of Bletchley Park that a sort of inspired amateurism was at work there. Recruits to the cause were not professional cryptanalysts; rather, they were brilliant minds in specific fields such as mathematics, who could bring lateral reasoning to bear on the problems before them. Similarly, the early days of wireless interception had a pleasingly ad hoc, informal flavour.

In the 1920s, interception was mostly carried out in an anonymous corner of the Passport Office in St James's Park. There was also, according to Geoffrey Pidgeon, a small station operating out of a riverside office in Barnes, south-west London. This location might not have been entirely random; there was a Marconi factory close by and, as Pidgeon points out, there were clear links between Marconi and MI6 in the years leading up to the Second World War.

Yet another secret listening post was located in the south London suburb of Denmark Hill. Here, within a large police station, listeners would covertly tune in to embassy wireless traffic. According to Pidgeon, this unit enjoyed a minor triumph in the inter-war years when it intercepted the communications of a 'subversive' Russian organisation operating out of leafy Wimbledon.

By the mid 1930s, there were prototype out-stations dotted around the world, keeping sharp ears out for Britain's imperial interests. One such station, in Beijing (then Peking), was operated by Edgar Harrison under the aegis of the Foreign Office. The intercept station itself was based in the city's British legation.

Young Harrison listened to Chinese communications at the time of the 1936 abdication crisis, and was fascinated by the widespread disapproval expressed towards Wallis Simpson. The station broadly handled diplomatic traffic, but it had a hidden, interior function too: that of closely monitoring Japanese wireless communications.

Added to this network was the establishment of a station in the British colony of Hong Kong. Elsewhere, another prototype out-station had been set up in Spain in the mid-1930s to keep close track of the conflict in the Spanish Civil War.

And the subject was a matter of growing interest among all the services. In 1934, Sir Charles Blount – Director of Air Intelligence at the Air Ministry – established a unit, operating out of an RAF base in Lincolnshire, to intercept radio traffic. This swiftly became so successful that not long afterwards, a strikingly eccentric young academic was drafted in from Oxford to work full-time on its intelligence gathering. This was Josh Cooper, then thirty-three years old; and before he attracted admiration at Bletchley Park both for his awesome abilities and his distractingly unnerving mannerisms, he was swept deep into the bosom of the Air Ministry.

For the purposes of the coming conflict, an American radio set known as the HRO (the initials were said to stand for 'Helluva Rush On') was identified as being the most suitable; it could pick up both Morse and human voice transmissions with ease and, with a certain dextrous rearrangement of components, had a very broad range. Initially about 1000 were ordered in. As the war progressed, these numbers would rise to some 10,000.

Meanwhile, down in Woldingham in Surrey stood an innocuous looking suburban bungalow with the curious name 'Funny Neuk'. Among the names on the electoral register for the property was one Hugh Sinclair – otherwise Admiral Sir Hugh Sinclair, head of MI6. This suburban structure, placed conveniently close to the North Downs and situated at a good height, served as the base for wireless transmissions.

*

A little more surreal – and perhaps foreshadowing the offbeat, eccentric feel of the 1960s television show *The Avengers* – was an intercept station set up deep within the tough prison of Wormwood Scrubs, west London, in the months before the war began. It was given the designation of the Radio Security Service (and because it was in essence an offshoot of MI5, it was also known as MI8). The purpose of the station was to intercept and track down transmissions from enemy agents working from within Britain. In one section of these unusual headquarters, the prisoners were moved out (to secure accommodation in the countryside), and intelligence figures such as Hugh Trevor-Roper (later Lord Dacre) moved in.

Trevor-Roper had been hauled out of a comfortable life as a young don in Oxford. Very poor eyesight meant that he would not be called up for regular army duties. Swiftly he was recruited by Walter Gill, the Bursar of Merton College. Major Gill was an intensely pragmatic enthusiast who, during the First World War, had worked in the fledgling field of wireless interception; when based in Egypt, it was said that he had had transmitters fitted on top of the Great Pyramid. Now, working deep in their incongruous prison wing, Gill and Trevor-Roper dedicated themselves to the business of detecting enemy radio waves directed towards agents in Britain; or indeed, radio waves emanating from those agents' sets.

The idea was based on an early anxiety about bomber raids; the authorities were concerned that enemy agents might be able to set up radio beams in such a way that the fighter pilots could home in on them as targets. In fact, in conceptual terms, this was not a hundred miles away from what later evolved as 'beam bombing', where pilots would use radio beams to triangulate the location of their targets.

HM Prison Wormwood Scrubs is – and was – a formidable and lowering structure, and one might easily imagine that the aesthetically sensitive Trevor-Roper would have baulked at having to work in such a place. His office was based on the first floor, near an iron walkway that clanged with every footstep. But why were he and his colleagues there at all? The reason was that this was a secure location in which captured spies could be dealt with in conditions of reasonable discretion.

Also working among the drab green tiles of Wormwood Scrubs were a number of smart debutantes, engaged in secretarial work in the echoing cells and corridors. Did Trevor-Roper shudder at the gloom? Not as such. In fact, far worse in his eyes was the area just outside: streets and streets of soot-blackened 'council houses', the drab and uniform avenues of East Acton. Nor was he especially thrilled to find himself living in rented accommodation in the nearby suburb of Ealing.

These quibbles aside, Trevor-Roper and Major Walter Gill proved to be brilliantly effective at their radio interception work; for, having accumulated a great number of German messages transmitted on certain frequencies, the two men took them home to the flat in Ealing and began decoding them. Gill had expertise in cryptography, Trevor-Roper a working knowledge of the German language. Just a few months into the war, they had stolen something of a march on the assembled cryptographers at Bletchley Park: after a great deal of analysis and effort, the codes began to unravel before their eyes.

As it happened, these codes were the ones being used by the Abwehr, the German secret service. Trevor-Roper felt that this was quite a coup. His superiors, however, were furious. Not only was it considered a grave and foolhardy security breach; there were also the layers of regulations and complication of hierarchies, along with the ever-present sense of resentment between different branches of the security services. The 'breach' was considered so serious that Trevor-Roper received a visit at Wormwood Scrubs from Alastair Denniston, now the director of Bletchley Park, and one of his long-standing senior cryptographers, Oliver Strachey (the brother of Lytton). The two men were emphatically not there to congratulate the myopic young Oxford don. And subsequently, it was Strachey who inherited the role of cracking the Abwehr codes harvested by Trevor-Roper.

Nor was his sojourn at Wormwood Scrubs to last long. The Radio Security Service – which was swiftly to prove so successful, with a growing team of volunteers based all over the United Kingdom and eagerly sending in their monitored logs of German radio signals – needed room and space to breathe, and so new and more salubrious premises were found on the northern tip of London in Barnet; the team moved from gloomy Wormwood Scrubs to a roomy and attractive nineteenth-century property called Arkley View.

Back in the late 1930s, along with various other senior intelligence figures, Richard Gambier-Parry was well aware of the urgency of his work. There was little question that the Germans' communications systems would be tightly run and technologically advanced. It was also the case that although Britain was wealthy and powerful throughout the world, its security arrangements were meagre. Few embassies were equipped with the most modern, easily used radio technology, and so the business of communications had – in some regions – a flavour of the nineteenth century about it, much reliant on ink and paper.

So, as Gambier-Parry recruited, he knew that he had to pull in the lithest and most agile minds in order to ensure that wireless security efforts were successful.

By 1937, even before Hitler's *Anschluss* with Austria and demands upon Czechoslovakia, the Y Committee realised – in the face of demands from the Treasury that it should instead make economies – that it would need yet more bases. The drums of war could be heard all over Europe; nevertheless, the Committee's plans unfurled at no great speed. Further academic appointments were made; established naval bases such as those at Chatham on the Kent shoreline and Flowerdown near Winchester, in Hampshire, were customised for listening purposes.

In the archives can be found a slightly pained account of the early
wartime days of HMS *Flowerdown* (sited on land but nonetheless
referred to in all the naval terms familiar at sea), written by an
anonymous senior chronicler:

> Equipment available was, to say the least, in very short supply.
> Four steel masts, 120 feet high, erected at the corners of a
> 260 foot square were available for aerial construction . . . The
> position in regards to spare parts . . . was critical. On many
> occasions, spares from civilian receivers were brought in to
> use as replacements, Maintenance, as such, was practically
> non-existent, comprising merely the repair of sets which had
> broken down . . . the compiling of records in the early days
> of the war was seriously handicapped by the shortage of staff.

The place would change quite dramatically as the conflict
gathered pace in the early 1940s; HMS *Flowerdown* was to become a
teeming hub of Y Service activity, with a crew of high-spirited young
Wrens and sailors. Veteran Marjorie Gerken recalls the surprisingly
egalitarian atmosphere that gradually evolved there; how Wrens
and sailors would sit side by side, radio sets before them, their work
monitored each shift, day and night, by two figures sitting on a
central dais. The receivers, by now shipped in from America, were
sleeker, with ultra-smooth dials and a smart black metal finish,
and the atmosphere of the establishment – from the hyper-serious
focus on the work, to the unstoppably exuberant nature of the
dances, plays, shows and sports matches that the young people
of *Flowerdown* participated in – were to make it one of the most
efficient and certainly happiest of bases.

But the initial shortages of equipment encountered by *Flowerdown*
just before the outbreak of war were by no means unique. In that
curious, thundery atmosphere of 1939, when everyone knew – yet
no public figure said aloud – that war was inevitable, the scramble
to prepare was universal. In 1939, several other listening bases

were added, including one in Hertfordshire and two in the wilds of Scotland. These were all to be staffed by the Foreign Office.

Meanwhile, the Navy, with its separate interest in wireless and signals, had been busy elsewhere. Small wireless interception bases were established across the world: from Wellington in New Zealand, to Singapore, to Malta, to Canada. They were now fast acquiring the latest high-frequency technology – radios that could transmit and receive signals refracted in the heavens high above, in the ionosphere, and bounced back down in far distant lands. These high-frequency waves were ideal for long-distance radio transmissions. What more natural use of Britain's many colonies and territories than to enlist them for the purposes of national security? Indeed, this particular advantage, this ability to set up bases on almost every continent, was an intelligence asset that was to last well into the 1950s and the Cold War.

There were wheels within wheels in the security services as well. Richard Gambier-Parry was detailed to run Section VIII – as distinct from MI8 – an MI6 offshoot that unusually had some independence from day-to-day Foreign Office interference. His role was partly to strengthen overseas wireless and intelligence links.

But there had to be proper headquarters for these wireless interception operations too. Just as the codebreaking activities of GC&CS were moved out of London from St James's Park to the Buckinghamshire town of Bletchley, so the Foreign Office settled upon two handsome properties – certainly much more handsome than Bletchley Park itself – just a few miles away. The first was Hanslope Park; the second a requisitioned country house – a rather fine Regency structure – called Whaddon Hall. The latter estate could very easily be made secure; and it had a range of outbuildings that could be adapted for all sorts of purposes. It was at Whaddon Hall that the security services built their first secret dedicated transmitter of the war, for the purposes of MI6 communications.

Not only that: in the stables to the side of the building was a secret factory which manufactured special wireless sets for the use of secret agents. Head of MI6 Admiral Sir Hugh Sinclair took the precaution of ensuring that the work of Whaddon Hall, dedicated as it was to communications within Intelligence, was kept free of interference from the Foreign Office. The transmitters of Whaddon Hall were, in effect, his own private fiefdom.

These two grand country properties, Whaddon and Hanslope Park – with the addition of Beaumanor Hall – would serve as the nerve centres of the wireless interception operations that were to come. Indeed, later on, as Hanslope gathered in transmissions from around the world, it became something of an attraction for the higher echelons of Allied command, according to Geoffrey Pidgeon: 'Hanslope was considered important enough for Lord Gort, General Alexander, Field Marshal Montgomery and General Eisenhower to pay it a visit . . . Never had there been such a large gathering of amateur wireless operators whose sole purpose was to eavesdrop on enemy wireless intelligence.' Like Bletchley Park, the work of the Y Service was hidden far from general view. Even from its early days, it also shared Bletchley Park's spirit of inventiveness and innovation.

3 The Human Computors

Just before war was declared, an anxious belief took hold among the staff of Bletchley Park that there might actually be a dramatic drop-off in radio traffic for them to intercept. This would – they imagined – be caused by the radio silence they presumed the Germans would impose. Such a thing had happened in the latter stages of the Great War, although the reason had not so much been security as the increasing prevalence of telephone landlines. Nonetheless, there was worry that if such a silence were to recur, it would cause immediate damage to codebreaking and intelligence opportunities.

And indeed, in August 1939, there was an ominous decrease in radio traffic in the days leading up to the German assault on Poland. However, once the attack was under way, it was found that volumes of signals rose dramatically once more. In fact, GC&CS found that there were more German signals than ever before.

But in those early, uncertain weeks of conflict, the security services were seemingly caught out rather badly, both by the enemy and by their own disorganisation. There was the notorious Venlo incident of 1939 when two senior SIS officers – in the process, so they thought, of trying to help disaffected German commanders stage a coup – were lured into a trap in Holland, and spirited over the border into Germany. Not only were the two men – with all that hideously valuable knowledge – now in the power of the Nazis, they had also been captured with some state-of-the-art radio equipment, the technology of which could also conceivably be useful. The British agents were imprisoned for the duration of the war.

It was apparent even before Britain declared war that the Y Service would have to be expanded dramatically. In military terms, as they stood at the start of the conflict, the main intercept station, manned by the Royal Signals, was at the old naval base in Chatham, Kent, on the Thames Estuary. This station picked up army signals. There were two big naval Y stations: one near Winchester and another up in Scarborough, on the Yorkshire coast. The main RAF Y station, meanwhile, was in Staffordshire, located on the moorland between Leek and Cheadle.

Even before the war, '[it] was quite clear that the Luftwaffe was the strongest and most menacing of all foreign air forces,' recalled Bletchley's Air Section head Josh Cooper in his diaries. Finding a way of listening to bomber and fighter pilots' communications would be crucial. But when RAF Cheadle began operations, it was all actually reasonably straightforward, remembered veteran Peter Gray Lucas in an essay. 'A Warrant Officer was in charge of the intercept operators' room . . . The operator wrote down everything he heard, including the procedural exchanges. Any formal message was passed into the teleprinter room and sent formally but without undue haste to Bletchley, where it was decoded, translated, edited and sent by teleprinter to the Air Ministry in London.'[1]

There was, though, according to Bletchley veteran and former director of GCHQ Sir Arthur Bonsall, one immediate setback: a shortage of operators fluent in German. So, in the first few weeks of the war at Bletchley Park, as the classicist academics and keen young undergraduates trawled from the universities began to materialise, such messages from the Luftwaffe were handled in a special hut by four people given the Wellsian designation of 'computors' – specifically spelt with an 'o', to signify that they were akin to those who worked on mathematical tables. On the face of it, this was not the most glamorous designation, especially for a Cambridge professor of classics. Perhaps even less glamorously, it was soon decided that the 'computors' should be sent from Bletchley to RAF Cheadle, thus doing away with the intermediate teleprinting stage.

There, wrote Peter Gray Lucas, 'they sat at a large table in the middle of the air-intercept room. The operators sat at their receivers ranged around the walls and handed their intercepts to the computors. The messages were immediately decoded, translated, and shown to the Warrant Officer in charge of the room, who passed them to the Commands as he saw fit.'

Living up to the chilly, Dalek-like efficiency of the term 'computors', this small team quickly became extraordinarily successful. Even though all signals were sent on to Bletchley Park, the computors became so familiar with the patterns and rhythms of the messages coming in from over the blackness of the North Sea that during any night, they could themselves quietly decode enormous amounts of material.

Arthur Bonsall, then very young, was sent to oversee their work in the initial stages. This involved a comic dispute as to his exact status: civilian or military? The authorities decided that for form's sake, he ought to be in the RAF. 'I spent a morning in the airship shed being catalogued and weighed and measured,' recalled Sir Arthur, 'and [I was] issued with a knife and fork and spoon. Before I had finished my lunch, I was told there had been a change of policy . . .' And so he had to 'retrace his route' and hand back the cutlery. For the duration, he was to all intents and purposes a civilian.

The human computors at RAF Cheadle slipped into their routine with remarkable ease. In the very early stages of the war, Luftwaffe pilots were lax about using the special codes and codewords provided; but even when they did so, the computors were swift to unravel them. Too swift, it seemed, to be believed by higher authorities. Sir Arthur Bonsall recalled an occasion when RAF Cheadle reported that German bombers were on course for the Forth Bridge in Scotland. Despite the clarity of the report, Fighter Command chose to ignore it. As a result, it was 'surprised' when the attack actually did take place. It is possible that Fighter Command simply did not believe the provenance of the information.

It is intriguing that the Cheadle computors were able to press on happily with decoding at a time when the Bletchley authorities were sharply tightening their grip on security; not only were the codes the business of Bletchley Park and Bletchley Park alone, but anyone outside found to be successfully decrypting would be severely dealt with (Hugh Trevor-Roper's nerve in cracking codes, as we have seen, earned him the lasting enmity of the Bletchley authorities). Later yet, there would be fresh and furious debate concerning the various out-stations abroad – from the Middle East to Asia – and the amount of material it was deemed proper for them to process and decode 'in-house' without endangering the great Bletchley secret.

Somehow, though, RAF Cheadle was the happy exception to these outbreaks of paranoia and jealousy. Just so long as the Luftwaffe signals were sent to Bletchley, as well as being decrypted in Staffordshire, all proceeded smoothly, and the computors enjoyed a degree of autonomy that few others were to be granted.

Also vital – especially in those early, sweaty days of the war when the fear of German invasion was at its height – was the work of RAF Kingsdown in Kent. As Sir Arthur Bonsall has noted, at a time when radar technology was in its infancy, RAF Kingsdown provided the closest that the British could get to real-time reports of the positions of enemy pilots: their take-off times, the courses they were flying, the heights at which they flew.

Bonsall added that 'Kingsdown and the other Home Defence Units came into their own during the Battle of Britain.' The Home

Defence Units he referred to were the many listening stations – ranging from small to minuscule – which were swiftly established around Britain's coastline, from Cornwall to Scotland. In the spring of 1940, the military authorities were still constructing this vast, complex operation. Sometimes there was a sense of ingenious extemporisation.

And of almost equal importance were the tiny ad hoc RAF stations – sometimes based in caravans, or in honeysuckled clifftop cottages – on the south coast. For it was of course the south coast that would witness so much of the action: the German fighter pilots zooming in across the Channel, the RAF pilots braced to meet the assault. In the early days of the conflict, these tiny stations could also gauge the immediate urgency of messages; although fighter pilots were supposed to communicate in code, the heat and terror of conflict meant that frequently, the listeners along the coast heard their voices; tense, terrified young Germans talking – or more often, shouting – in plain German. There was almost a form of perverse intimacy in the relationship; the young women listening in to what were frequently either moments of crisis or occasions of exhausted triumph.

RAF Kingsdown operative Peggy West recalled that the station lay in what was termed 'Bomb Alley'. Otherwise, though, it was a happy base, presided over by 'Miss Conan Doyle, the daughter of Sir Arthur'; 'Wing Commander Budge', described by West as 'a wireless wizard', was their 'respected and dedicated commanding officer'. Even at the very start of the war, they picked up some nifty tricks:

Initially the radios used were rather awkward boxes whose coil changes [tuning components that could be changed in order to receive different frequencies] were needed at the most inappropriate times . . . But when small compact radio sets began to arrive from crashed German aircraft, or via clandestine routes, you can imagine we found those

36   The Secret Listeners

German sets were ideal for us too. These covered the whole spectrum of frequencies used by the Luftwaffe by rotation of one comfortable dial with precise tuning capabilities.[2]

Elsewhere, in the earliest stages of the war, Gordon Welchman – senior cryptographer and Bletchley Park's great organisational genius – had forged close links with the staff at the Chatham naval base. They would ensure that communications received were bundled up and sent at top speed by motorcycle courier, even on icy, wet winter nights, to Bletchley Park, where round-the-clock shifts could immediately start decoding and analysing them.

Motorcycle couriers were not the only means of transmitting information but quite often, in those early days, they were the most reliable. Also in place was a system of teleprinters; but in 1939, there were neither enough telephone lines nor enough teleprinter operators to make the technology work effectively. At Bletchley Park, a small number of WAAF operatives, referred to affectionately as 'Tele-princesses', were based within the main house; by the time the technology became more reliable and the machines were used around the country and around the world, they numbered around forty in total.

Elsewhere, the Radio Security Service was settling comfortably into Arkley View in Barnet. Here, according to Pat Hawker, were to be found 'analysis, intelligence, direction finding control and various administrative departments'. Rather like Bletchley Park, huts were built in the grounds, the better to accommodate equipment such as teleprinter terminals. Dispatch riders were always at hand to take intercepted messages directly, and at top speed, to Bletchley Park.

It was understood – even in the generally unprepared atmosphere of 1939 – that a great many wireless intercept operatives were going to be required. The work could not be left to clutches of individuals hunched by radio sets for hours on end. Having said that, the story of recruitment to the Y Service shows that the net, though cast carefully, was also cast wide. The selectors were not merely going to rely on military personnel at secluded coastal bases. Just as the authorities at Bletchley Park had sought out mathematicians, chess champions and crossword lovers, so the Radio Security Service was fixing upon Britain's ever-growing numbers of wireless enthusiasts, many of them quite young.

Radio was – and possibly still is – a fundamentally male hobby. And part of Arkley's remit was to take in not merely intercepts taken down by professionals, but those also picked up by a small but substantial army of gifted amateurs. These amateurs were known as Voluntary Interceptors.

One such operative – or VI – was teenager Ray Fautley, who had been utterly fascinated with the science of radio since his earliest years, showing a precocious talent in constructing his own receivers. And though this enthusiasm was to lead him into years of extremely hard work, it is clear that he would not have begrudged one moment of it.

Seventeen-year-old Ray was still living at home with his parents in Mitcham, south London. Since the age of fourteen, he had worked for radio firms, including Marconi, with a zeal that his employers must have found extremely heartening. In 1939, he was co-opted into becoming a listener. Not from any secret premises, but from his parents' front parlour. There, a radio set was installed inside a bureau, where it could be hidden from sight when Ray was not using it.

'I was with the civilian Y Service, you could say,' he explains. Though Mr Fautley was not to know it until a great many years later, the frequencies allocated to the Voluntary Interceptors to tune into were those used by the Abwehr, the German secret service. His instructions were to tune in on bands 'from 7 to 7.5 megacycles per second, or megahertz, as it is now. But what I listened to: they gave me no clue whatsoever. All they said was, write down any Morse signals you hear and send them in to us.' And that is what he did: Mr Fautley would tune into the frequencies within the bands given and, simultaneously translating from Morse (a precious high-speed skill that he shared with all other Y Service operatives), would scrupulously note down, upon specially provided stationery, the letters that he had decoded. So how was this young lad drawn into such specialised war work?

'This chap at Marconi's was the bloke who had put my name forward for the work. And he knew about it when the vetting man came to my house.' The visitor who materialised on his doorstep one afternoon proved to be the archetypal hush-hush Man from Whitehall – much to the consternation of Fautley's parents, who were not allowed to know what was going on. 'There was this chap in a bowler, with an umbrella, he was doing background on me,' says Mr Fautley with a chuckle. 'Asking me where my parents were born, where my grandparents were born. I told him exactly where they were born. They were all Brits. The furthest away was born on the Isle of Wight. Most were from London. I myself was born in Camberwell.'

As can easily be imagined, while this serious, confidential talk was going on, Ray Fautley's parents were in the other room, bewildered and anxious about the mysterious visit. 'When this Voluntary Interception gentleman, with his bowler hat and umbrella, was leaving, I said to him: would you please say just a few words to my parents?' Young Fautley of course was not allowed to do so himself – the vow of secrecy was imposed with immediate effect. 'I said, "They'll think I've done something awful and that I'm going to be taken away and locked up . . . I don't know what they'll think."

'The man said, "All right." And within my hearing, he said to my parents: "Your son will be doing work of very great national importance to this country." I thought, what on earth . . . I'm no secret agent . . . what on earth could I be doing that was so important?'

The background to this thrilling opportunity is a sharp snapshot of a long-lost world of engineering skill and knowhow. For even as the war broke out, young Fautley, who had built his own radio receiver at the age of twelve, had moved from Marconi and was a junior with another big radio firm of the day.

'I got a job with the Mallard Radio Valve Company in Mitcham Works,' he says. 'The little laboratory I worked in was on an island in the middle of the River Wandle. You had to approach on a footbridge. I joined the firm in December 1939. The senior engineers took to me, because I was like a sponge. The stuff I learned from those senior engineers in about the year that I was there – well, I don't think there's a single piece of equipment I've seen from that time on that I couldn't use.'

The War Office was very keen on this level of expertise. Not least because, while waiting for further interception stations to be established, it needed experienced and skilled listeners to monitor any kind of illicit broadcasting. The man at the Ministry co-ordinating this voluntary effort was Lord Sandhurst.

Much like his RSS colleague Brigadier Richard Gambier-Parry, Sandhurst had a jovial side that would manifest itself in comical newsletters sent out to the Voluntary Interceptors. In these, he would refer to himself as 'T W Earp'. He once wrote a morale-boosting poem – aimed at the radio specialists, with all their frequently impenetrable jargon and acronyms – that concluded:

> If you can dodge the blinking German Army
> Or copy AOR through thick and thin
> And you can copy VIOLET's QRX's
> You're a better bloke than me so
> BUNG IT IN!

Indeed, certainly in the early stages of the war, the (sometimes very young) Voluntary Interceptors were rather more adept at the work than many operatives either in the services or the Foreign Office. Like the computing whizz-kids of today who seem to have an instinctive aptitude for the technology, a youthful generation of radio fanatics had swiftly mastered this new and fast evolving science of valves and coils and receivers. Certainly, young Ray Fautley – who was required to do all this on top of his demanding day job, and a stint in the Home Guard too – took to it with relish. Even the extra tasks laid on by the War Office.

'There was a whole lot of stuff: the responsibility I got for designing – aged eighteen – a set of coils for a transmitter which the War Office wanted. It had to be manufactured out of components that were to be found in any radio factory used for making radio wireless sets.

'From that time on, I knew exactly what type of wire to use for any particular frequency. I proudly presented the senior engineer with the set, and he used it.

'I didn't want to let him down, I was going to do this job. Even though I had no idea what to do to start with. It's stuck with me ever since.'

When he started as a VI, Ray Fautley found that the Radio Security Service was to issue him with a kit. First came the receiver itself, which was to be secreted within the Fautley front parlour. 'I had made my own set,' he says. 'But then they loaned me a thing called the AR88. Now that really needed two men to lift. I couldn't lift it myself now. It weighed an absolute ton.'

Together with this cumbersome equipment, older than the sleeker HRO receivers that were coming in, was paraphernalia that would not have seemed out of place being given away with a boy's comic of the day. 'I got a parcel, with message forms and the log sheets, and stamps. And there were some lovely envelopes stamped "Secret" in red – and some slightly larger plain envelopes and some gummed stickers marked *PO Box 25, Barnet, Herts*, which I used to stick on the plain envelopes.

'All my logs went inside the "secret" envelope, and then that was put inside the other one. All very cloak and dagger.' The very idea of 'PO Box 25, Barnet' is a tribute to the Post Office of that era. Is it remotely possible to imagine trusting such correspondence to today's service? 'But this is how the Voluntary Intercept Service operated,' says Mr Fautley. 'Eventually, there were about 1500 to 1600 of us – all over the UK.'

Indeed, according to wireless veteran Pat Hawker, the system evolved piecemeal, with a spirit of improvisation about it:

> Throughout the early war years, hams (including at least one woman) were recruited on a regional basis. A Captain in the Royal Corps of Signals was put in charge of each section . . . Many radio amateurs holding pre-war licences, who also belonged to the Radio Society of Great Britain, received a letter from Lord Sandhurst. The amateur was then subjected to a security check by the police and was interviewed by the Regional Officer . . . the V.I. was enrolled after signing a declaration under the Official Secrets Act . . . The V.I. couldn't, of course, explain why he was unable to take part in duties such as fire-watching or the Home Guard because he didn't have any time to spare. Sometimes a small room in the house was used as the listening post or . . . a shed in the garden, suitably blacked out.[3]

Like many young radio enthusiasts, Ray Fautley had already learned the intricacies of Morse code. 'I learned from my colleague at Marconi's when I was an apprentice in 1935 because when he knew I could already do a bit of Morse, he brought a Morse key in and an oscillator and a pair of earphones.' The aim was to improve Fautley's ability and, crucially, speed. 'In the lunchtimes, he used to send me Morse messages out of the newspaper, just plain language, and in three weeks I was doing twenty words a minute, much to my amazement and to his.'

Until the war, Fautley had never made use of his skill. But now it was very much called on. As well as doing a full day's work, the Voluntary Interceptor was expected to go home in the evening, have some tea, and then put in two hours of concentrated radio work, five nights a week. Fautley settled into it quite quickly.

'One of the first things I found when I started listening was that there was a consistent signal which I heard every night every time I was on exactly the same frequency, and [which was] quite obviously machine-sent Morse. Perfect spacing, perfect lengths to dots and dashes, you couldn't imitate it because it was so perfect. It used to rattle along at twenty words a minute.' Everything Ray copied had to be in block capital letters, which was harder than transcribing in normal, flowing handwriting. 'The reason I had to copy everything in block capitals was because if it was done in longhand, you could get confusion between Us and As, Vs and so forth.'

Even in these early months of the war, Mr Fautley was gaining both valuable expertise and passing useful material on to the top secret PO Box in Barnet, north London – not that he could ever know it as he took down the coded messages. Of the station that was sending automatic Morse, he says, 'I sent it in with the log and they came back and said: "This you can use as a frequency marker."' In other words, it was a German frequency that he could not only monitor but use as a fixed reference for tuning to others. 'And so on my calibration mark of 0 to 100, I knew exactly what that frequency represented. That helped me calibrate the whole scale.'

'Automatic Morse is the same, whatever machine sends it. It's regular, exact. A human being does not send regular, exact Morse.' The irregularity of the human touch, however, could itself be of terrific strategic value to the listeners. The individual rhythms of those operating the telegraph keys, tapping out those 'dit dit dahs', were very distinctive. As a result, if you could recognise the style of a particular German Morse operator, you would know you had hit the correct frequency.

And so it was that Mr Fautley began slowly to identify many different German operators simply by their individual styles of transmission – their 'fists'. Once a German radio operator could be identified by his own unmistakable style, the listener could home in on his individual quirks and working habits; small slips in operating procedure which on the face of it wouldn't mean much

– but which allowed the codebreakers a way to crowbar their way into ciphers. Slips such as the repeated use of a girlfriend's name as a test, or simply the use of 'Heil Hitler' at the end of every message.

'Every operator is slightly different,' says Mr Fautley. 'They may be similar but they are never exactly the same. When I send Morse, the dashes I send are probably not all exactly the same length. I was listening to a particular station and it had a three-letter call sign, and I copied all that down. And what amazed me was at the end of the transmission, they quite often sent [the numbers] 7-3. Now that's amateur radio parlance for "best wishes". In any language.

'I thought: "This must be a German amateur operator sending that." Because if this was actually the German military and his officers had seen that going out . . . he'd probably have got court-martialled. Anyway, on the same frequency, at the same time, the station would come up with different call signs. Still three dashes but different. But the fist was the same. So I put on my log: "same operator".'

Indeed, as the war progressed, many Y Service operators formed a strong impression of their German counterparts: like themselves often youthful, with that same zeal for the science of the wireless. Behind all the elongated dots and dashes were oddly recognisable human beings. Obscene though the Nazi regime was, there did not seem to be many cases of Y Service operatives feeling terrific animosity towards their immediate German equivalents. In a few cases, there was respect.

As Mr Fautley settled into his grinding though fruitful listening sessions, his anonymous superiors in Barnet were very pleased with his efforts and – pleasingly – felt that he should know. 'They came back with "Well done" because this helped them enormously. All this stuff was being card-filed.'

And Mr Fautley was not alone in doing outstanding work; as a whole, the VIs succeeded in picking up – often on very faint, hard-to-hear frequencies – some golden intelligence. Any messages from such an important source obviously gave vital clues to

operations, tactics, strategies, manoeuvres. In the early stages of
the conflict, the Voluntary Interceptors – and senior analysts at
Arkley View in north London such as Hugh Trevor-Roper – became
so good at identifying certain operating procedures that those very
procedures gave the cryptographers at Bletchley Park some of the
first clues they needed to smash their way into the Enigma codes.

VIs would sometimes overhear the German operators discussing
changes in codes, and telling each other about cipher updates in
order to keep each other up to speed. As a result, the garrulous
German wireless operators were helping Bletchley Park to keep up
to speed as well.

The Abwehr codes were to prove particularly useful to the Arkley
View analysts; as the conflict progressed, they were able to focus
on these in detail, thus yielding invaluable information about the
enemy's entire communications systems. And, thanks in great part
to the Voluntary Interceptors' perceptiveness in distinguishing
between different German operators, other advantages were
gained. Against the grain of national stereotypes, German radio
operators were much more gossipy than their Allied counterparts;
when establishing contact with each other, they were much more
prone to casual chattering. This very chatter was as individual as
fingerprints. And the practical use of such information enabled
staff at Arkley View to record systematically on index cards the
details of each operator, where roughly they were based, and
the sorts of military manoeuvres that they were reporting on.
According to Geoffrey Pidgeon:

> Box 25 received up to a thousand log sheets daily from V.I.s
> and full-time interceptors. These had to be examined to
> identify new Abwehr services and to sort the familiar ones into
> their allotted groups . . . If the operator sent in a previously
> identified station the details were sent to the relevant Group
> Officer, located in the next hut, who would then advise the
> operator whether it was 'already covered, thanks' or 'still

wanted' . . . A large wall map was kept in the Group hut with coloured wool stretching between points showing the location and working of the various stations. To prevent a casual visitor from seeing the extent of British discoveries, this map was covered with a curtain that was activated by an electric motor.

It was not just 'fists' that were of tremendous use to the Barnet crowd. 'Another useful aid in identifying stations which changed their call signs regularly . . . was by noting the peculiar and tune-less notes which some of the primitive transmitters produced.' Metaphors for these notes, heard in the background, included 'a croaking frog, a fly in a bottle, a clucking hen, an Epsom salts note and a painful and pathetic note'.[4]

The country was divided up into regions, each allocated to an officer who made it clear to the VIs that 100 per cent accuracy was of the essence. Nevertheless, the officers also tried to ensure that two or more VIs would cover certain frequencies, so that if the odd mistake was made, it could be checked against the other VIs' transcriptions.

There was also what might have been seen as healthy competition with other listeners – particularly the radio operatives of the General Post Office. Used to working only with the highest quality signals, GPO operatives were rather stumped by the fainter sort that the VIs became so expert in following. One RSS official commented: 'We have continually wiped the eye of the Post Office over it and I am very anxious that we should wipe it cleaner.' Indeed, by March 1940, when the Germans made their move into the Low Countries and France, it was the VIs who succeeded in hearing agents in those countries being sent secret messages to alert them to the coming invasion.

Away from the excitement and the achievements of Arkley View, life in Barnet was occasionally rather exasperating for the high-minded fox-hunting aesthete Hugh Trevor-Roper. His leisure hours would ideally be bound up either with his passion for wild countryside or his equally strong love for the classics, but his attempts back at home to concentrate on scholarly pursuits or even work on his amusingly self-conscious and ornate diaries would be thwarted by the garrulous landlady of his billet, who frequently attempted to engage her young lodger with lengthy monologues concerning 'theosophy', feminism, the ancient secrets of the Great Pyramid, the significance of dreams, the legends of Atlantis, and the possibilities of a new psychic dimension. Trevor-Roper's Radio Security Service workplace was thus not merely a satisfying outpost of intelligence, set aside from the venomous bickering of MI5 and MI6; it was also invaluable sanctuary from a talkative landlady.

In the meantime, Ray Fautley's early training – and his natural love for the medium of radio – ensured that his initiation into the realm of secret listening was reasonably straightforward (even if he was later mistaken for a spy, as we shall see later). For many others, including the thousands of young women drafted into the effort, the process was more trying.

Owing to family connections, Shirley Cannicott (née Gadsby) found her initial experience of wireless interception rather more glamorous than the rough and ready training that immediately followed. She was keen to do her bit, she had languages, and her father knew someone with Admiralty contacts. This resulted in an interview with Lady Alexander, wife of the First Lord of the Admiralty. 'It was quite an experience to go in by the front gate of Admiralty in Whitehall,' wrote Mrs Cannicott, 'and after polite enquiries made by a liveried porter, to be conducted along long, low-ceilinged corridors, lit by anciently-shaped lamps.' After this, she was required to visit 'the citadel', the great concrete mass on the side of Horseguards Parade, where she sat a test. Having passed, in the following days she found herself dispatched to north London:

> I was sent up to Mill Hill where we were given – was it a week or two weeks? – very perfunctory training.

We were never given any instructions about the 'insides' of radios or anything of that kind . . . just a brief chat on what a radio wave was and what it could do . . . Headphones on, set on, swivel the dial ever so slowly forward and back, forward and back, overlapping a portion of the dial each time, until the whole sweep was covered . . . to hear a noise, a voice, something other than the swish of 'radio silence'. We were a generation of young who had done this same thing nightly on our parents' wireless sets, searching for foreign stations with dance music late into the night after Auntie BBC had closed.[5]

For Sybil Welch, the culture shock was rather greater. Leaving Glasgow University to sign up for her new duties in the Wrens, she found herself being sent to the Royal Naval College, Greenwich. As she wrote:

This training course was a somewhat unnerving experience. It seemed a long way from Goethe, Grillparzer, Hebbel, and other pillars of German literature to the deep baritone voice of Lt Freddie Marshall shouting: 'Achtung! Achtung! Feindliche Zerstorer and Steurbord!' This, he taught us, was the sort of thing we might hear from a German E-Boat near the English coast, and which we would have to intercept and send to our nearest intelligence centre.[6]

Even for young women from London – where one might some-how expect slightly greater insouciance – the experience of being pulled into the vortex of war was disorientating and unsettling. In early 1939, Iris Sugg – together with her friend Betty Miller – had recently left school. They found work as clerks in the Post Office headquarters at St Martins le Grand. As war broke out, Mrs Sugg recalls, 'a circular was passed around the office asking for female staff to apply for training in the "Post Office Wireless Service", which was vital for the war effort. Betty and I decided we would fill in the application forms.'

They applied, attended interviews, and passed; then they were given a rather curious briefing. After having the importance of the Official Secrets Act impressed upon them, the two young women were additionally told ominously that 'if the war did not go well, and the very worst happened, we would not be associated with the Post Office, we did not exist.' This clearly had quite an effect on their youthful imaginations, but they pressed on.

'Soon we were passed on for training in London, learning the Morse code and radio procedure,' recalls Mrs Sugg. 'We were now qualified "wireless operators" and waited for our postings.' As it happened, the two young girls were not required to travel far; twenty-five miles at most. Even so, they were still daunted; this was an age, as many veterans testify, when girls in particular were seemingly less worldly than their modern-day equivalents. Travel was a rarity, as indeed was straying far from family. 'The great day came telling us we were posted to St Albans and enclosing rail passes and other documents,' says Mrs Sugg. 'On our arrival there, we were to be met by a local police constable who would find a billet for us. Thus two teenagers who had never been away from home before were off on an unknown adventure to help the war effort.'

The billeting procedure was striking enough for the two young girls. In the company of a 'fatherly' policeman, they were taken to a local housing estate. The constable then simply started knocking on doors, asking the houses' occupants how many bedrooms they had, and whether those rooms were occupied. A few householders during the war years would happily fib in the face of officialdom, for fear that the adult billetees or child evacuees – complete strangers both – would turn out to be unruly, dirty, infectious, flea-ridden or completely uncontrollable. The policeman had to knock on quite a few doors.

Then one woman told him that her husband was serving abroad, and that she only had one small child and four bedrooms. According to Mrs Sugg, the policeman said 'Right. These two young ladies will be billeted with you and you will be hearing from Social Services about your payment.' She remembers, 'The owner had no choice. We were force-billeted and the policeman's job was done.

'Mrs Haymer – for that was our host's name – was super. She became a second mum to two bewildered and frightened teenagers and we stayed with her during our posting at the radio station at Woodcock Hill, St Albans.'

Spring 1940, and in the Surrey household of eleven-year-old Geoffrey Pidgeon, the family had been much impressed by the advent of two mysterious yet cheerful billetees – Wilf Lilburn and Bob Chennells, young men engaged in unspecified war work to do with wireless technology. The pair were friendly, polite and well mannered, but the nature of their work – and their frequent absences – was shrouded in secrecy. One day, Geoffrey got a clue as he walked into Lilburn's room to tell him that he was wanted on the telephone. 'He'd got an ordinary wooden Philco [radio] set, wooden frame, fretwork on the front. He'd turned it round and he'd taken out a handset,' says Mr Pidgeon. 'And he was talking to someone. I looked at that – I was astonished, I sort of backed off. All they said was that they were working in the wireless station.' Actually, it was a great deal more than that; they were right-hand men of Richard Gambier-Parry and in those early days of the war, they were running extraordinarily risky missions back and forth across the Channel.

'These two chaps were coming and going a lot – sometimes they would be there and sometimes they would be away for a week,' continues Mr Pidgeon. 'Wilf disappeared one week and when he came back, my mother said to him: "Oh, have you been back to London?"

'"No," Wilf said, simply, "I've been to Holland."

'Now of course at that time the British Expeditionary Force was there. My mother said to him, "How did you get into Holland?"

After all, there were destroyers up and down the Channel. But it was just a throwaway line. It just came out. Then I realised.'

Lilburn and Chennells were running replacement wireless sets to agents in the field. They were going back and forth, through Bordeaux, Belgium and Holland, and then returning to the ordered, calm simplicity of Caterham.

But their very presence in the Pidgeon household was to have a transformative effect, not least on young Geoffrey himself. At that time, his father, the owner of an upmarket West End ticket agency, was also carrying out his duties as an ARP warden. 'Wilf and Bob had to go,' says Mr Pidgeon. 'But then weeks later, in April or May 1940, Bob Chennells phoned my father and asked if he would like a job with their organisation.

'None of us knew what it was apart from something to do with wireless. Father was asked to go to 34 Broadway, near St James's Park. When he got there, he was taken into a room and there were components of a wireless set: condenser, resistor, valves – and he had to name the various parts. And they said, "All right Mr Pidgeon, you'll hear from us."' As it happened, Pidgeon's father was a skilled amateur radio enthusiast who had built his own sets. The work was an ideal fit.

'He had to give references,' adds Mr Pidgeon. His father was in the unusual position of being able to supply references from an extraordinarily gilded source: in his professional life, he had regularly escorted relatives of Queen Victoria – residing at Kensington Palace – to the theatre, having arranged the seats for them. 'You can't get more impressive than that, can you?' says Mr Pidgeon. 'So father – about a week or so later – had a letter saying would you please travel to Bletchley Park and when you get there, phone this number and you will be met. He was also told to catch a certain train, which he did. He was driven in a Packard to Whaddon Hall and there was Bob and Wilf. He was asked if he would like to run the wireless stores, which were in their infancy, for the organisation. And he said yes.

'It was a civilian job. But then of course Dunkirk had happened – this was now early June. The country was in a terrible state. Troops were coming home. Every regiment under the sun came up a gangplank. And so father was quickly fixed up in a place called Stony Stratford. He was billeted with a family called the Crows.' Not long after this, the Pidgeon family would find themselves at the heart of Britain's top secret wireless operation.

4 The Listeners at Large

The Nazi war machine was tearing its way across western Europe: and to many in Britain in the summer of 1940, the fearful question was when – not if – those same forces would cross the narrow strip of sea that separated the country from its deadly enemy. The British Expeditionary Force, caught hideously by surprise when the Germans made their lightning advance through France, had been forced into a retreat that was dressed up to look like a pyrrhic victory. But Dunkirk if anything underlined the apparent vulnerability of the nation. Not one country had yet succeeded in standing in the way of Hitler's forces. Was Britain really prepared to do so, all alone?

On top of this, recalled Bletchley codebreaker Peter Gray Lucas, signals 'were read during the land campaigns of 1939–40 but it is unlikely that they yielded any usable intelligence. The only recollection that survives is the excitement among the computors [at RAF Cheadle] when a corrupt signal that they had rendered as "harass refugees" was read out in a BBC bulletin.'[1] Clearly the term 'harass' was early evidence of the shocking ruthlessness of the enemy. But on this occasion, the computors, normally so efficient, had got it wrong. The signal had in fact stated 'protect refugees'.

However, it was too late, recalled Lucas; it was out there. And the BBC did not broadcast a correction.

Further to the south of England, however, the Y Service was to notch up one vital victory; and that was the crucial support that it supplied throughout the Battle of Britain. As Sir Arthur Bonsall pointed out, the Wrens based at RAF Kingsdown in Kent, and at the tiny listening stations dotted along the coast, were providing the sort of intelligence about bomber formations – the scientific advance of radar was still very much in its early days – that was to prove utterly invaluable. The Bletchley Park official history states:

> Information from the Home Defence Units . . . using German-speaking WAAF and Wrens staff on high frequency radio intercepts from the pilots and their ground controllers, was sent direct to the local RAF commands as well as a HQ Fighter Command at Stanmore . . . With growing regularity and accuracy as the battle proceeded, the organisations exploiting the Luftwaffe signals traffic [were] able to give advanced information about the purpose, type and scale of the enemy's attacks.

Lisa Ison had just completed her Wrens special duty course and was dispatched to the listening station at Dover. 'A very slow journey as the train kept stopping as there were dogfights overhead,' she wrote. 'The Battle of Britain was in full swing.' She described 'watching German fighters shooting down the barrage balloons over Dover Harbour, which looked like fun. Another time seeing the elite Goering squadron flying back very low over the cliffs, close enough to be able to see all the markings on the planes – even the pilots' faces.'[2]

Some tiny coastal out-stations were to be very fondly remembered by the Wrens who had worked in them. In 1940, Daphne Baker was sent to Dover as a cipher officer. In the early days, in a small room on Marine Parade, life was good fun – not least because she was able to see friends, and her parents only lived a few miles away. But then came Dunkirk, and suddenly Dover was at the centre of the evacuation. 'The nights were clear,' she wrote. 'The harbour was so crammed with vessels of all sizes that you couldn't have dropped a pebble between them, let alone a bomb.' She was among those who helped the soldiers off the little ships, and noted how they walked 'like automatons'; clearly the men felt that this was a defeat, rather than the triumph it would later be portrayed as. But for Daphne, this was where the war acquired deadly seriousness and urgency, with the odd extraordinary moment of redemption.

'We were on night watch,' she wrote, and reports of sinkings were pouring in, including the ship of the husband of a fellow cipher officer. 'We whisked the signal away so that she couldn't see it but were heartbroken for her. Early in the morning there was a sudden scuffle and a figure in a French blue smock burst into the cypher office and clasped this girl to his bosom. I don't know how many times he'd been sunk and picked up that night, but there was her husband, and one happy ending.'[3]

Imogen Ryan was posted to Harwich after an incongruously idyllic summer of 1940 in which her Suffolk garden 'burst with fruit and vegetables'. Even in that moment when the Nazi threat was at its sharpest, she recalled that life at Harwich was 'fun'. 'Most of the people I was lucky enough to be working with were highly intelligent and very good company and we were, of course, all "Nice Girls",' she wrote. 'This is to say we all came from comparatively comfortable backgrounds and conformed to the current rules of good behaviour.'

For others, there was a curious mix of fresh sea air with a grandstand view of the Battle of Britain, and the Blitz that followed. Elizabeth Agar was posted to Portland Bill in Dorset and found herself working in a small cottage:

It was up a hill about one hundred yards from the road – a struggle with suitcases and provisions. It looked out to sea on three sides. There were rocks to climb and the walks along the cliff were glorious – walks spoiled by the strict requirement that we take our tin hats and gas masks with us . . . on one occasion, I remember our cook coming back from a walk during which a low-flying aircraft had let loose a burst of indiscriminate gun fire. She got down behind the only available shelter, a small gorse bush. She came back very shaken, saying, 'I didn't know which end to put my tin hat!'[4]

These exposed coastal positions brought all sorts of hazards. With Dover having gained a deserved reputation as 'Hellfire Corner', Daphne Baker's small team was moved to an abandoned lighthouse nearby at South Foreland, no longer working because a cliff had collapsed almost on top of it. They also operated, higher up, from a nearby empty windmill, which gave a wide view across the Channel. 'In those early days it was terrible to see our ships being sunk by Stukas and Dorniers right in front of us,' she wrote. 'We were stuck to our sets listening on the aircraft frequencies, and I was relieved to see that mine wasn't the only hand that shook as we wrote.'

And there was the terrifying matter of enemy fire. 'By now the shelling had started and for several reasons we came in for a lot of it,' wrote Mrs Baker. 'Firstly a lighthouse and a windmill made a good practice target even if the Germans didn't know we were there. Secondly, if Dover Harbour was being bombed, ships would scurry out as close under our cliff as possible.'[5]

The nature of the work acted as a sort of alert in itself. In one coastal station, a Wren intercepted a message stating that her hut was being targeted, and indeed that the missile had already been launched, which gave her and her colleagues about half a minute to get out. The projectile fell short – but the fright was comprehensive.

For those who lived in Dover, the shelling became almost a matter of macabre routine; with the German guns just eighteen miles away across the water, and with the strategic importance of the port and its military HQ, the townsfolk became almost inured to regular explosions, as well as the incendiaries from air raids. There was a local shelter but many were wary of using it, fearing that the ground above might be hit and everyone within buried alive. According to one local woman, many townsfolk instead favoured 'the caves', the network of tunnels that ran beneath Dover Castle.

As summer gave way to autumn, Elizabeth Agar, in her Portland Bill eyrie, faced ever more hazard from German bombers. She wrote in her diary: 'I was in Weymouth with a couple of others in the car and on the way home, the sirens went . . . I was driving, and we had just got on to the road across Chesil Beach when the planes came to bomb the oil tanks at the other end. Once on to this narrow road, turning was impossible and stopping unthinkable . . .' She drove on through the dark with only her side-lights, in a state of terror. This gave way to a moment of pitch-black comedy as she was then pulled up by a sentry, who refused to let her continue as a result of an unexploded bomb: her reaction was one of wild indignation, as it meant reversing, and going back all the way into Weymouth in order to pick up the necessary pass documentation from her superiors. Bullets and incendiaries were one thing; the grinding wheels of British bureaucracy were another.

Aileen Clayton, based in Hawkinge on the south coast, recalled in her brilliant book *The Enemy is Listening* some of the curiously intimate relationships that the listeners would develop with the German pilots with whom they had become familiar:

The pilot of one of the aircraft engaged on . . . perfectly legitimate reconnaissance, had become quite a friend of ours, and we quite frankly looked forward to him 'coming on the air' to give his reports. His callsign, I remember, was 'Amsel Eins'. He assumed that we were listening, and he would chatter away to us in English. 'I know, you English listening station, can you hear me?' he would cheerfully declare. 'Would you like me to drop a bomb on you? Listen – whee! – boomp!' and he would chuckle into his microphone.

'But war makes the most savage demands, and the day had to come when we were instructed to let No. 11 Fighter Group know . . . a flight of Spitfires [jumped] him, and he was shot down in flames. He was unable to get out and we listened to him as he screamed and screamed for his mother and cursed the Fuehrer . . . We heard him all the way down . . . I went outside and was sick.[6]

In those febrile months, there would inevitably be panics that the Nazi invasion was already under way. Up at Sleaton Sluice in Northumberland, Jane Fagg and her colleagues were given a 'mother-of-pearl revolver' to be on the safe side; on the Isle of Wight, the listening Wrens had been given blue overalls in case of emergency – in the event of the Germans landing and taking over, they could pretend the listening station was an orphanage. A curious idea – yet in Dover, Daphne Baker recalled an even more bizarre back-up plan that she had received in the form of an official directive: in the case of the Nazis landing, she was to walk to Bristol from Dover, taking with her a tin of tuna fish as sustenance.

Elsewhere, Geoffrey Pidgeon's father had been spirited away to Buckinghamshire and Whaddon Hall to begin his confidential radio work, but the rest of the family were still living in what was fast becoming an extremely hazardous zone; in Surrey, the war was being fought directly over their heads. After a few close encounters with German bombers, it was clear that the Pidgeons would have to join their father as quickly as possible, even though for them, as for all the other boys of Surrey and Kent, the pyrotechnics in the blue skies were hypnotic. 'Biggin Hill was bombed,' says Mr Pidgeon. 'We were in a triangle – Croydon was about six miles north, Biggin Hill was about five or six miles east. And the runway at Kenley was less than two miles from our house. So when the German fighters were coming back, they were right over our heads, a hundred feet up. There were dog fights were going on overhead.

'On Thursdays, our mother worked in a mobile first aid unit – an old single-decker bus. And after one battle, they went to Croydon. There were a lot of injured – and killed I suppose. The bombing was pretty bad. Our house was hit but not very much. Shrapnel, a dozen big holes.

'Also we were very close to the newly built Caterham bypass, and they were trying to bomb that, and the roundabout was a perfect spot, because all the communications went through there. When the bombing stopped, we went out in the fields behind, with all the bomb holes, and smoke, and we collected bits of bomb. The bombs had hit a gas main the other side of the bypass and that was shooting a forty-foot flame in the air.'

Not long after that, the family joined their father near his clandestine work in the Midlands countryside.

For those who concern themselves today with the security of electronic communications, it is noteworthy that the government had been taking a keen interest in the interception of messages even in the earliest days of radio. 'The Official Secrets Act of 1920 had required all cable operators to supply copies of their traffic to the British Government,' wrote Nigel West, GCHQ chronicler. At the time, this would largely comprise telegraph communications. Any intercepts that were then deemed to be of potential use to the security services were copied and distributed. The mighty company Cable and Wireless, which by the outbreak of the Second World War operated almost half of the cable network crossing the planet, was assiduous in passing material on. Alastair Denniston, the director of Bletchley Park, declared: 'Between us and the companies, there has never been any question as to why we wanted the traffic and what we did with it . . . I have no doubt that the managers and the senior officials must have guessed the true answer but I have never heard of any indiscretions through all these years with so many people involved.'

The shock of the Nazi assault on western Europe was concentrating military minds, especially in the case of the anticipated assault on Britain. In terms of interception, Y Service personnel had already ventured into the field, and across the Channel.

One such officer was Kenneth Maynard, whose ability with wireless technology had already been spotted. Although he has left no diaries, his daughter Alison Trelfa picks up the story of the first part of his extraordinary war: 'My father was an only child and tended most of the time to amuse himself. His main hobby, when a child, was as an amateur radio enthusiast. He spent hours communicating with other enthusiasts from all over the world.

'He was a member of the Radio Society of Great Britain and as such he was extremely proficient at Morse code. He also spoke fluent French and a smattering of other languages. In 1938 the Air Ministry approached the Radio Society of Great Britain to help form a civilian wireless reserve. My father was sent to France in November 1939 and although his service record says that this was as part of the Advanced Air Striking Force I know that he was working in a listening station at this time.

'He was at this time intercepting messages and trying to decrypt those which had been encoded. He served there until the fall of France in May 1940. He used to tell me that he escaped from France on the back of a motorbike, driven by a colleague from the listening station.

'They drove to Dunkirk and were unable to escape so they managed to get to St Nazaire where they got on the last boat,' adds Mrs Trelfa. 'I don't know what happened on the boat but apparently he was terrified. He asked my mother never to ask him about it so she never did. It wasn't until after his death that she told me this part of the story, and how scared he had been.' A few weeks afterwards, Maynard would be posted abroad again, this time to a more exotic, even luxurious environment.

One region of the world about which the British seemed to have done a lot of forward thinking was the Far East. Even in the early months of 1939, the Far East Combined Bureau – which dealt with all cryptographic and wireless matters in the region – was preparing to move out of Hong Kong to the more strategically sensitive region of Singapore. Just a matter of days before the conflict began, the move was completed, although such an upheaval could not come without teething problems. The immediate difficulty was recruiting the extra personnel that would be needed on that side of the world.

The Bureau's Captain F. Wylie recalled that the difficulties involved 'the effect of having to expand during a crisis, train staff and keep abreast of current work – all with a transplanted organisation'. On top of this, he added, there were unexpected physical side-effects suffered by some of the older officers who sailed there from more temperate climates. Mainly because of the ferocious and exhausting heat, 'Retired naval officers so far sent out are not able to stand up to watch-keeping and energetic duties.'

Nonetheless, the successfully transplanted Bureau was joined, in the early days of 1940, by a Special Liaison Unit (SLU) from Bletchley Park. The notion of these units sprang from the nimble brain of Captain Frederick Winterbotham, an MI6 man based at Bletchley who today is equally well known for the fact that he wrote the pioneering book on Ultra (as the top secret intelligence harvested from the Park's codebreaking triumphs was designated). The idea was that Bletchley operatives – quite often officers and sergeants – were specially trained to deal with, and decrypt, much material generated by the Y Service.

'The officers and men of the Special Liaison Units . . . had to learn to study a long silence,' wrote Ronald Lewin. 'In war, this was essential: they carried Ultra in their hands.' He went on to observe how swiftly this branch of intelligence had been deployed. 'In 1940 . . . SLUs were established at the headquarters of Gort's British Expeditionary Force in France . . . to pass on such Ultra as might be available from Bletchley and Vignolles.'[7]

Care was taken that officers were never too senior, for such figures would have attracted attention and speculation. The idea of SLUs was that no one should really know that they were there. As Captain Winterbotham wrote, the Special Liaison Units were to play a crucial role in the Bletchley intelligence operation:

> The SLU officer was responsible for personally delivering the Ultra message to the commander or to a member of his staff designated to receive it. All messages were to be recovered by the SLU officer as soon as they were read and understood. They were then destroyed. No Ultra recipient was allowed to transmit or repeat an Ultra signal. Any action taken by a commander on the information given by Ultra was to be by way of an operation order or command or instruction which in no way referred to the Ultra signal or could lead the enemy to believe that his signals were being read . . . No recipient of Ultra could voluntarily place himself in a position where he could be captured by the enemy.[8]

The role of the Singapore Special Liaison Unit was to closely monitor the movements of the Japanese military. Again, showing some forethought, the Government Code and Cypher School had been working hard on the intricacies of Japanese cryptography; Colonel John Tiltman and senior codebreaker Hugh Foss had been swift to immerse themselves in the challenge, and to impart to others what they found. Of course, as the Singapore station was to find later in the war, forethought is not the same as a crystal ball; but despite subsequent shortcomings in intelligence, it was remarkable that such a bureau was operated so speedily and efficiently. According to historian Peter Elphick, Cable and Wireless was prevailed upon to helpfully tap cables; and very soon, there appeared a platoon of about thirty Wrens, specially trained in certain Japanese uses of Morse.

They could also monitor significant German movements; such

as when the pocket battleship *Graf Spee* sailed from the Atlantic into the area of Madagascar in the Indian Ocean. The HF/DF (high-frequency direction finding) receivers – nicknamed Huff-Duff – were extremely powerful. But hearing the messages was one thing. Correctly interpreting them was quite another.

In the Middle East, the secret listeners were equally swift off the mark. Early in 1940, it had been decided to broaden the listening operation in order to allow decrypts to be relayed directly to officers in the field; to this end, codebreaker Freddie Jacob had been sent to Cairo to open a station that became known as the Combined Bureau Middle East. Jacob helped to set up base in the pleasingly incongruous setting of what had been the Flora and Fauna Museum at Heliopolis, not far from Cairo. Second Lieutenant Donald Shirreff had the job of supervising the erection of the complicated masts nearby, which was carried out by roughly 100 Egyptian workmen.

The mobile arm of the Y Service was soon picking up recruits from a variety of sources. One man selected to work out there was Alison Trelfa's father Kenneth Maynard; after his adventures in France, he was called upon to widen his experience in Cairo.

'By July 1940, Bletchley Park was making progress in reading the new high-grade Army and air-force cyphers and by August, a steady stream of decrypts was reaching Cairo,' states the official Bletchley history. 'BP increased the number of cryptanalysts in Cairo to ensure that as much of the traffic as possible would be read locally.' There had been an encouraging start to the work there too. 'The British had been expecting the Italian attack from Libya into Egypt on 13th September 1940, although the decrypts did not give the actual date. The arrival of Italian air reinforcements in Albania had been revealed by decrypts and so their attack on Greece on 28th October was no surprise.'

The official history is if anything a shade too modest. In that September incursion, Italian troops occupied a strip of coastline, posing an immediate threat both to Alexandria and to the security of the Suez Canal. In the days and weeks following, the work of the codebreakers and the Y Services was an early triumph; they broke into almost all the ciphers used by Italian military formations. The British commanders on the ground were soon apprised of crucial strengths and weaknesses, and were able to exploit them.

By December, the British counter-assault upon Italian forces was launched. In the midst of this, a British field army Y section continued to provide a torrent of successful decrypts from Italian codes, prompting a senior Bletchley Park figure, Nigel de Grey, to describe this as 'a perfect, if rather miniature example of the cryptographer's war'.

It also happened to be a perfect, if rather miniature example of the tensions that existed between the various services and their cryptography operations. After these initial successes, a memo sent out from the Admiralty stated: 'Major Jacob, who is head of Military cryptographers in Cairo and has had twenty years experience in Government Code and Cipher School, should be appointed as head of Bureau . . . he should be authorised to communicate direct with head Government code and cipher school on technical matters connected with cryptography.'

For reasons of security, there was a maze of bureaucracy around the work of Bletchley; if you did not absolutely have to know, then you wouldn't. In this sense, Major Jacob (despite all his years of experience) was honoured. The historian and codebreaking veteran Ralph Bennett was witness to the delicate cat's cradle of responsibility, and how Bletchley Park assumed its own role:

Hut 3 [of Bletchley Park] was suddenly empowered to signal useful intelligence direct to Wavell in Cairo. This was an unprecedented step. Not foreseeing what they were letting escape from their control, it is to be presumed, the War Office and the Air Ministry allowed a Secret Service organisation, hitherto staffed mainly by civilians, to handle operational

intelligence. Who was to judge what the Army and Air Force
in Egypt might find useful, and who was to compose the
signals? Small parties from the two services, closely linked
to the War Office and the Air Ministry by telephone, were
already attached to the translation watch and so the work
naturally fell to them.

Or, more precisely, to Bennett himself:

A new member of the military section, a young Cambridge
don with four months in an Officer Cadet Training Unit as
my sole remotely military experience, my German acquired
during a year's study of medieval history at Munich University
– I was ill-qualified for the task which thus unexpectedly came
my way . . . we (and the other Air and Military Advisers) were
now to be the channel along which passed the intelligence
which was to transform the basis of all operational planning.[9]

A little further down the line, however, and even in the midst
of the desert war there would be a series of spats among those
involved in the work of Heliopolis.

Captain Hugh Skillen was among those who worked in the
field – that is, among the soldiers in the desert – in specially
dedicated units. 'In the field with the "Y" sections . . . [it] was a
male society of four or five score individuals, thrown together for
long periods of two to three years,' he wrote. Moreover, familiar
comforts and diversions supplied to other troops were denied to
these wireless men for much of the time. 'There was no ENSA and
no entertainment at all for them, for security reasons and because
more often than not . . . they were isolated from other military
formations on a high piece of ground in order to obtain good
reception conditions.'

Out in the field, their duties involved an odd mix of claustrophobia and agoraphobia: situated in an empty landscape, yet

cooped up in the backs of specially adapted vehicles, mostly vans – close, cluttered spaces where two or three wireless operators would work at their HRO receivers, headphones clamped on, desks and chairs jammed next to one another. Accommodation for their off-duty hours was scarcely more comfortable: equally cluttered tents.

These spartan souls, added Captain Skillen, had to be resourceful in keeping their morale up. 'Without a book, newspaper or radio they made their own entertainment, finding kindred souls and minds . . . their society becoming an extension of the common room they had vacated . . . with long debates on philosophy and history, religion and art.'[10] All this was in the face of the jeopardy that they had to face – from the 'bomber and the minefield' to 'the scorpion in the tent'. No theatre of war is ever comfortable, but the more cerebral Y Service recruits, some drawn from the cool echoing cloisters of academe to the desert war, had to face an unusually alien and harsh environment.

Back amid the noise and the bustle of the city alleys and market-places, though, the young people sent out to Egypt at the behest of Bletchley – 'extra cryptographic staff will be made available and sent to Cairo as soon as possible' stated a confidential Admiralty memo in 1940 – were also, without knowing it, witnessing the final days of a world that would never be seen again. For these over-whelmingly young recruits, some of whom had never left Britain before, this was the Middle East in all of its rich, dazzling wonder. From the glimpses of the Pyramids in the distance to the hiss of water spray on embassy lawns, from the lazy fat grey flies that had continually to be swatted to the pervasive smell of offal and urine, this in some ways was a meeting place for peoples of the world; and in others, a world of its own.

The Cairo operation also demonstrated the skill and flexibility of Y Service operatives. 'The lesson had been learned the hard way in Belgium and France . . .' wrote Hugh Skillen, 'to have effi-cient and speedy means of transmitting the intelligence to the military commanders and to send back enciphered Enigma to

Bletchley Park by means of SLUs . . . using Type-X machines, similar to Enigma machines but more secure.' Staff were also willing to swap roles between cipher operations when required. Indeed, the entire Heliopolis operation was planned, down to the 'Natives' who would be required to perform other tasks: as a memo from the time suggested, there would be a need for '2 cooks, 2 waiters, 1 labourer and 1 messenger'.[11]

In Britain, meanwhile, the Army had established its chief listening base at Beaumanor Hall in Leicestershire, while the RAF set up its equivalent just a few miles away at Chicksands in Bedfordshire. The main Chicksands building was a handsome Gilbertine priory, founded in 1147 and rumoured to be haunted by countless nuns. It also boasted some fourteenth-century stained glass (which was removed in 1940, to be on the safe side). But the RAF establishment ran into difficulties almost from the start. 'In July 1940,' states a memo in the archives, 'a detachment of about 30 airmen under a flight lieutenant was sent to Chicksands Priory to set up an intercept station . . . At that time, the building was occupied by the Navy under the command of Rear Admiral Millar, and a little later the Army were to send in a detachment and make it an all-services station.'

The result of this, some time later, was apparently a great deal of tension and perhaps even hysteria, especially among the Wrens who were to be posted there. Before that, though, there were other causes of ill will, as another early memo stated:

I have the honour to submit that the question of the organisation of Chicksands Priory should receive attention. At present, this station is shared by the three services. A Paymaster Captain is in command and the staff in the station consists of Naval ratings and Admiralty civilian personnel . . . members of the WRNS, the ATS and the WAAF . . . it is situated in a country district with only small villages in which it is difficult to find billets. At present the billets are extremely over-crowded and 12 of the RAF personnel are sleeping two in a bed, a state of affairs which cannot be continued.[12]

Quite apart from the reluctant bedfellows, the building had to be customised in such a way as not to attract the attention of German bombers. Even so, the complexity of the equipment meant that the place could not help but look rather striking. 'As all of the work had to be carried on in the upper rooms of the Priory,' wrote the careful and anonymous historian, 'masts were erected all round the building and from insulated triatic stays dozens of straight wire aerials of 70 to 100ft in length, conveyed to the upper windows, until the whole must have looked like a large spider web.' Later, there was the addition of a vast – and in its way, aesthetically pleasing – arrangement of masts not far off in the shape of a vast circle.

Elsewhere, on the Yorkshire coast at Scarborough, the naval listening station established long before the war was tuning into shipping signals in the North Sea and beyond. In the weeks after the war ended, its commander wrote for government record purposes a history of the work done there. 'I think it safe to say that before histories were written, there were "Y" services in existence,' he noted wrily. 'I have mentioned the above mainly to indicate that . . . we did appreciate the value of "Y" at sea . . . Training of personnel for those duties was started and built up at Scarborough . . . where approximately 2,500 ratings were trained, including Canadian, American and Polish ratings.'

In keeping with many other wartime establishments, Scarborough had got off to a rather shaky start: back in 1934, in terms of equipment and technology, it was all looking extremely shabby. 'I found on arrival that "Y" was a "Cinderella", the wireless transmission and electrical equipment could only be classed as "junk" and my operators were of the opinion that the material read was destined for the waste paper basket.' His job was to persuade them that their role was absolutely key; as he added drily:

Hitler's accession to power in Germany at this time, [followed by] the Japanese seizure of Manchuria, Mussolini's Abyssinian conquest and the Spanish Civil War indicated the 'Y' was of value.

I doubt if I can find words to appreciate the work and zeal put into this job by the original crew of 25, who took my word that their time was not being wasted and upon their experience and knowledge, a 'Y' personnel ashore and afloat, whose number ran into thousands, was built.[13]

But by the time the war was under way, Scarborough fast picked up a reputation, especially among Wrens, as an attractive posting. Y Service veteran Ray Pelan wrote of the establishment:

A mixture of ratings, Wrens and ACSWs made up the watch – about 60 or 70 . . . The main receiving room . . . was virtually underground in that it was a large rectangular brick and concrete building with a secondary blast wall. The whole thing was sunk halfway below ground level and covered by a mound of grassed earth . . . Constantly ready in the watchroom were two ratings with small attache case-sized boxes, whose task was to seize any urgent (and presumably exploitable) signals and literally run with them . . . to the teleprinters building where Wrens were ready and waiting to signal them to various British and American authorities.[14]

For the young women who found themselves posted here, there was at the very least the distraction of the beautiful coastline and countryside (to say nothing of an occasionally rumbustious nightlife – in a period in which young people seemed disproportionately keen on dancing, Scarborough offered a great many opportunities for lively hops). The work, though, could be appallingly tedious. WAAF Ursula Smith, a Y Service Special Operator, expressed her deep frustrations in wry verse:

> We sit and twiddle our young lives away
> We twiddle all night and we twiddle all day
> They say it's for victory, we wouldn't know
> But search every frequency, high, medium, low
> We fiddle with knobs, adjust Audio Gain
> But somehow we know it will all be in vain
> For do what we will, Activity's nil.

She went on to give an evocative verse account of the gruesome working conditions:

> The wind howls around us, the hut fills with smoke
> Our eyes are red-rimmed, we splutter and choke
> There are things more heroic and valiant by far
> But it's our contribution to winning the war.

There is something poignant about even a verse that is meant to be comic. For part of the tension of the job – and one of the causes of the occasional nervous breakdowns suffered by the operators – was the idea that despite listening to beeps, fast and slow, for hour upon hour, one might hear nothing of consequence.

Added to this were occasional misunderstandings with local people. Mrs Margery Medlock, then a Wren based in Scarborough, remembers her own particular resentment. 'We worked in a three-watch cycle of duty. For the midday watch, two "United" single decker buses could be seen waiting outside of our hotel to transport us to the country. I well recall someone writing to the local newspaper to complain: "Why is it, that at the height of the war, the Wrens, every afternoon enjoy being taken on a picnic?"'

Mrs Medlock's response to this is still salty: 'Some picnic!'

The work was highly concentrated; the women worked '8 hour marathon sessions transmitting coded signals by teleprinter and other machines on a direct line to Bletchley Park. We had special machines for U-Boat and E-Boat bearings, and three Western Union cable lines to the United States.' Yet, despite the up-to-the-minute technology, and in quieter periods, it was difficult during the more humdrum shifts for Mrs Medlock or any of her colleagues to know the precise value of the contribution that they were making. For them, it was a matter of sitting in inhospitable, remote places, and having to concentrate at unholy hours on monotonous signals. They did not even have the solace of listening to voices.

But they were also key when it came to the fast developing art of direction finding. This, in broad terms, was a method by which the positions of U-boats and other vessels could be tracked down via their radio signals; it was a form of triangulation. And the Wrens and others at Scarborough were soon at the centre of the effort. As Y Service veteran and wireless expert Peter Budd now says, they were at the very heart of the conflict:

'Direction finding in the Atlantic was responsible for as many U-boats being sunk as radar – possibly more. Imagine an escort vessel: when it transmits, the signals either go up to the ionosphere, or travel for eighty miles – what we call a ground wave.' Importantly, so too did the signals of a submarine that had surfaced. 'If you were on a frigate escorting the convoy and you heard a U-boat – because you were listening out for it directly – then that U-boat would also be heard from Scarborough.' But for the Huff-Duff operatives, it was a swift, skilled business. A U-boat would – obviously – spend as little time on the surface as possible, and transmit any necessary messages with super-brisk efficiency. In other words, the listeners would have to be fast to get a lock on the vessel's position before it dived back down into the deep. The Allied escort ships and the Scarborough operatives would both get a fix on the U-boat signals bouncing off the ionosphere and between them be able to effectively plot a position.

It wasn't necessary to know the content of the U-boat messages – although for the Scarborough operatives sending this material back to Bletchley, some communications turned out to have terrific value, as they enabled Admiralty to plot direction and progress, thus ensuring that convoys could take evasive action in good time. However, it should also be borne in mind that HF/DF operators were monitoring a vast expanse of the North Sea. Their senses and reactions had to be acute. 'The U-boat starts sending a weather report or convoy sighting report, and if you're a good operator, you can tell from the strength of signal that there's a U-boat on the surface transmitting,' says Mr Budd. Then, 'it's all about accuracy and a race against time.

'And it was the job of those at Scarborough to warn all the shore stations around the country. They developed the ability – via the breaking of Enigma – to be able to tell the Admiralty where the U-boats were going, what their position was.' To take a random example, says Mr Budd, 'the Admiralty would know that four U-boats were going to follow Convoy U81. And they would warn the convoy that there was a wolf pack closing in on them. So the convoy would change direction.'

There was an ironic twist that gave these lethal cat-and-mouse games an edge of even greater jeopardy. 'The Germans had broken the British codes before the war,' says Mr Budd. 'So you'd have the situation of us intercepting the information that the wolf pack was coming – and the convoy changing position as a result – but then the Germans would tell *their* naval HQ that the convoy was changing course. And then our interceptors would hear *that*.' In some cases, a grimly farcical circle developed: the enemy instantly gathered that the Allies had somehow sensed their threat (though, crucially, the Germans did not believe that the Allies had cracked Enigma) and taken evasive action. The messages went back and forth. 'And it went on until Bletchley Park was able to convince the Admiralty that the Germans had broken our codes – something they initially wouldn't believe.'

Because, for ordinary recruits, the absence of information or feedback made the work all the harder, the commanding officers of some stations shrewdly used a mix of psychology and humour to lighten the atmosphere. Anne Stuttford recalled of the Forest Moor station in Yorkshire: 'Our lieutenant, Hancock was his name, fashioned a medal. It was a hideous thing made of cardboard with red squiggles on it and a red ribbon. As one of us found a missing group [lost frequencies], so the medal was stuck on her [radio] set. So fierce was the competition for this medal, it could have been made of solid gold . . . I wonder if Hancock realised what a clever ploy that was, so many spirits kept up by a small circle of cardboard.'

But at Beaumanor Hall (the courtyard of the nineteenth-century house was adorned, bizarrely, with a ship's figurehead depicting Admiral Cornwallis, which had for some reason been transported there all the way from Chatham Docks), the young women and men were slipping into a way of life that, although free of immediate hazard, put its own pressures on morale.

For those of a slightly more sophisticated background arriving from London – even a London completely blacked out – there was a dread that the provincial acres of Leicestershire would prove unendurably dreary. One officer in a letter to his wife expressed the forlorn hope that there would at least be 'a billiard table'. His arrival late at night surprisingly provided a lift to his morale after he ingested a quantity of tomato and pilchard sandwiches, coffee and two whiskies. Then, taking in the house, decorated in what he considered questionable taste, he began to see the possibilities for fun; and that even though the duties would be intense and focused – with several cryptography officers setting up their operations base in an antique bathroom, with a board across the bath – the property itself held out some possibilities of country-house party pursuits such as tennis.

For a serious young man like Chris Barnes, brought up in Kent and having been given months of Morse and wireless training at Fort Bridgewood (a base near the Royal Dockyard at Chatham), Beaumanor was not an immediately attractive proposition, even though he found that he had been posted there with a great many other intelligent young chaps from his part of the world, apparently gathered in with terrific zeal by a Kent educational committee. 'We were mainly from Chatham, Rochester, Gillingham and Maidstone. I was a little bit further out at Sittingbourne . . . There were quite a lot of older people at Beaumanor when we got there, they'd worked before in Chatham and Chicksands and also the Post Office. So when we – a younger lot – came in, there was quite a sharp age gap. And there were very much senior ones in charge.'

But the wartime Midlands lacked a certain something. 'I found myself dumped in Loughborough, which was not the most cheering of places,' says Mr Barnes with a small laugh. 'In those days, it was a bit run down – it had been a bell foundry place that had gone over to munitions during the war, and for me, it was a bit of a shock after coming from rural Kent.' Happier amid bucolic tranquillity, Mr Barnes set about fixing the situation. 'Soon after that, I moved to Woodhouse Eaves. I've always preferred living in villages. And immediately started on shift work.'

There was no breathing space, and the rotas were unforgiving. 'It was intense. You sat down at a receiver, with a pad in front of you, and you struggled to hear the often very weak signals. Which were then fed to Station X.' This was the shorthand intelligence term widely used for Bletchley Park (though the actual Station X was in reality a tiny MI6 radio room in the house's attic, next to the water tank). 'We didn't know anything about Bletchley Park at that time,' says Mr Barnes. 'And you struggled to read these messages. You vaguely knew where they were coming from but you didn't know what they were about at all.

'You were normally given the frequency because you were watching specific tasks. Some people on each watch were trying to find them, but most of them were specifically listening to targets that they knew would come up at certain times. The most important thing we tracked was the U-boats . . . I think we knew that they were U-boats, but we didn't realise the importance of it.'

They also listened in on 'military structures in France and on the Russian front'.

'It was straightforward, but it was arduous, and required patience and perseverance. The main problem was interference. Artificial noise, and sometimes deliberate noise, because the Germans jammed the signals.'

Mr Barnes's need to live somewhere other than a grey, nondescript town went rather further than aesthetic fastidiousness; he badly needed a strong contrast in his leisure hours in order for him to be able to shake off the work and to rest properly. The village of Woodhouse Eaves certainly had the tranquillity he was looking for, not to mention a homely little pub to which he and his great friend Ted Sandy would repair, making pints last for hours, much to the vexation of the landlord. Indeed, the only real drawback of the place was that Messrs Barnes and Sandy were not popular with the locals; because their work was highly secret, they could not breathe a word even to their landlady about their role. As a result, the villagers merely saw a pair of able-bodied young men not in uniform, and seemingly without any adequate explanation for this state of affairs.

'They didn't like us much,' says Mr Barnes. 'They thought we ought to have been in uniform. Our landlady didn't like Ted and me much anyway. There must have been some compulsory billeting going on in that area simply because there were so many of us. And the villagers as a whole: you had to keep very quiet. The secrecy was just as tight as it was at Bletchley Park.'

There were obvious consolations, though, especially for a keen walker such as Mr Barnes. 'It was lovely country. You never think of Leicestershire as being a very beautiful county but round the Charnwood Forest, it was.'

In a wider sense, another dread for Beaumanor operatives, in common with other listeners around the country, was the irregularity of the work itself. Even though the hours were absolutely rigid, the radio traffic fluctuated and on some days and nights there would not be much to listen in to. 'Repetitive Strain Injury had not at that time been discovered,' wrote Maurice de la Bertauche. 'On many occasions, one might spend the whole eight hour watch doing absolutely nothing except searching on a specific frequency.' He recorded a rueful poem on the subject:

> They also serve who sit and wait
> I serve, my trousers shine like plate.

'Night duty was tolerable if one was busy,' he added, 'but interminable if there was no wireless activity . . . occasionally, a sadistic, childish trick was played upon any [wireless operator] who dozed off. Some diabolical fiend – probably one of the younger members – would withdraw his headphone jack, plug in his own headset, and search around to locate some insufferable signal, preferably a noisy teleprinter.' The jack would then be half-replaced and the set volume wound up to maximum. The prankster would wake the victim – who would be in such a panic that he would swivel round, wonder about the noise on his headset and plug the jack in properly. Then he would 'spend the rest of his shift scraping his brain off the ceiling and walls', added de la Bertauche with unkind relish.[15]

Joan Nicholls's experiences on the quieter shifts at Beaumanor tended more towards the caring and sharing. 'We used to play noughts and crosses, do crosswords, tell our life stories, and plan our futures; and some who were particularly naive would be told the facts of life, especially when marriage was looming.'[16] Such talks, however, had to be held with a close eye on the door. Anyone caught gossiping on duty would be severely reprimanded.

Rene Pederson also remembered the Herculean efforts necessary to stay awake during Beaumanor's quieter shifts. 'The night duty was a devil as very often we had not had much sleep before midnight and sometimes had in fact been out on the town in the evening,' she recalled with admirable candour. 'I think we all smoked. I can remember burning my elbow to keep awake once at least.'

Arriving at Beaumanor at a rather more senior level in 1940 was Hugh Skillen, who had already been through military training at Sandhurst and inducted into the world of intelligence. 'I was sent to see Major Crankshaw who was to become an authority on Russian affairs after the war,' wrote Skillen (indeed, Edward Crankshaw gained invaluable experience of Soviet affairs when in 1942, he spent weeks in Moscow negotiating with paranoid military officers about the sharing of certain aspects of Y work; after the war, he wrote books on Russian history). 'He told me nothing about the work I would be engaged in, apart from making it appear quite mysterious, and he accepted me for training in the Y service.' Skillen's introduction to the service, as it turned out, was brilliantly, Britishly comic.

He was first posted to No. 1 Special Wireless Group at Harpenden. 'I was to be met by a black car at a railway station . . . but for some reason, probably the train running late, there was no black car when I arrived and I had to go to the postmaster at Harpenden to ask for a secret location as I had only PO Box No. R100 as a reference.' Happily, the postmaster was perfectly well aware of the top secret location in question. It was Rothamstead Manor, and it was here that Skillen was acquainted with the 'Y Handbook', in which, as he said, 'I felt considerably lost.' After this came his transfer to Beaumanor.

It was still early days, and the place was a little on the quiet side. 'The big house was empty and a lone teleprinter chattered away from time to time with no operator in sight.' In a moment of boredom, Skillen 'sat down at the keyboard of the teleprinter wondering if it was connected at the other end. There must have been someone on duty at the other end because when I began to type "the quick brown fox" . . . the typist at the other end began a conversation with me. This was my first acquaintance with a teleprinter and I used to practise for a few minutes each evening . . . and the operator would chip in again at the other end.'[17]

Not long after, Skillen was transferred to nearby Chicksands Priory, where he was to fall in with some startling and colourful company.

5 The Blitz and the Ghost Voices

For a young Voluntary Interceptor like Ray Fautley, the Blitz was not merely a time of terrific apprehension; it was utterly exhausting. Throughout this period, there was an unspoken expectation that life simply had to stumble on, as normally as one could manage. So young Fautley's nocturnal VI duties continued, even as the bombs were falling from the night sky. Yet it is striking that it would not have occurred to Fautley to do otherwise, and this was not for reasons of virtue. For him, as for everyone else, such things passed beyond a conscious sense of duty and somehow became ingrained, second nature.

And there was one day – rather than night – in which Fautley was extraordinarily lucky to escape with his life. He was now employed at the Philips radio factory in Balham, a few miles south of Westminster. 'I was in the canteen – I was doing a bit of fault finding on the R107, an army receiver,' he recalls, quite cheerfully. 'I was sitting there, working and having my lunch about midday. No air-raid siren noise or anything – yet the next thing I knew, I was lying flat on top of a young lady.

'I was covered in plaster dust, brick dust, broken glass and money. What had happened? A small bomb had landed only fifteen feet from me. Luckily for me, there was a brick wall between. On the other side of the wall was the drawing office, and it killed two draughtsmen outright. The blast took me off my seat and smashed me right through the glass kiosk where the girl was taking the money. I finished on top of her.'

Luxuries such as dignity were in short supply during the Blitz. 'It was a bit frightening,' Mr Fautley says drily. 'After we stopped coughing and the dust settled, we searched around and found what money we could and put it in a tin. It was a mess. And then – back to work. From one till six! No counselling or anything in those days; it was just a bomb. Everyone had bombs.

'We both got up and dusted each other down and felt all right, nothing broken, all OK.'

But the postscript illustrates vividly what urban populations were expected to live through during that time without complaint.

'I got back home – I was living in North Cheam then, tube from Balham to Morden, then got a bus – and when I got in, my mother took one look at me and said: "You're filthy! What have you been doing?"

'I said, "Oh, we had a bomb at work."

'And she said, "Oh, you'd better go and have a bath. You look awful."

'I got my five inches of water, because that's all we were allowed during the war. I started to undress and I got a nasty shock – my underclothes were soaked in blood – mine. It was very frightening. It had all dried. There were lacerations everywhere. I hadn't noticed anything because I had a jacket on.

'Every item of clothing I wore that day ended up having to be destroyed. They all had fragments of glass in them, even the shoes. After all this, I got in the bath, and thought to myself: "What's that in my back?" I shouted to my mum, asked her to come and have a look and see what was wrong. She came in and said "You've got chunks of glass sticking in your back."'

With a practicality that some might now find rather gruesome, Mother took direct action. 'She pulled these chunks of glass out and I screamed – because boy, did that hurt. She got six bits of glass out of my back. With muscley bits. It bled when she pulled these fragments out. Frightening, the way it might have gone. But I didn't bother going to the doctor. It all healed up, I heal quickly . . . I had never felt it before because I was leaning forward when working.'

Mr Fautley was young; and he had both a sense of obligation and a burning love for the role that he had been assigned. So, as the raids continued, his work tuning into those faint German frequencies went on. Yet, he insists, there was nothing unusual about that – the miracle of the capital was that everyone kept trudging on, as though the bombs were little more than a trifling inconvenience.

'London was burning, every night. Yet the post office was still able to deliver. They wouldn't now. Everybody was working. They wanted an end to this blessed war. Some were saying it would be over by Christmas 1939. Of course it wasn't. I used to go out to Croydon Airport to watch the dog-fights, the Spitfires. And then if you saw something falling, you ran. Looking back, I realise now how unique the situation was.'

Unique, and galvanising too. Early in the evening on which the London Blitz had begun – 7 September 1940 – future wireless operator Betty White was at the Holborn Empire, watching comedian Max Miller perform; for some reason, either those inside failed to hear the air-raid warning, or it simply did not get through. Seventeen-year-old Betty and her companions were aware of some noise, but, as she says now, 'we thought it was distant thunder.' It was only when everyone emerged from the theatre and heard the terrible sound, some five miles east, of the old docks being bombed, that they realised what it was.

At that time, Betty was working in the civil service and was obliged to continue to do so even as her office was evacuated to the seaside resort of Bournemouth in Dorset. Eventually, though, in the face of the relentless onslaught – not just the bombs in London, which saw her parents' house flattened (her parents, miraculously, survived) and a tram on which Betty was travelling 'clipped' and tipped over, but also the unexpected fighter attacks on Bournemouth – Betty and her sister became desperate to join up. 'I volunteered for the Army,' she says. 'I was told, no, they're not taking anyone. So then I took an IQ test for a place with the air force.' But the authorities looked at the impressive result of the test and instantly decided on a different course for Betty, especially when she answered in the cautious affirmative to the question: 'Can you stay awake all night?'

Another crucial factor was that Betty's brother had, a couple of years back, taught his little sister Morse code. It was clear where Betty White was needed most.

In Caterham, Surrey, young Geoffrey Pidgeon and his brother had watched the Battle of Britain being fought above their heads; but one particular day, when a local airfield was bombed, settled the matter as far as their father was concerned. Having himself been drawn into the secret wireless world at Whaddon Hall in Buckinghamshire, he was determined that his family should join him, even though the billeting space in Stony Stratford was uncomfortably tight.

After a journey from London crammed into a car, the family were introduced to their new hosts. 'We were all packed up with the Crows. The Crows said, "Your bedroom is a big one, Mr Pidgeon. You have to have you and Mrs Pidgeon in the big bed, and your three boys on the floor."

'So there were five of us in one room. And we stayed there – I think we were only moved out around the time of the Coventry raid. Because thanks to the successes with Enigma, and the Bletchley recruitment, the area was filling up like wildfire. Billeting was jammed all round the town. You couldn't get a hotel, you couldn't get in a billetor's home.' But finally came a rare opportunity. 'Joyce

Crow worked for a builder – Cowley and Sons – and they had just refurbished a flat over a butcher's shop in Stony Stratford High Street,' says Mr Pidgeon. 'It was supposed to be for Mrs Canvin, the butcher's wife. But she didn't like it. So it was given to us. Thirty bob a week, I think it was.

'It was fantastic! Mother and father had a room. Older brother had his own room, and younger brother Trevor and I had a room. And there was a lounge and a kitchen/dining room. So – how lucky we felt, when everyone else was crammed, doubled up. We got moved into somewhere that was almost palatial.'

But the move away from Caterham public school was also to change the gravitational pull of Geoffrey Pidgeon's life, bringing it closer to the exquisite intricacies of the secret work of Whaddon Hall.

The Blitz was, for others too, a very effective catalyst. It propelled a sixteen-year-old GPO telegraphist, Robert Hughes, into the war. He was too young to be conscripted but the nightmarish destruction all around led him to request 'early call-up'.

Mr Hughes had left school at fourteen and gone to work for the Post Office; this gave him a skilled grounding in the science of wireless telegraphy. He lived with his family in London near the City Road, Islington, a district that was particularly badly hit. 'The bombing there was horrendous,' he says with feeling. 'At one stage around that time, I had a goitre, a great lump on my throat, and I had to go to Barts Hospital.' This was situated near St Paul's Cathedral. 'My ward was three floors up. One night there was a tremendous air raid. The staff pulled our beds away from the walls. The beds were bouncing with the bombing. Next day I just walked out, went walking round the City.' It was a kind of aftershock. 'My father came to visit the hospital, saw the empty bed . . . well, they couldn't find me anywhere. That bombing went on every night for six months.'

Despite the trauma being inflicted upon both the city and its inhabitants, there was a genuine effort to keep things moving as normally as possible. But the nightly onslaughts also triggered a potent blend of rage and helplessness, as young Hughes and his colleagues were expected to operate in the Stygian darkness of unlit winter evening streets, the bombers like angry hornets above their heads.

'There were bombs all night but we had to go to work all day,' he adds. 'In the post office, we worked eight in the morning till eight at night, twelve-hour days, delivering government telegrams. And you'd go out in a complete blackout. They never gave us torches. We knew the streets but we didn't know the numbers. It was pretty intense.'

This led to his request to join up immediately. It was granted. And this young man who had scarcely even left London was soon to find himself sent off to the Mediterranean, not only to experience a world more vivid than even those he had seen on the cinema screen but to live a life that could be as hilarious as it was hair-raising. It all started prosaically enough, however, within the grounds of Butlins holiday camp in Skegness, where he and hundreds of other young lads were sent for their basic military training. After intelligence tests, Mr Hughes was marked out to be a Special Wireless Operator. He had originally put in for a naval position. And here it was.

Then, after a transfer to the more intensive and technical training centres in Brighton and Eastbourne, came the harder months: the focused learning of Morse. 'We were trained for very high speeds – twenty-eight words per minute,' says Mr Hughes. 'The original intention was that they were going to recruit men thirty years old or thereabouts to be Special Operators – but they found that they couldn't hold the high speed for any length of time. Because the brain's not so adaptable or flexible as it is with eighteen-year-olds.' In fact, he arrived in Alexandria in Egypt to find a couple of the older operators still there. 'They must have discovered after the first influx that they would be better trying out younger men. Twenty-eight words per minute is quite a speed. And obviously,' Mr Hughes adds drily, 'you couldn't ask the German operator for a repeat of the message.'

On the south coast at Hawkinge, the relentless autumn campaign of bombing was also having a profound effect on personnel. Aileen Clayton recalled:

> During the long and busy winter of the Blitz, I became so weary that the time eventually came when I had to ask my doctor to prescribe Benzedrine to keep me awake while on watch and sleeping pills to knock me out if and when I did get a chance to rest. Living as I did mainly on a diet of black coffee and cocoa, the dark circles under my eyes made me look like a panda bear and yet I hated to go to my billet in case I missed any of the action.

And, as she recorded, the intensity of the situation understand-ably took its toll on other officers:

> One day, when the bombing and the shelling had been rather noisier than usual, one of the men in the unit cracked under the strain. I was senior WAAF on duty . . . and I could see that one or two of the girls were already on the verge of tears. Lack of sleep and the constant bombing were beginning to tell, and I could feel that hysteria was not far off. I had to act quickly, and so for the first time in my life, I slapped a man across the face hard, and several times. It had the desired effect. Unfortunately the hysterical man was my senior in rank.[1]

The Blitz throughout the autumn of 1940 was spreading to every major port and city in Britain. Though London received the heaviest bombardment, cities such as Southampton and Plymouth were also subjected to horrific damage, possibly intensified because they were very much smaller than the capital.

'I was posted to Plymouth with six or eight others to operate a teleprinting room in the naval fort at Egg Buckland . . .' wrote Wren Imogen Ryan, 'we spent a certain amount of time chatting to our friends in other teleprinting rooms scattered along the English coast, chatting to the people in the plotting room next door to ours, doing the Times crossword.' But this amiable atmosphere soon gave way to something rather sharper. As Ryan recalled with a certain wryness: 'Air raids began in Plymouth a few days after we arrived and made life frightening and uncomfortable for a bit. As our quarters on the Hoe were uninhabitable, we were told to find our own digs where we could, and this did lead to enlarging one's experiences quite a bit. I, for one, had never met an alcoholic before, and found it quite alarming.'[2]

Others were equally matter-of-fact about the risks. Fellow Plymouth Wren Jean Campden recalled:

Among out-standing incidents would come being bombed out of our quarters . . . the night before I was due to be posted to Dover. It happened in the middle of the night, there was a fearful noise, the building shook, plaster and bits of glass flew around and we were ordered out into the road where there was an enormous crater where a bomb had landed . . . I proceeded to Dover the following day where I found my suitcase full of fragments of glass lurking among my clothes, also that I had picked up an appalling cold from standing about in my night-attire the previous night.[3]

For Ray Fautley, tirelessly tuning in from the front room of his parents' house in south London, there was another sort of hazard to be faced than falling bombs: that of other people misunderstanding exactly what he was doing. 'My listening period was usually from 8 p.m. to 10 p.m. for four or five nights every week, and so I told my girlfriend, Barbara, that it would be best if we only met at weekends. That didn't go down very well at all because I wasn't allowed to tell her why.

'Even so, one Wednesday evening, Barbara called at my house with one of her girlfriends, and my parents foolishly let them in.' It should be recalled that even though Mr Fautley's parents had had a brief chat with the bowler-hatted man from the Radio Security Service, they still did not know exactly what their son was listening in to. And when the young women walked into that front parlour and saw Mr Fautley crouched over the half-concealed wireless set, jammed into the bureau, they immediately leapt to a terrible conclusion . . .

'I was concentrating on writing down what I was receiving,' says Mr Fautley, 'and then they came in. I don't know who was most shocked – the girls or me! I babbled that I was doing some tests at home for Marconi's, but the look on their faces indicated that they didn't really believe a word of it. My girlfriend clearly thought that I was a spy!' Indeed, so convinced was she that she immediately took her friend, dashed out of the front room and out of the house up the street. Mr Fautley was obliged to give chase. 'I had to stop her because I knew she was looking for a policeman. But even then, I still couldn't tell her what it was that I was doing. Well, what could I say? Many, many years later – when Barbara was my wife – I was finally able to tell her what I had actually been doing.'

Ironically, though, Barbara might have found out much sooner had she paid close attention to the *Daily Mirror*, which during the Blitz inadvertently gave the game away about the Voluntary Interceptors on its front page. Given the well-worn maxim 'careless talk costs lives' – plus the need for absolute secrecy when it came to monitoring messages delivered via the Enigma code – this clumsy and inadvertent breach of security was astounding.

'Spies Tap Nazi Code' screamed the *Mirror*'s 1940 headline, with the byline 'By a special correspondent'. 'Britain's radio spies are at work every night,' declared the article. 'During the day, they work in factories, shops and offices. Colleagues wonder why they never go to cinemas or dances. But questions are parried with a smile – and silence. Their job isn't one to be talked about.' Except by the *Daily Mirror*, it seemed. The 'correspondent' added: 'Home from work, a quick meal, and the hush-hush men unlock the door of a room usually at the top of the house. There, until the small hours, they sit, head-phones on ears, taking down the Morse code messages that fill the air.'

One such volunteer helpfully provided a quote concerning the expressions of gratitude he received from his secret headquarters. And astonishingly – given the extreme lengths to which Bletchley Park had gone to keep the nature of its work secret – the volunteer seemed quite happy to burble on: 'Naturally we have no idea of the codes used by German agents. But it is a great thrill to feel you might be getting down a message which, decoded, might prove of supreme importance.' According to Nigel West, this colossal security blunder caused 'tremendous agitation at Bletchley'.

Unsurprisingly so. By this stage, Bletchley Park codebreakers had made substantial headway into the seemingly impossible task of taking the Enigma codes apart. But if the Germans – who considered Enigma completely unbreakable – were ever to learn of this triumph, they would instantly increase the complexity of their encryptions, sending the codebreakers back to the very start. The repercussions would be incalculable.

The story is just one illustration of why there was anxiety among so many codebreakers and wireless operatives that matters of the gravest secrecy might be blurted out by accident. As the *Daily Mirror* had proved, it was all too easy to do. A later memo, sent out by Bletchley's director Edward Travis to personnel in all stations, stated:

It would be a reflection on your intelligence to suppose that you do not realise that spies may, and indeed do, exist in this country; and that an idle piece of boasting or gossip on the part of any one of you may reach circles outside of your control whence it may be passed to the enemy and cause, not only the breakdown of our successful efforts here, but the sacrifice of the lives of our sailors, soldiers and airmen, perhaps your own brothers, and may even prejudice our ultimate hope of victory.

Travis cited a couple of examples that had recently been brought to his attention; instances when the gossipers in question were lucky not to find themselves facing criminal charges and had only avoided doing so thanks to his personal intervention. One woman 'employed in responsible duties disclosed their nature within her family circle, thinking no doubt that the secret was safe there . . . What she had disclosed in the family circle was repeated by one of its members in mixed company, actually at a cocktail party, whence it was duly reported to me.' And though she and other transgressors escaped prison, the stress 'and humiliation to which these proceedings will have subjected them and their families, no less than the realisation of the dangers to which they have exposed their country will no doubt be some, if not equal, punishment'.[4]

As to Travis's dark warnings of spies being at work in Britain, this was the assumption within the War Office even before the war had begun, and the Radio Security Service throughout had been diligently seeking out any such elements. As it would later transpire, the department attended to this job with great success, although there were never quite as many spies as Whitehall had feared. Indeed, there appear to have been more agents passing information to the Soviets at that stage than to the Nazis.

Nonetheless, tremendous care was required and the Official Secrets Act applied universally across the Y Service; for even though the Germans would of course understand that the Allies were working to the very highest standards of wireless interception, they would be sufficiently confident in the complexity of their codes to keep up an unrestrained flow of traffic. So while they knew the messages were being picked up, the Nazis continued to believe that any communication encoded through Enigma would remain unreadable.

The secrecy was almost glamorous for those who worked at Bletchley Park; it was less so for those who worked in the out-stations. This was particularly the case for the young women who listened in to encoded Morse messages from aircraft and shipping, and whose role was simply to send on these random jumbles without any proper idea of their significance. It was difficult for some to feel motivated, since on the face of it, they seemed to be little more than invisible cogs.

This may well have been one of the factors that were to lead to so many upsets at RAF Chicksands as the war progressed: a combination of the monotone, anonymous nature of the work, and the fact that the women could release none of that pent-up frustration because they were forbidden to discuss what they were doing. For Hugh Skillen, though, the atmosphere in the earlier days at Chicksands seemed more conducive than other places he had passed through, including Beaumanor. Chicksands Priory was, he wrote, 'a delightful old house' with a dining room from which an old carp pond could be seen. 'The legend was that carp had been there for centuries since the time of the monks.'

Skillen was rather taken with the small officers' mess. 'There was a fine table at which a dozen could have been seated very comfortably but we were usually four in number at lunch or dinner. At the head of the table was a Rear-Admiral or some very senior naval rank . . . opposite me was a young, very attractive Wren officer, who was [the Rear-Admiral's] secretary or aide-de-camp.'

There was also a figure who would later go on to find global notoriety in the Cold War. 'On my right was a handsome debonair lieutenant in the Intelligence Corps: Guy Burgess. After dinner, we sometimes played darts in the mess, Burgess and I with the Wren, and Burgess and I would go to a pub in the evening for a quiet drink.'

Those drinks took place on days off. Skillen's colleagues, though, would endeavour to make his lonely nocturnal tasks a little more bearable. 'When I was Night Duty Officer, the butler would place a plate of beef sandwiches on my desk covered with a silver tureen. But I was to be disappointed more than once to find that [Major Jolowicz] had given them to his Alsatian. At any rate, there were only a few crumbs left on the plate.'[5]

A number of wireless operatives and Auxiliary Territorial Service girls (the ATS was the women's voluntary army, the equivalent of Wrens and WAAFs) found a sometimes attractive element of chaos at Chicksands. The historic nature of the building had – when they considered their work – a pleasing incongruity. 'The Priory – its quiet and peacefulness – the formidable figures that parade its corridors, rings around their arms and under their eyes,' wrote an ATS satirist in a staff magazine. The anonymous comedian continued:

> Legend has it that a nun, who did what none should have done, wanders through the grounds in the not-so-still of the night. I understand she didn't live long enough to become a Mother Superior . . . I doubt whether our presence within its walls will go down in history, yet surely history has been made for I cannot recall having heard where the two women's services [the ATS and the WAAF] have worked in such close co-operation. Many thought it impossible, but the age of miracles is not past, and women do not have their claws out all the time.

The modern world had caught up with the Priory: 'There were long aerials stretching for hundreds of yards in the direction of Libya and Egypt,' wrote Skillen. There was also a growing card index, slightly less innovative, though no less effective. But tension

had begun to boil in Hut 6 of Bletchley Park over the quality of
the material being sent from Chicksands. A memo in the archives
from August 1940 points up 'the new and relatively inexperienced
Air Force station at Chicksands', going on to underline acidly:

> We have compared the actual decoded messages taken both
> by Chatham and Chicksands on the same day and we find
> that Chicksands made in all from two to three times the
> number of errors made by Chatham . . . Moreover, the more
> coarsely graduated dials used on the Chicksands sets impose
> an additional handicap on their operators, making it difficult
> for them to distinguish between different groups, and also
> making them more liable to imagine different groups when
> in fact only one is concerned.

It wasn't just a matter of airwaves filled with different code
groups from multiple branches of the German war machine.
Apparently small matters such as the dials were actually crucial,
for various reasons. For instance, on the popular American HRO
receivers, which came to be used throughout the Y Service, the
dials were intricately and exquisitely engineered along with the
radio's other complex components – a labyrinth of 'spring-loaded
split-gears' and other tiny parts. The result of this was pinpoint
dial accuracy, especially vital if an operator had subsequently to
find the same frequencies again. And it went beyond a merely
technical issue. The work was already demanding enough: in an
already pressurised atmosphere, the damage to morale caused by
having to work with equipment that was not up to the job could
have been crushing.

A little later, Group Captain John Shepherd, who had just
returned from Africa suffering from yellow fever, was told that
he had inherited command of Chicksands. The prospect was
painted for him in bright colours; he was told by a friend at the
Air Ministry: 'It's a diverting job with 2,000 acres of shooting.'

Chicksands monitored Luftwaffe signals from north Africa and much of Europe and, a little later, the Russian front; it also transmitted messages – disguised in the form of sonnets or even simple greetings – to Allied secret agents working in France. So the complexity of its work could not be underestimated.

But Captain Shepherd wasn't told of a vast reorganisation which was turning the place upside down and creating tremendous ill will. As he was to recall:

> Colin [his friend] had not told me that an embryo operation there already had to be expanded something like ten times by the day before yesterday . . . we built a camp for airmen – and airwomen – and a technical site to replace the spooky old Priory, and we trained a thousand or so wireless operators to provide Bletchley with some of the enormous mass of German Air Force high-grade ciphers.[6]

One did not have to have supernatural foresight to anticipate that there might be personnel problems. A number of the WAAF recruits trained and sent to Chicksands were as young as seventeen; many had never before lived away from home, and the initial conditions were at best primitive. 'At first they had to share billeting, ablution and latrine arrangements with the men until two self-contained and separate living camps were constructed,' wrote Hugh Skillen.

Among all staff, the paramount need for accuracy – whatever the state of the Chicksands equipment, or indeed the state of morale – was not some matter of abstract perfectionism; lives depended upon it. As Skillen wrote:

> Even far removed from the battlefield, many suffered from stress because of the exacting and precise nature of their duties. While an Intelligence Officer in the field might have a recurring nightmare that he had missed an enemy

tank strength – a routine report of prime value to the
Allied commander . . . the wireless operator suffered from
nightmares that he had slept in, had been late reporting for
duty, or had missed his rendezvous with his opposite number
on the Morse key on the enemy side . . .[7]

But equally, these nightmares were not in vain. In May 1941, the
staff of Chicksands played a key role in the symbolically momentous
sinking of the German battleship *Bismarck*. After a lengthy cat-and-
mouse pursuit in the freezing waters of the Atlantic, the ship's
captain, Admiral Lutjens, broke radio silence on the morning of
25 May. It was the listeners at RAF Chicksands who picked up this
crucial transmission. And it was from this that, ultimately, it became
possible to deduce in which direction the vessel was heading.
The desperate pursuit continued, and the *Bismarck* once or twice
managed to swerve past the British vessels. But by the morning of
27 May, the British – who, after the Chicksands transmission, had
never quite lost the battleship's position – closed in and delivered
the final blow.

RAF Chicksands is not alone in being able to claim credit; for
according to wireless veteran Peter Budd, whose own war consisted
of tracking Japanese submarines, the young women based in the
station at Scarborough were also instrumental in running the great
vessel down, and indeed, might have got there before everyone
else, were it not – avers Peter Budd – for blunders made higher up
with the information that they had provided.

'They had *Bismarck* on radar. They knew exactly where she
was, they were shadowing her,' Mr Budd says. 'But then they'd
lost her. No one knew where she was. Then the admiral in charge
of the *Bismarck* broke radio silence for an hour to send messages
back to Berlin and everywhere. Can you imagine those operators
in Scarborough – fifty of them who normally get just seconds to
hear any kind of message from a German vessel – hear someone
transmitting plain language? All the direction finding stations

around the Atlantic – Britain, Iceland, Newfoundland, Ascension Island, west Africa . . . attained perfect positions.

'Scarborough sent this information to the Admiralty, the Admiralty sent it to the Commander in Chief on HMS *Anderson* Home Fleet. The position was apparently given to an RN's navigating officer – and then he transposed it on the wrong chart, 200 miles north of where it was. The whole home fleet turned around and steamed away from the *Bismarck*. I've always wanted to know what happened to that bloke. The most perfect fix that had ever been given to anyone.' Not that anyone at the Scarborough base could have known. In contrast to Chicksands, life there continued as amiably and high-spiritedly as it had done before.

Some miles away, the listening station of Beaumanor, part of the War Office Y Service, was developing its own distinct character as a community. 'Much of this must have stemmed from the isolation brought about by the inability to talk about their work, even to spouses or close relatives,' recalled veteran Philip Blenkinsop. 'It is also apparent that the mixture of social backgrounds contributed to the atmosphere of the place. Equally clear,' he added tartly, 'is that the quality of intellect was considerably above that of a conventional military unit . . . largely because of the need for technical skills.'

'The personnel [to begin with] were male civilians,' wrote Hugh Skillen, 'radio operators recruited from the Royal Navy, the Merchant Navy and the Post Office . . . If he possessed the necessary skills, [an operator] would be rewarded at the rate of 80/- per week . . . and then by annual increments to 96/- as an Experimental Wireless Assistant.'

Because of the War Office designation, Beaumanor became referred to as War Office Y Group or – in one of those acronyms so beloved by the military – WOYG. The staff knew themselves as 'Woygites'. 'Other terms in common use at the time,' recalled Blenkinsop, 'included "Beaumaniacs" and "Manor Beaus" for some of the more dashing male members.'

There were three types of Woygites. First there was the Army. Then there were the 'Hard-Cores', or Experimental Wireless Assistants, dressed in civilian clothes – despite being part of the forces – and billeted in and around the local villages. A few single operators found accommodation in the old manor itself.

Finally, as the establishment grew, ATS girls were drafted in and billeted en masse in several large houses around the area. Two such young ladies were Mrs Gladys Earle and her sister Hazel Webbe, who received their initial ATS training in 1940 in the Butlins Ocean Hotel in Sussex. They were both asked by the authorities if they had ever seen a typewriter. When both answered in the affirmative, they were told that this made them 'born teleprinter operators'. The first time they actually clapped eyes on such a thing was at the next stage of training in Chatham.

Judging by the more exuberant magazines and newsletters that they managed to put out, this mix of people proved from the start to be both lively and cheerfully cynical. Like their intellectual counterparts at Bletchley Park, the team at Beaumanor had a music society, staged their own concerts, and even had their own version of the Proms. And again like Bletchley, the manor house found an alternative use on a regular basis as a ballroom dancing venue.

But all this was vital, says Beaumanor wireless veteran Chris Barnes (himself a civilian there), because otherwise the intense nature of the work could have had a corrosive effect: 'You had to relax – you had to shut it off completely.' First of all, this meant going straight home to bed after a shift to ensure proper sleep. The rest of the time, it was very important to get involved socially.

'The other activities that you did formed an important part of contrasting with the work,' Mr Barnes says. 'There was a rambling club. There was a cycling club. There was music appreciation, which definitely introduced me to classical music.' The latter society was run by musician Harry Dodd, himself a 'Woygite', and Mr Barnes has fond memories of both Dodd and his music appreciation group. There were 'not very many members, probably only about 20, but that included a number of lifelong friends that I made.' Each meeting would start off 'with a chap introducing the piece' – the music that they were to listen to and discuss at that session – then 'playing it on an old record.' Dodd contributed an article to the Beaumanor magazine in which he gave a delightful potted history of the orchestra. 'Several of the leading British symphony orchestras pay frequent visits to Leicester,' he advised, 'and a number of Woygites often take the opportunity of hearing a fine orchestra "in the flesh", an experience which the broadcast concert or the gramophone recital, however enjoyable, can never replace . . .'

As Chris Barnes explains, 'It was culture, and we needed it.'

In addition to music, there was dancing: unlike Bletchley Park, which seemed to be teeming with ballroom experts, the Beaumanor crew were unskilled enthusiasts. To this end, dancing classes were arranged, and taken by a staff member happy to be known as 'Victor Silvester' Carrington. 'The social life was very important,' says Mr Barnes. 'Without it, the intensity and monotony would have got us all down.'

Unlike the more cerebral Bletchley codebreakers, the Beaumanor community was also extremely sporty. Active football, hockey and rugby teams were formed almost immediately. And, as Philip Blenkinsop noted after a conversation with a former ATS girl there, 'life was more Radio One than Radio Three . . . More informal entertainment seems to have centred around The Pear Tree, The Curzon Arms and other local hostelries . . . A major product of Beaumanor in those days was gossip . . . Liaisons, both innocent and otherwise, undoubtedly took place and the wives of (wireless operators), often living far away and not knowing the nature of their husbands' work, must have felt grounds for concern.'

As (then) Corporal Harold W. Everett of the Intelligence Corps recalled, there were also moments of high comedy. All the wireless work, he observed, was 'housed in a very big country mansion and was as closely guarded as any present-day atomic weapons research establishment'. As a result, the local people, from Leicester and the surrounding tiny villages, would sometimes speculate fruitlessly on the nature of the work being carried out there. One line of thought – prompted by the forest of tall radio aerials – was that each and every aerial was directly connected to a British secret agent, and it was from Beaumanor that these brave spies were receiving their instructions. Another local rumour heard by Everett was that the house was being used as Rudolf Hess's prison and interrogation centre and that he was tortured for information there 'on a daily basis'. 'I doubt between all of us, we should even have got a toenail each,' reflected Everett on this idea.

The secrecy was extended, magnificently, to the most inconspic-uous of tradesmen; on one occasion, the large old house, with its smoky, spluttering fires, urgently required the services of a chim-ney sweep; and a local gnarled old figure duly presented himself at the gates. It fell to Everett to shadow the man as he carried out his tasks. There was a terror that, left alone in a map room or opera-tions room, the sweep might see things that he was not permitted to see; only with Everett there could he be safely kept from a temp-tation to nose around.[8]

Everett clearly found this episode very amusing, although with a moment's reflection, we might wonder if the military paranoia was actually quite justified. For the presence of the military, together with all the aerials, would indeed have made Beaumanor an intriguing prospect for a spy.

In a wider sense, though, we might only refer back to the spy fictions of William le Queux (or the ingenious detective stories of G.K. Chesterton) to find the source of the notion that the man you were least likely to notice – chimney sweep, milkman, postman – would be exactly the figure for such an agent to disguise himself as. In any event, as Everett noted, after being tailed all over the house and then escorted to the gates, the chimney sweep 'waved me goodbye and hurried off no doubt to the local pub to share the joke with his cronies. But no matter,' he concluded wrily, 'Britain had survived another critical test. Like a nun's habit, the sheets remained unlifted.'

In contrast, when other figures – superior personnel and VIPs – paid visits to Beaumanor, the panic was less about security than about tidying the place; filing papers and scooping up the tea things, which were frequently left lying about as if in some students' common room. But for all the apparent chaos, the seriousness of the institution was never compromised. Indeed, perhaps surprisingly, the actual conditions in which the operators worked were to become the source of union trouble. Tea things left lying around were one matter: but other forms of carelessness could make life distinctly uncomfortable.

'The union made representations about conditions in the huts,' says Chris Barnes. As at Bletchley Park, much work at Beaumanor was carried out in plain wooden huts in the grounds, which were apt to be stuffy in the summer and freezing in the winter. 'Those huts were pretty terrible sometimes. The ventilation was very poor. There was inadequate heating. And in those days, everybody smoked and that made ventilation dodgy. But I suppose that as a result of those union representations, things were improved.'

That was about the extent of union success, though, as Mr Barnes recalls, 'I don't think the union cut much ice there. I don't think [the base's officer in charge] Commander Ellingworth had any regard for unions. It was the Civil Service Radio Operators Association we belonged to. I think on the whole we must have been rather wasting our money.'

The very idea that unions would have been allowed to operate within such a vital establishment at a time of war now seems extraordinary, regardless of how much or how little they achieved. But such safety valves were necessary, for the pressure of the work was liable to produce outbreaks of tension, here as at Chicksands. According to Chris Barnes, though, Commander Ellingworth, was a unifying figure in the old-fashioned way. 'He was very autocratic.

People were a bit scared of him. And it didn't do to argue with him. Whether you were civilian or in the services, it didn't make much difference. But I don't remember myself being involved in rows or tensions. I think people got edgy at night. At three in the morning, you can have a row with anyone, can't you?'

In the coastal listening stations, the coyly styled 'Home Defence Units', the operators – once they had gained the experience – were becoming adept at recognising and understanding the jargon used by German pilots. The knowledge was crucial because certain pilots were quite loose-tongued and conversational, and were thus apt to give away details of forthcoming raids. In this way, the RAF could anticipate some of the Luftwaffe's moves.

The men and women operating from RAF Kingsdown, meanwhile, were perfecting a novel type of dirty trick that not only demonstrated mastery over German signals, but also threw that knowledge right back at the Luftwaffe. It was a tactic known poetically as 'Ghost Voices'. The idea was that expert linguists could tune into pilots' frequencies and pass themselves off as German Flight Command, as Wrens and WAAFs stood by making notes of the pilots' responses. By doing so, the linguists could give the pilots fake co-ordinates, false targets, send them on fuel-sapping wild goose chases, lose them over the Channel, fool them into believing that the land beneath them was Belgium and not Sussex . . .

'Specially selected men and women began annoying voice interference on the 3–6 [Luftwaffe] megacycle range,' recalled Kingsdown operative Peggy West. 'Pseudo controllers . . . gave false fog warnings to get aircraft to land, read poetry, or relayed Hitler's speeches to disrupt and frustrate, and gave direct, contrary orders to cause confusion.'

The tricks sometimes led to moments of hilarity. 'A German controller was trying to direct his aircraft to Kassel,' remembered Peggy West. 'Kingsdown's "ghost" was trying to stop them and told them not to take any notice of the Englander who was trying to confuse them. After an exchange or two, the German became pretty agitated, lost his temper, and swore. Our "ghost" replied, "The Englander is now swearing" and was met by an infuriated shriek from Germany: "It's not the blank Englander who is swearing, it's blankety-blank me"!'

And the presence of women on the airwaves also led both to some ingenious double bluffing, and also – even in situations of high tension – to even greater heights of amusement. 'When a 101 Squadron Lancaster with an ABC Special [a jamming transmitter] was shot down over Berlin, the Luftwaffe assumed Kingsdown's "Corona" voice interference came from that ABC equipment,' said Peggy West. 'They reasoned, correctly, that the RAF would not allow women to fly operationally over Germany and switched to women ground controllers. Since we had anticipated that, we did the same. One of our girls got into a similar battle of wills, the only difference being that both women ended up laughing with each other and had to shut down. We all enjoyed the incident very much – but did wonder what happened to the lass over there!'

In broader terms, the trick's effectiveness could not last for ever. Having become wise to it, Luftwaffe flight command issued new 'friend or foe' codes that the pilots would employ before receiving further instructions. It is a terrific example, though, of just how proactive and game a number of the Y Service operatives were, and how skilled with language. As the conflict progressed, their skills and their tricks – for a few personnel, extending deep into the realm of espionage – were to develop dramatically.

6 Heat, Sand and Ashes

According to society figure Robin Stuart French, Cairo in 1940 was 'A filthy, Frenchy, modern town – an ancient, elegant, primitive city.' For British newcomers, it could be disorientating. Quite apart from the obvious sights, it was a clamouring cacophony of 'horse-drawn vehicles, trams hung about with people, army trucks', where an attempt to get anywhere was a struggle. The Musqi was a maze of poverty-riddled streets in which upper-class women came to browse and buy among innumerable shops, piled high with silks and rugs and perfumes, while metal-workers hammered out jewellery. It is difficult to imagine a sharper contrast between this intensity and colour and noise and the muted provincial greyness of Bletchley in Buckinghamshire.

For Bletchley codebreaker Henry Dryden, dispatched to help with the successful new interception service in Egypt, the journey itself was something of an induction into this extraordinary new life. His first voyage, sailing out from Glasgow, met with disaster: 'The fire alarm sounded, followed a quarter later by "abandon ship stations",' he wrote. 'The fire, caused by the bursting of an oil-pipe under the boilers, got out of control . . . The following Sunday, I got back to [Bletchley Park], soaked in sea-water and oil, to be greeted by John Tiltman with: "Hullo old boy, haven't you gone yet?"[1] The lightness of Mr Dryden's tone distracts the attention from the fact that any voyage during this period – when the waters of the Atlantic and the Mediterranean were being ruthlessly patrolled by the U-boat wolf packs – was a profoundly unsettling business.

One rather disquieting aspect of life in Cairo was the seemingly porous nature of secrecy. 'Security is almost non-existent,' wrote Hermione, Countess of Ranfurly, herself working in the office of the Special Operations Executive there and later branching into what she vaguely described as 'cipher work' in Jerusalem. 'If you give our address to a Cairo taxi driver, more often than not he'll say "oh, you want to go to secret office".'

The Countess was there under extremely unusual circumstances; after her husband was posted to the Middle East, she set off in pursuit of him, defying every rule and regulation in the way that only the smarter, better-connected, wealthier women could. Her extraordinary adventures took her all over the continent of Africa. Seeing her chance to come to Egypt, she somehow, against all the odds, secured herself a position in order to replenish her fast-diminishing funds.

'It was exciting flying in over the pyramids,' she wrote of her arrival by flying boat. 'We landed elegantly on the Nile and little boats came out to meet us. Captain Mountain came ashore with us and told Customs and Immigration officials that I was a special passenger and must be helped in every way possible . . .'[2] From here, on the last of her money, she managed to find the address of some friends of her husband living outside the city. In terror that she would be arrested and turned back, she presented herself at the door of distinguished expat Pat Hore-Ruthven; he and his wife, and their guests, were extremely amused.

In the years to follow, the indefatigable Countess's duties were punctuated by some extremely colourful adventures; for it hardly needs to be added that she was socially connected with all of the leading players in the region at that time, from General Wavell – the man in charge of Middle East command – downwards. She also stands now as an emblem of the determination of women to get involved in the war effort; the experiences that she and WAAF Aileen Clayton had are sometimes startling, in the sense that our distant view of women's role in the war is that they were kept very firmly away from jeopardy. Clayton's introduction to Egypt seemed similarly exciting:

> We flew south to Lagos, where those of us who were urgently needed in the Middle East were told we would be flying overland via Kano, Maiduguri, Fort Lamy, El Geneina and El Fasher to Khartoum, while the others went on by flying boat via the longer Congo route. Half an hour out from Lagos our Lockheed Lodestar developed engine trouble and our pilot, Captain Bowes-Lyon, a cousin of the Queen, had to return to make an undignified landing in a mangrove swamp on the edge of the airfield. We finally reached Khartoum a few days later, where I had the awe-inspiring honour of being asked to dine with the Governor at the splendid Government House.
>
> The following day, we joined a flying boat coming up from South Africa, and after a brief stop for lunch at Wadi Halfa, few on to Egypt, skimming down just as dusk was falling on the Nile at Rod-el-Farag, where I was met by Rowley Scott-Farnie and Kenneth Jowers, the Commanding Officer of the Y set-up at Suez Road, Heliopolis. It had been a fascinating ten days' journey.[3]

One slightly reluctant Cairo 'cipherine', to use her deliberately vague term, was Barbara Skelton, later to marry writer Cyril Connolly. In London, she had been keen to avoid being propelled into the Wrens, hoping instead for what she grandly termed 'a proper job'. But a continual inability to be punctual led to those 'proper jobs' – secretarial positions – disappearing from beneath her. As very few other girls did at that time, however, she found herself in the Café Royal in Piccadilly one evening, and bumped into an old acquaintance of hers – Donald Maclean, at that time a young diplomat, whose name would become rather better known in the 1950s as one of the Cambridge spies. 'He suggested I offer my services as a cipher clerk to the Foreign Office and said he would be my sponsor,' she wrote drily.

The result was an intensive three-month training course deep in Whitehall. Then, she recalled, she was offered a choice about her destination: Guatemala, Sweden or Egypt. So Egypt it was.

As well as the usual hazards of travelling in convoy – all such journeys across the oceans had been made in convoy since the start of the conflict – she found that the voyage presented other unexpected complications, such as the sexual jealousy of the purser who, vying for her favours with a young Frenchman, wooed her with 'French tart scent' and 'vanishing cream'. The conflict between the two men grew so intense that, one night, they both came to blows, the Frenchman fell overboard, and Skelton had to raise the alarm to have the man rescued. Later, the same Frenchman was himself driven into a passion of sexual jealousy, and he banged Skelton's head against an engine and threw two of her combs into the sea.

Initial impressions of Cairo were not appealing. It was, she wrote, 'oppressive, dusty and colourless'. Her arrival at the Embassy was no more cheering:

> The embassy was grey and deserted. The cipher room was on the ground floor with steel bars across the windows . . . Lipsticky cups of half-drunk tea were scattered about among used carbons, despatch books, partly chewed slabs of chocolate and countless cigarette ends. Then I was put into another taxi and driven to the Continental Hotel where another cipherine showed me to my room.[4]

It was clear that whatever magic the city was to hold for Skelton, it would not be found anywhere near her work. She was greeted at the office by a wispy red-haired youth in an Eton tie, and entered the office to find herself posted with a 'phenomenally fat ex-naval commander who sat surrounded by tiny dish-cloths used to mop the sweat from his eyes. Each day, fresh mops were brought to work in a satchel containing pencils, pens, and an India rubber attached to a string. We worked on shifts and got picked up and taken to work in a kind of cattle truck.'

At the Heliopolis station, to which Skelton had been posted, it was also clear that the conditions would be trying, for the volume of work was growing ever greater. 'The intercept station . . . was largely engaged in covering high-grade networks,' wrote Henry Dryden, 'the Enigma messages carried on them being relayed by radio or cable to Bletchley Park for processing.' Equally, messages were relayed to Services Headquarters in Cairo. 'Because of their sensitivity, the messages were shielded from the eyes of the cipher officers by being encoded in a simple substitution before encipherment and dispatch from the United Kingdom.'

Heliopolis, after its early successes of 1940, was to come further into its own in 1941. In January, the British mounted an attack against the Italian forces occupying Eritrea, Somaliland and Ethiopia. The precise date for the British assault had been selected because the Heliopolis interceptors had been listening to Italian plans for movement back from Sudan. And as the British forces closed inexorably on the Italian army in Ethiopia, the Italians were virtually helpless: the Cairo listeners and cryptographers picked up every single order, plan and communication between the Italian military leaders. Just a few days later, the British and Australians entered Tobruk and 25,000 Italian troops were taken prisoner.

Then there was the triumph of General O'Connor, commander of the Western Desert Force; his attack not merely drove the Italian army back but also crippled a good part of it. The figures were stark: some 20,000 Italians were killed or wounded in the pincer movement, and about 130,000 were taken prisoner. But this victory 'could hardly have been achieved without the excellent and copious intelligence information that was available to General Wavell', states the official Bletchley Park history. 'This came primarily from decrypts of . . . Italian cyphers at BP and at the Central Bureau Middle East in Cairo. The brave dash across the desert would have been foolhardy in the extreme had it not been known from the many intercepts that no significant enemy forces stood in its way.'

But the war in the desert had only just begun. In the early months of 1941, Britain was receiving stark intelligence that the Germans were massing military forces in Romania. Since the immediate strategic threat these forces posed was to Greece, in one sense the British were now concerned with coming to the aid of an ally. But there was another consideration too; that any German conquest of Greece would bring Hitler's armies uncomfortably close to the British strongholds of Palestine and Egypt, as well as to the strategically vital Suez Canal.

So, in March, around 60,000 British troops were ferried from Egypt to Greece in preparation for such an assault. The consequence of this, however, was that when Rommel and his Afrika Korps – who had arrived in Tripoli in February – started to push east, there were fewer British forces available to mount an effective defence. By April, the British were forced to withdraw from Benghazi; Rommel and his troops marched into the vacated city. Nor was the British withdrawal especially dignified, as mobile Y Service veteran G.A. Harries, who was in the thick of the scramble, later recalled: 'Things got pretty desperate as we were chased out of Libya . . . We made a night-time stop . . . just over the border with Egypt. We were well south in the desert all this time.'

And indeed, Harries and his comrades were having to maintain the highest levels of concentration to home in on the enemy's signals; from their range and frequency, the Y section was able to tell just how close the Germans were getting. 'We moved again, finally leaguering at about midnight,' he continued. 'We went to sleep with our boots on that night. We had only been asleep a short time when we were awakened by engines being started up and found ourselves brightly illuminated by flares. There was only one word for what happened and that was panic.'

According to Harries, everyone took off at great speed, including his wireless intercept car (such specially modified cars, crammed with equipment, were widely deployed). He and his comrades made it back behind the Alamein line, but in the general confusion, Harries was then informed that he was to be posted back into the desert with another operator. Orders were orders. They drove off, with a mass of interception equipment, in a 'battered 3-ton truck with badly broken springs', their instructions to link up with another wireless unit that was still operational in the desert.

Harries recalled the extraordinary sight that confronted him and his comrades; as they drove westwards along the coastal road, theirs was the only vehicle headed in that direction. Passing them eastwards in an endless convoy was, as Harries put it, the Eighth Army in full retreat and 'heading towards Alexandria'. He recalled that there were occasional isolated groups standing by the side of the road, without any form of transport and desperately thumbing lifts. Harries and his comrades presumably did not drive very far west.

The German army's push towards Egypt continued, its pursuit of the British seemingly ineluctable. Alison Trelfa recalls from reading his accounts that her father, Kenneth Maynard, was sent out to Cairo at around this time. Called upon to widen his experience after his adventures – and Steve McQueen-style escape from Nazi forces – in France in 1940, he was sent to Heliopolis in May 1941. His daughter now says: 'In a magazine printed for the old boys of his school during the war, my grandfather wrote about my father: "In May, 1941 he was specially selected to go out to Cairo to help to organise a unit there, and he has been there ever since." Whether he was specially selected and whether he was helping to organise anything, or whether it was just a proud father speaking I don't know.

'Where my father stayed whilst in Cairo I am not sure, but I do know that the officers were allowed to use the swimming pool at the Mena House Hotel. This is a lovely looking hotel which is still existence today. I know that he disliked Cairo as a place and always said that after spending time there in the war he didn't ever want to go abroad again. I do remember clearly what he used to say about it, but it's probably not for sharing!

'I got the impression that he was quite bored for a lot of the time that he was in Egypt and there was a lot of sitting around – presumably when not on duty. He was very modest though and not the sort of person who would glorify or exaggerate things. I have a huge number of his books, mainly history books which he read when he was out there. He was certainly never allowed anywhere near the front line. He used to carry a piece of paper stating "This officer is not allowed within x miles of the front line (on land) and considerably further than this when in the air."

'He was issued with a gun at the beginning of the war and six bullets,' Mrs Trelfa adds. 'I'm not sure that he ever even took it out of its holder, but I do remember him saying that he had never put the bullets into the gun.

'He also had a least one girlfriend – a friend who was a girl? – when he was in Egypt, despite being engaged to my mother. My mother often used to tease him about this. According to my mother, this girl was in the ATS and was "very posh, the daughter of a Lord or something". I love the telegram which he sent to my grandparents when he returned from Egypt. It says simply: "Fatted calf required Monday or Tuesday".'

But while some were able to maintain a sense of insouciance, surrounded by girlfriends and favourite books, others in the Y Service in Egypt had a rather more rigorous time of it. Hugh Skillen wrote of the Middle East campaign:

In the field off-duty there was no recreation, no amusements, no pub, just a muddy field or a scorching desert and the fear of scorpions in your bedroll or in your boots and the incessant distant thunder of guns and the danger of enemy bombers.

With no respite, not even weekend leave in eight months, it is no wonder that there was even suicide among the young 19 and 20 year old Oxbridge graduates . . . A nervous consequence of concentration on weak signals through 'mush' – interference – resulted in operators suffering from deafness and I remember visiting several in hospital in Tunisia when the campaign ended and many of them became temporarily completely deaf.[5]

No such reference to suicides appears either in contemporary documentation or the various post-war accounts; but, given the sensitivity of such a subject, that is perhaps not surprising. What did seem to be more obvious, however, was a fractious atmosphere in the Heliopolis Bureau. As various officers struggled for dominance, the tension began to percolate through to the operators. Aileen Clayton wrote of the Y operation in Heliopolis:

The structure had evolved from a quasi-civilian organisation, but by 1941 it had developed into a heterogeneous assortment of civilians and civilians disguised in uniform, several of whom had little or no sense of military discipline, and even less desire to understand it. They all worked with or under career and conscripted Army and RAF personnel, and this inevitably led to some frictions and misunderstandings.

These frictions and misunderstandings reached boiling point in the middle of that year; it is instructive that even in the heat of conflict, there was still time for officers to compose lengthy, elegant memos of an increasingly acidic nature. One such man, senior officer Lieutenant-Colonel Walter Scott, was furious about what he was and was not apparently allowed to know about how the codes were being broken and what messages they were revealing. He was also frustrated about the output from the Heliopolis station, and about which officers decided what codes got priority.

The reply that Scott received from Major Wallace, commanding officer of the Y unit and Heliopolis offshoot known as 5 Intelligence Signals (5 IS), drove him to further heights of indignation. Wallace wrote to him: 'I recognise that [your] notes are made with a view to seeing what can be done to produce more from the Y resources . . . than you do at present. But . . . priority of work on high-grade cipher is for final decision by the head of the Government Code and Cypher School.'

Scott appealed to Major Jacob, and in barbed fashion, mentioned 'muddles' caused by decryptions from the Heliopolis bureau, alongside an occasion when he was 'badly let down about the security of map reference codes by the HELIO experts, and on two occasions, our amateur efforts . . . had proved their advice to be wrong'. In other words, this was a face-off between Army codebreakers and their civilian counterparts. Moreover, Scott had been told that 'my question as to whether research would be done in the UK or at HELIO on a new military high-grade cipher which had just appeared in the Balkans was like a "red rag to a bull" to the Director. I had no right to ask such a question, and it was no business of mine.' Again, in other words, he had been told that the business of ciphers was above his pay grade.

The anger felt by the military concerning code-work that appeared to be out of their control, and yet had a direct impact upon their operations, was understandable. So too, however, was the need for such control to be kept as tight as possible. Major Jacob's smooth reply to Scott's outburst – in a memo addressed 'Dear Walter' – is an attempt to explain both the security constraints and the great ingenuity and expertise which Scott apparently could not see at work. '[Major Wallace] is . . . definitely in a position to say, knowing the individual capabilities of his own staff and the intricacies and interconnections of the ciphers themselves, which of his staff should, given new requirements, work on any particular cipher and furthermore, whether it is better to concentrate at Heliopolis or whether to put some of his staff temporarily afield . . .'

Jacob went on to add, with a dash of vinegar: 'I do not think that I am likely to prejudice the production of Military, Naval or Air information by using my powers of pooling the staff in an improper manner . . . In my position as Director, it is unthinkable that I should obstruct any one section.' Quite so.

The disputes over these and other seemingly small-scale matters were to boil up again a little later in the year, resulting in a flurry of incandescent memos that – incidentally – also throw a good deal of light on the workings of the Y Service. 'But through the sheer enthusiasm of the staff,' wrote Aileen Clayton, with silky diplomacy, 'and their desire to pit their wits against the enemy, somehow the system worked.'

And possibly one of the reasons it did was that – unlike rainy Leicestershire or Bedfordshire, where young WAAFs were struggling to focus on impenetrable messages while at the same time dealing with the frustrations of basic accommodation and severe rationing of items like cigarettes and chocolate – Cairo was a dazzling world: colourful and intense and overflowing with sensory stimulation. As Aileen Clayton wrote:

Officers of all the Services who worked on the headquarters staff [in Cairo] lived out in private accommodation – in flats, pensions, and hotels around the city. Until I was able to find my feet, Rowley Scott-Farnie [a wing commander and signals officer] had booked me into Shephards Hotel, which in those days before the great post-war revolution, was sheer Edwardian opulence.

There seemed to be myriads of Egyptian and Sudanese suffragis flip-flopping around the hotel in their heel-less slippers, clad in white galabiyahs, and red cummerbunds and fezes. The food, after the deprivations of England, was good and plentiful, and the service was so impeccable that it was not difficult to understand why the troops roughing it in the comfortless wastes of the Western Desert referred to the 'fleshpots of Cairo' . . . The plentifully stocked shops and the gay night clubs were all a far cry from the battles that were raging in the desert.[6]

There was another side to this, as one young woman posted from Bletchley Park in 1941 was to discover. Cherrie Ballantine was twenty years old when she made the voyage out from England; the Cairo that she found, while utterly wonderful and eye-opening, also triggered in her an occasional stab of guilt. She recalled, for instance, that the nightlife in the hotels had its own heightened elegance, and that there were dances that the young people very much enjoyed. But it was also on these occasions that she would think of people back in Britain and throughout Europe; the men who were fighting. As such, it was a life that was extremely difficult to resist yet one that could also leave one feeling just a little queasy.

But what Mrs Ballantine would also have found were extraordinary social networks; not merely of the smarter kind of person but also literary and artistic types. While the Countess of Ranfurly and her husband Dan were effortlessly plugged in to the military hierarchy and the other aristocrats, people such as Barbara Skelton and novelist Olivia Manning represented the more bookish end of the scale. As an expat society, it was gossipy and close-knit and in a curious way hermetically sealed from the rest of the world.

Skelton recalled a near hallucinatory social whirl; one glittering figure was a 'Coptic playboy' known as Victor: 'During one summer leave in Alexandria, he showed me all the class beaches,' she wrote. 'The lowest grade consisted of nothing but boulders. Victor had a beach hut among the wealthy Egyptians who never entered the sea but were to be seen lunching on the sands under vast parasols being served by white-robed servants.'

She also noted: 'Many old friends turned up in Cairo, including (Feliks) Topolski, in his role as war artist. We made a memorable trip to Luxor and had the tombs to ourselves but for a guide who brought along a donkey that I mounted when overcome with fatigue.' Ahead of this, though, in the glamour stakes, was the evening she met King Farouk, while dining at a restaurant called the Auberge des Pyramides.

The king was, according to Skelton, seated at the next table and was in excessively playful mood, flinging coloured pom-poms around his fellow diners. This encounter in turn led to an invitation to some of the embassy staff to attend a royal house party in the desert. Skelton and the other guests were conveyed there by private train, and that night, there was further playfulness as the bewildered guests were summoned to sleep on mattresses on the roof.

Skelton caught Farouk's eye; and he had more surprises for her. During the course of this multi-evening party, the King noticed her earrings. When she awoke the next morning (in a bed, this time), she found a jewel box under her pillow. The earrings had been copied in gold and emeralds.

The nature of this continuing relationship is something Skelton discreetly chooses not to divulge. But their affair caught the eyes of others. She wrote: 'One day I was summoned by the First Secretary at the Embassy, Bernard Burrows, who said that if I went on seeing Farouk, I would have to leave Egypt. Then Burrows gave me two weeks leave which I spent hitch-hiking around the Middle East.'

For those stationed hundreds of miles out in the blinding sands, such things would have seemed a world away. For some of the military operators, there was the Experimental Armoured Division; in essence a unit receiving and sending messages and codes while on the move across the desert – and while under attack – in specially designed armoured cars. 'Each armoured car functioned as a separate unit,' recalled G.A. Harries. 'As the interior of the cars was limited, all [soldiers'] kit was carried on the outside, including bedrolls. When I eventually returned to base, I found much of my clothing useless, riddled with shrapnel holes.'

And despite enemy fire – the booming guns of the tanks, the howl of incoming bombers – the life of a wireless operator had to proceed with full concentration and complete accuracy. As Harries recalled:

> Traffic was usually 5-letter Enigma groups except under battle conditions when messages were sent in a simpler 3-letter code . . . When it was necessary to move at night, which was quite often, we forged across the flat stoney desert just like a naval convoy. One of the operators off watch would stand in the turret to watch for any hazards or obstacles. Incidentally, I found it impossible to operate while on the move, as we were required to do. The operator on watch would be so bounced about at the back of the car that he would have to hang on to the table and I do not think that anything worthwhile was received while the car was in motion. The sets had a rough time too – but seemed to stand up to the arduous conditions.[7]

The HRO sets in question were clearly sturdy constructions. Not only was there 'bumping about' to contend with, there was also the ubiquitous sand, all those particles whipping through the wind, nightmarishly pervasive for man and machine alike. The fact that the radios withstood this battering suggested they had a touch of indestructibility. It is little wonder these old models are still so adored by ardent radio enthusiasts.

In April 1941, it became clear that despite the many triumphs of the Y operatives in Heliopolis, there was one weak spot: while they had done a brilliant job of unravelling the Italian codes, they were less successful with the complexities of German radio traffic. Some decrypts had shown quite clearly that not only had the Italians declared war on Greece, but the Germans were preparing for an invasion of that country; however, there had been a concomitant underestimation of Rommel's plans for north Africa. Added to this was a certain inexperience about handling the sort of information that would prove most effective when passed on to General Wavell and his forces.

None the less, it was in no small part thanks to the Y Service that some 50,000 Allied soldiers were successfully evacuated from Greece when the Germans' aerial onslaught began in April 1941. In the weeks before that, a small mobile Y unit had been established there – in essence, a one-man operation carried out by young Edgar Harrison of the Royal Signals. Having joined up in the 1930s and spent time in China, Harrison was an expert in his craft. Yet his mission to Greece was to be unexpectedly hair-raising.

In the early months of the war, a top secret memo had been circulated around the War Office concerning what was expected of the Y Services in the field – and also, what was not to be expected. 'In the field and when in contact with the enemy, concentration is impracticable,' the memo stated. In other words, a secret listener jammed into a car with headphones on while under bombardment was hardly going to be able to pick up much. 'Interception from the short range stations used by the enemy is only made possible by the provision of interception units in the forward area.'

But Edgar Harrison's mission in Greece as a one-man interception unit was all about getting a head start in what was to become a battlefield. And indeed it turned into an extraordinary struggle to stay ahead of the enemy. Harrison was initially summoned to Whaddon Hall and MI8 HQ to be briefed by Brigadier Gambier-Parry and found himself dispatched to the Mediterranean the following day by flying boat.

After a brief stop-off at the station in Cairo, Harrison joined the British Military Mission in Athens (and Major-General Gambier-

Parry, who happened to be the Brigadier's brother). There, at the Grand Bretagne hotel, Harrison immediately took to the roof and found that it was perfect for his needs. He set up an aerial; within a matter of hours, he was transmitting signals and information.

Harrison also had at his disposal an equipment-packed vehicle – a Packard. This, according to his memoir, constituted a Special Liaison Unit; by these means, he was able to receive high-grade signals intelligence – both from local sources and from London and Cairo – and pass it on to his field commanders.

Not long after Harrison established himself, he was informed by his immediate superior, Colonel Casson, that the Germans were poised to attack Greece through Yugoslavia. Just as Harrison prepared to leave the British Army base in the town of Yannina and return to Athens, the Germans launched their strike. The Greek army, which had held out against the Italians, were effectively helpless in the face of the far superior Nazi onslaught; they had no choice but to capitulate. And despite the brave efforts of the RAF, the Luftwaffe could not be held. The British forces had to retreat.

And in the middle of all this chaos and carnage, Edgar Harrison, the one-man Y unit, took to his Packard and drove at speed from Yannina to Athens – a terrifying journey throughout which the car was bombed and strafed by the planes above. As the Germans moved through the country, it was clear to Harrison that he had one, immediate, desperate priority – to destroy all his radio and cipher equipment, to prevent even a scrap of information getting into German hands. To do this, he would have to move in and out of Athens at top speed.

According to his own account, when he got there, the city was eerily quiet. There was certainly no one for him to report to. Knowing that he had very little time, he went to his base at the Grand Bretagne hotel; having dealt with the equipment there, he shot across to the British Embassy in order to destroy its wireless sets too. This done, he abandoned the Packard and boarded a train to Corinth. So began a harrowing odyssey south towards the port city of Kalamata, to join other British troops waiting to be evacuated. Only so many vessels could get there in time, though. With the Germans fast closing in and the beaches still full of troops, the full-to-capacity rescue boats that had made it through had no choice but to sail off; and the officers and men left behind at Kalamata were left with no option but to surrender to the advancing Nazi forces.

Except Harrison. Because of the clandestine nature of his SIS work – and the hazard that someone else who knew of it might inadvertently talk – he knew that if he were to fall into German hands, his life, as he put it, would not be worth living. As a result, he had to take himself into hiding.

With some resourcefulness, Harrison embarked on a fugitive life, moving along the Greek shoreline and sleeping in caves. Before the evacuation, he had taken care to supply himself with enough money so that, even though locals were suspicious of him, he was able to obtain food and water. But these days must have been utterly ragged with fear and apprehension. After a period of moving along beaches, Harrison found a rowing boat. He took the bold decision to put out to sea, with a store of food and water.

Yet Harrison's good fortune was to hold. Having spent a night and a day bobbing about on the Mediterranean waves, he and his tiny stolen boat were spotted by HMS *Kandahar*. The ship's captain was utterly bewildered by what he saw as Harrison's act of nautical insanity. But Harrison was amusingly insouciant. 'I knew the Navy would pick me up,' he said.

And so it was that Harrison, safe, sound, and now properly fed and watered, was delivered to his next destination: the island of Crete. This was, of course, to be little more than a breather . . .

On Crete, Harrison joined up with the Special Liaison Unit, under Captain Mike Sandover. The team was kept very busy with a huge amount of Ultra traffic and Harrison's proficiency was appreciated in the small team. But just days later, on 20 May, came the almighty – if not entirely unexpected – assault from the skies, as German dive-bombers and other planes launched their assault on the island, the prelude to a vast paratroop invasion. As the relentless bombardment went on, Harrison once again, this time together with his comrades, set to work on destroying the cipher equipment. And as before, there was no possibility of surrendering to German troops, for their secret knowledge would mean they would be subjected to terrible interrogations. Once again, retreat was the only option; Harrison and his colleagues were placed on board a naval vessel and taken to safe harbour at Alexandria, just as Crete finally fell to the Nazis.

Although in a wider sense, events in Greece and on Crete were unlikely to boost British morale, they did at least pleasingly demonstrate that the Y Service was effective and accurate. Edgar Harrison was not quite alone in providing signals intelligence; there was another small mobile unit as well. Meanwhile, at the highest level, information from decrypts in April concerning the forthcoming German invasion of Greece had been passed to General Freyburg, commander of the Allied forces on Crete, but – as was common in that relatively early stage of the conflict – Freyburg was not told the true provenance of this miraculous stream of intelligence. The secret of Ultra was hidden even from the generals. Instead, Freyburg was informed that this information was coming from a brilliantly well-placed spy in Athens. And so, as the Axis powers advanced through the country, the small Y unit and Bletchley Park were able to keep in contact, and thus to pass back and forth decrypted messages of great value concerning the enemy's latest positions. Were it not for this stream of information, the retreat from Greece and Crete could have been dramatically more disastrous.

As it was, the Crete operation led to terrible losses, particularly of naval defences – to say nothing of the horrors perpetrated upon the civilian population by the invading Nazis. The atrocities committed in Crete are the source of continuing echoes of hostility even today. But the effectiveness of mobile Y intelligence had been emphatically demonstrated. It has even been suggested that a little later on, while out in the Western Desert, General Freyburg asked casually whether that 'brilliant spy' who had worked so well in Athens was still operating.

7 A World Wide Web of Intelligence

One of the bleakest, coldest, most northerly of the British Y stations was sited just outside Murmansk, on the north-western tip of Russia; a seaport in the Arctic Circle that stood not far from the borders of Norway and Finland, and which could boast a harbour that was free of ice. The station was established in 1941 in order to give aid to the Arctic convoys sailing through those freezing, treacherous waters, pursued by the U-boat wolf packs and by German battleships.

In the wake of Operation Barbarossa – the German invasion of Russia – and with it the violent end of the Molotov/Ribbentrop pact (the always fragile non-aggression treaty between Germany and Russia that had also contained clauses concerning the appropriation and carving up of eastern Europe), the port of Murmansk was also a means by which the Allied convoys could deliver urgently needed goods to the Russians. In this sense, the Y station suited the Soviet purpose, at least for a time. But the Russians had an extra use for it too; according to the official Bletchley Park history, it gave them valuable information about German naval transmissions. Intriguingly, also according to the official history, the paranoid Russians at one point demanded that the station be closed down, for fear that the British were spying on them; but when this was done, the Russians found that they missed the intelligence that the station generated. Soon afterwards, normal service was resumed.

Shipboard wireless telegraphist Ron Charters was sailing on HMS *Bellona* with the Russian convoys near the Arctic Circle at the time when the Allies were attempting to give careful support to the nervy Soviets. Charters soon became familiar both with the harshness of that region of the world, and the danger that lurked in the icy waters of the Arctic. 'I well recall my almost stunned realisation when receiving my first U-Boat . . . message,' he wrote. 'There was little time to identify [it] and at the same time take a bearing on the signal.' He had no idea how he succeeded on this first encounter but it did, he said, teach him to be fully alert. However, he was having to perform such feats of focus in appalling weather. 'We were not allowed to sling hammocks while at sea and it was a case of using an inflated life-belt and sleeping fully dressed on any part of the deck that was free,' he recalled.

In the midst of such conditions, the young sailors on the frozen ships did what they could to keep spirits high. On one occasion, when two ships were berthed at a Russian port in the darkness of midwinter, the rival crews set up a football match in a square that was 'covered with ice and snow'. 'With no available changing facilities, I, with 21 other "braves", changed into our football strip in the open,' said Mr Charters. The Russian locals looked on 'more with amazement than admiration'.[1]

But the Y station at Murmansk was not perceived as the most attractive posting. One veteran wrote bitterly of his sojourn there: 'Mosquito-ridden north Russia is as inhospitable as its communist inhabitants.'

A few months later, the British made great efforts to tackle the simmering distrust that clearly existed in Anglo-Soviet relations, to the extent of sending a senior military commander out to Moscow to talk directly with his Russian Y Service counterparts. There were delicate diplomatic issues: not least of which was the importance of not letting the Russians know that the British had succeeded in cracking the Enigma codes. On top of this was the barbed issue of Russian security; it was all very well the British sharing some of their valuable Y intelligence, but how could they be sure that the Soviets would not accidentally leak such intelligence to their enemies? This was later to become a diplomatic matter requiring almost superhuman skills of negotiation.

Secret listeners were also quietly active in neutral countries, picking up transmissions from enemy spies. The nature of such missions – often given not to highly trained British secret agents, but simply to young men with a firm grasp of radio expertise – was filled with intrigue and risk, and proved an invaluable means for these men to grow up very fast. One such man picked out very early for such duties was Morse and short-wave radio expert Bill Miller, who was designated a Section VIII operator.

Having completed three months' military training on the south coast, Miller was approached quietly by his superiors and asked if he would be willing to put himself forward for special duties 'involving overseas service'. As if this were not thrilling enough, he was then given the old cloak-and-dagger injunction not to tell any of his friends in the regiment what he had been offered. He was also told that he was to be posted to a place in Buckinghamshire called Bletchley Park.

It was here that the James Bond-esque life began in earnest, and the way Miller related it exudes a sort of quiet, carefree pride. Like Edgar Harrison before him, Miller was fully briefed by Brigadier Gambier-Parry. His mission, he was told, was to 'proceed to San Sebastian in Spain near the French frontier.'

There, his cover story would be that he was joining the staff of the vice-consulate. Miller's real business, however, was to set up a wireless out-station and transmit reports back to Britain on a daily basis. It went without saying that this had to be a top secret operation. German operatives transmitting from neutral territory would be slightly more lax about short-range material, and might not even bother enciphering it. For this reason, it was vital that they should not suspect that anyone in the locality was listening in on them. Furthermore, the neutral countries were extremely reluctant to allow the gathering of any form of covert intelligence on their soil; neutrality was a tricky balancing act, and the pressures upon them were great. To be caught could create serious repercussions, and cause substantial damage to related secret operations.

So, before travelling out to San Sebastian, the young and relatively inexperienced Bill Miller was sent for a short but intense course of advanced cryptography training 'with a couple of nice young ladies', as he put it, from MI6 HQ in Broadway Buildings, St James's Park. This gave him a grounding in both encoding and deciphering.

One such code he had to learn with extreme care was his personal one. It was based on one of the brand new paperback books from Penguin, *Poet's Pub* by Eric Linklater, and involved 'the [book] page number and a line number to choose a couple of words or a phrase from which a grid was formed'. Miller also had to familiarise himself in painstaking detail with German officers and units, their military equipment, their tanks and guns and vehicles. In other words, he was required to take on board a very great deal in a short space of time.

At last, in early 1941, came the flight to Lisbon, and the start of his adventures. He departed from Bristol; and the world in which he landed was a far cry from everything that he had known. In Portugal there 'was no blackout, no war, and the shops were full of fruit that had not been seen at home for a long time', wrote his friend Geoffrey Pidgeon. 'He could not get over the brilliant lighting everywhere, the streets, the shops, the crowds of people sitting in cafes and restaurants . . . A man from the Embassy took him out to dinner at a restaurant one night. During the meal, he muttered: "Take a discreet look at those chaps over there . . . they're from the German embassy."'[2]

This was just the start of it. Miller was then required to establish himself in Spain, which was quite a different prospect from Portugal. In the aftermath of the Spanish Civil War, the ruling dictatorship of General Franco might prove amenable to the Germans at any point, so it was vital for Britain to know of any Nazi manoeuvres in the vicinity. The naval fleet around Gibraltar would have to be given sufficient notice to set sail in the event of German troops crossing into Spanish territory; British diplomatic interests, too, would need advance wireless warning in order to be able to burn their secret papers before the enemy arrived.

Young Miller found himself posted, with a minimal cover story, to the British consulate in Bilbao, the staff of which clearly had no wish for him to be there. The Spanish authorities had recently set down extremely stringent rules to do with forbidden wireless interception and transmission; it seemed to the consulate staff that it was altogether too obvious what Miller was, and what he would be doing.

Miller was counselled not merely to keep himself to himself, but also to avoid the attentions of young women; this was a matter of deep practicality. Of all the catches a female counter-intelligence spy might make, a wireless operator was among those of the highest value. Like all secret agents, Miller was also advised not to frequent the same bars or cafés repeatedly; it was important that he should not be noticed, or attract attention. And so this very young Englishman, operating almost independently, set up his equipment in a small back room, and began the long vigils listening in on German signals.

Young radio experts were also needed to transport vital equipment to strategic locations in Europe in order to help with the struggle against the Germans. These men would need an unusual blend of talents: both the raw bravery of the Special Operations Executive and the technical knowhow of a back-room scientist. One such man, a talented young wireless buff known to his friends as 'Spuggy' – real name Arthur Newton – had, after his recruitment in the 1930s by Richard Gambier-Parry, been instrumental in devising wireless equipment that could be hidden and buried in strategic locations in the event of a Nazi invasion of Britain. His love and feel for the technology made him an invaluable innovator and by 1940, he was working for the Auxiliary Intelligence Organisation under Captain Peter Fleming (the brother of Ian).

Spuggy had also designed a mobile two-way station that could be used in a Dodge car. In the early weeks of 1941, he was required for a rather more hazardous mission: carrying valuable, up-to-the-minute radio equipment to Belgrade, Yugoslavia. This meant somehow crossing a continent dominated by the Nazis and Italians. The route, of necessity, would be circuitous. Quite how circuitous no one could have predicted.

Newton's journey involved sailing from Greenock, Scotland, and for reasons of evasive action, heading towards the North Pole. This part of the voyage was not only, as he wrote to his wife, 'B****** cold!' but also fraught with menace from the patrolling, invisible U-boats. Eventually the ship was able to set a more southerly course. Some weeks later, with its engines failing, the vessel reached the harbour of Freetown on the coast of west Africa; from there, Spuggy, still caring for his precious radio cargo like a mother hen with chicks, was obliged to load everything on to a rickety plane that was to sweep his party across the Belgian Congo. An encounter with a tornado forced the pilot to ditch the plane miles off course – the emergency landing clipping the tops off trees – and Spuggy and his equipment found themselves in a wilderness near Stanleyville where they were taken in by missionaries.

This accident-prone journey across Africa finally came to its conclusion in Cairo, as a rather crusty Spuggy, always on the lookout for somewhere to get a proper wash, made preparations to sail to Athens on a boat filled with New Zealand soldiers. Some days later, in April 1941, Spuggy was established in Athens (passing ships, as it were, with his fellow Y Service operative Edgar Harrison, though of course Spuggy's mission was onwards to Yugoslavia): at that time, Spuggy wrote home to his wife to inform her of his excruciatingly slow progress to Belgrade. The letter gives a vivid flavour of the near-anarchic atmosphere of Mediterranean Europe as the Nazi shadow grew longer:

The days after Yugoslavia told Germany to go to hell, impris-oned the Government, turned out Prince Paul and started mobilising, I had to go to Belgrade. Had stacks of baggage too! Caught a train Monday 4.30 a.m. and arrived in Salonika at 2 a.m. the following day. Went to hotel – had two hours sleep – then up again to catch another train for the Greek/Yugoslav frontier. Got across border and changed for Belgrade.

Arrived . . . 4.30 p.m. Wednesday after a nightmare journey. Train was packed with troops with women and children crying in the corridors. There was no food.

I delivered all the bags (with the valuable radio equipment) but was told to get out fast and to take the midnight train out from Belgrade to Greece. It turned out to be the last train. Crossed the Greek frontier at Salonika before Jerry invaded Greece.

As it happened, Spuggy's timing was acute; with the Germans advancing, Athens was in a state of near collapse. It was vital that he get out. But how? As an air raid started, he hurried down to the docks, thinking he might be able to hop on to a destroyer that was scheduled to be there. The ship in question did not materialise and time was running ever shorter. Spuggy managed to find a place on a refugee boat that was sailing for Alexandria, his fellow passengers terrified children and women.

'Had loads of bags and equipment and had to load this myself,' he wrote to his wife, 'which meant heaving out a derrick, tying all my boxes on to the end of the guy and then running up the ship and working the winch.' All of this very much against the clock. 'After sweating and struggling for half an hour in the boiling sun, I was a mess.'[3]

Ever preoccupied with hygiene, Spuggy 'managed to scrounge a wash' from the ship's engineer. Then it became apparent to him just how terrible the conditions on board were for the petrified evacuees: on a boat designed to carry six passengers, there were now 200 people with 'no food', 'limited water' and – at best – sparse lavatorial arrangements. Thankfully for Spuggy, there was the solace of some smuggled spirits; and he found himself a corner under a lifeboat cover. The boat was strafed by German fighter pilots, who dive-bombed and fired machine guns at the open deck; miraculously, there were no casualties.

The ordeal at sea went on for three days and three nights; when Spuggy and his shipmates arrived safe in port at Alexandria, he was able to return to Cairo and deliver the diplomatic bags and equipment that he had picked up in Belgrade. One might think he would be grateful for this deliverance, and for the relative peace of Egypt. But he confided to his wife as soon as he got there that he was 'fed up to the teeth' with it.

But what impresses now is the idea of a young man from Durham moving through this war-ravaged world with such apparent insouciance; his genius clearly lay not merely in the art of radio communication, but also personal communication. This ability to extemporise – while remaining completely imperturbable – was shared by some of his other radio-minded colleagues.

For Harold Everett at Beaumanor, a young corporal with 110 Wireless Intelligence Section, the prospect of Egypt loomed somewhat unexpectedly. 'Six of us were being sent to Cairo from our highly secret and closely guarded intelligence school in the Midlands,' he wrote. Not only that: for reasons of security and discretion, they were being sent via warship, rather than the more basic troop carrier. The six men clambered aboard HMS *Shropshire* at Glasgow; they were to find the interregnum at sea both extraordinary and a little like a dream.

For these young men and women, such voyages marked transitional moments in their lives. Because the nature of the work they were to do was cerebral rather than physical – and because there was not much they could do throughout the course of the long journeys but relax – they had time to reflect, while at the same time their eyes were opened to the wider, more colourful world beyond Great Britain.

Everett described moments of comedy:

> When we reached a specified latitude, the order was issued to don tropical kit. We soldiers emerged in the sartorial splendour provided by the War Office. We caused quite a stir as I imagine that the uniforms were left over from the Battle of Omdurman. Long, narrow, tight fitting jackets with high collars and real drain-pipe trousers for evening wear and some enormous long baggy shorts for daytime. These shorts [were] known as Bombay Bloomers.

Such voyages were, nevertheless, naturally jagged with jeopardy. There was alarm on board HMS *Shropshire* when it appeared that the biggest and most feared German battleship, the *Tirpitz*, was bearing down upon the convoy. In the end, it turned out to have been a misread signal (highlighting in a small way the need for complete accuracy). But Everett also noted that in an enclosed community like a warship, rumours were rife, and spread like lightning. The ship sailed to Sierra Leone, where one RAF passenger suddenly, and without warning, became manic with a clasp knife; the man had to be overpowered, sedated, and taken to hospital in Freetown.

Everett and his colleagues were then transferred to another ship for the next leg of their increasingly exotic journey:

We had no duties, the weather was glorious and the sea calm. I remember lounging in a chair on the foredeck in the hot sunshine reading a book I had found on board and watching the flying fishes. One day we were hit by a tropical storm – lightning of an intensity I had never seen before. Some chaps stripped off and enjoyed a refreshing shower in the cascading rain.

They arrived at the Gold Coast, where 'we were reminded that the Empire "on which the sun never set" was still a reality, as demonstrated by the sight of Government House with the Union Flag waving proudly from a flagstaff'. The voyage continued around the west coast of Africa, until finally it was time for a spell on a flying boat, which took Everett and his colleagues over the 'dark green impenetrable mass' of the jungle, a sight that he found 'unutterably sinister'.[4] By the time he arrived in Egypt, this quick-witted, good-humoured young Englishman was almost a citizen of the world.

Another young man who had his eyes opened to a hitherto unsuspected world during a voyage through the Mediterranean was eighteen-year-old Victor Newman, who hailed from Weybridge in Surrey. After Mr Newman's months of training in the arts of interception, he was at last to set sail with twenty or so of his squad on board HMS *Gambia*. This voyage to the Far East took in pit stops that he remembers with almost lurid clarity even now.

'We stopped off very briefly in Gibraltar, and then Alexandria. We only had about five hours ashore in Alexandria.' This was enough time to establish the sort of English presence – young men in a tight-knit group – that is greeted with wariness by so many Mediterranean bar owners even today. 'There were five of us in a gaggle, and we walked around the place, and then we realised we had to get back to the docks so we got this horse-drawn buggy and it took us down to the docks. But we didn't have any money. A terrible argument ensued with the driver when we told him we didn't have any money. The sergeant at the gate had to get involved.'

Nor did the tale end happily. 'The driver didn't get any money,' says Mr Newman, with a shade of remorse in his voice.

'Then we sailed through the Suez Canal,' he continues. 'We sailed the Red Sea and for some reason, we hove to for a while there. We were told then that we could go swimming if we wanted, so we did – swimming in the Red Sea!'

Meanwhile, a bus was sent to pick up Harold Everett and his fellow operatives from a transit camp on their arrival in Cairo. It took them to MI8 HQ in Heliopolis. Everett had been travelling for weeks. But, as he wrote, 'I was not destined to stay there very long. Many journeys lay ahead of me in many countries. My odyssey had really only just begun.'

Throughout the late autumn of 1941, the drums of approaching battle were sounding ever louder in Malaya and the Far East. The British colony of the Malayan peninsula held much that the Japanese needed: not merely was it in an excellent strategic position, it was also a land rich in rubber and metals – Japan of course lacked so many vital resources of its own. In order to fight a war successfully, to have a land such as Malaya within its grasp would have been invaluable.

According to various accounts, only a very few within the British ranks understood exactly the nature of the threat to Malaya and Singapore; and these few were countered by stubborn colonial diehards who waved away any suggestion of imminent danger. Nor, from the wireless interception point of view, was there any concrete clue as to the enemy's intentions. Certainly the listening station and Special Liaison Unit in Singapore were tracking messages to do with an ever more restless Japanese navy, while contending with ever-shifting ciphers. But even a decrypted message cannot always convey clarity. In some cases, the Japanese navy disguised the meaning of their communications by assigning certain operations code words from weather reports. Thus if a cryptographer were to receive a naval message that apparently said simply 'Westerly winds, rain', they could not be expected to guess that 'winds' and 'rain' were special terms used to denote the British, and Japanese intentions towards them.

For a young woman hailing from a quietly prosperous English provincial town like Norwich, Singapore was not an easy posting. Even without the looming catastrophe to come, this part of the world offered a great many challenges. Joan Dinwoodie had signed up for the Wrens and undergone the usual wireless telegraphy course, as well as lessons in rudimentary Japanese. Then came the voyage, which was punctuated by more than one fraught episode. 'I shared a cabin with three other girls,' she recalled. 'A few days after leaving, we were attacked by a Focke Wolf aircraft. Expecting to be sunk, two of us rushed back to our cabin and ate a whole box of Black Magic chocolates, as they were so hard to get.'

Then there was the station at Singapore itself:

> The working conditions . . . were dreadful. We worked in four hour watches in wooden huts with no windows and very little ventilation. It was extremely hot and humid and the perspiration ran down our faces, arms, bodies and into our shoes. Personnel from all three services worked together gathering and intercepting Japanese naval signals, coded and plain language signals and passing them on to Bletchley Park . . . One of the thunderstorms that were a regular afternoon feature blew four of the wireless sets and killed two of the Chinese coolies. After this we were double banked with experienced operators and had to adjust to Morse as the Japanese sent it.

It had to be admitted, though, that life was not unremittingly grim; such colonies held out a few exotic consolations. 'Although we were working very hard in difficult conditions and with different watches we still managed to have a very full social life,' remembered Mrs Dinwoodie. 'We visited the hotels – namely the Adelphi, the Rex and of course Raffles for dancing and dining. We visited rubber estates, toured [the city of] Johore Bahru, attended a Tamil wedding, and the Tiger Balm Botanical Gardens.' These, it must be reiterated, were experiences that would never before have been open to young women from such a background; in years past, only the very rich would have been able to tour and take their leisure in this way. Joan Dinwoodie was among the very first women from a more staid middle-class background to see such things.

> We also swam, played tennis and sailed whenever possible. We also went to the cinema and some of the films we saw included, 'First Love', 'Edison the Man'. During this time I met a Royal Air Force pilot named Rich and we started spending a great deal of our free time together. On one of our outings, on the 4th December 1941 we visited King Albert Park where Rich proposed to me.[5]

Tragically, the change in the air could already be sensed. Even before 7 December – the day when Japan launched the lightning, murderous assault on Pearl Harbor – everyone from the Wrens to the commanders was almost subliminally aware of a gathering feeling of oppression and menace. As Joan Dinwoodie remembered:

> The Japanese air raids were now becoming more frequent and it became very obvious that as we were the only intercept station in the far east that the authorities could not risk us being captured so we would soon have to leave. At first it was suggested that we would be sent to Australia but this changed and we were told that we would be going to Colombo in Sri Lanka (Ceylon).

Yet when Japan struck Pearl Harbor, it did so with an aggression the breadth of which had scarcely been imagined. The American fleet was almost completely destroyed. There had also been attacks on other US Pacific strongholds. And throughout Malaya and in Singapore, Japanese air raids had begun to increase in both frequency and ferocity.

In late December the decision was finally taken to remove the Far East Combined Bureau from Singapore; as Joan Dinwoodie said, it was shifted to Colombo in Ceylon. Memos in the archives reveal that there had been a great deal of heated debate, illuminating both the limits of communications technology and the extent to which certain aspects of the war were a matter of discussion, and indeed of miniature power struggles. Not only were the three services constantly jostling for primacy, there were also cliques within cliques in intelligence; the wishes of Bletchley Park operatives, for instance, straining against those of military intelligence. Even with Japanese fighters strafing Singapore, and the countdown to the invasion ticking by, there had been quarrels about what to do with the wireless interception services, and where best to send them.

'It was clear,' states one document for the attention of Bletchley Park's deputy director, Nigel de Grey, 'that following the outbreak of war with the Japanese, the Sigint party at Singapore would have to evacuate somewhere . . . [some] thought Australia would provide better facilities . . . An emergency meeting of the "Y" committee was called in London and the question of Melbourne was raised.' Also on the table was the possibility of relocating to India, to join up with Captain Marr-Johnson's Y operation. And what of Kenya, and the out-station site at Kilindini in Mombasa?

Australia continued to seem the most attractive option; but this idea was stymied by the certainty that 'communications between Australia and the UK were likely to go at any time and it would not be possible to get any raw material either "to" or "from" Australia.' Meanwhile, the most obvious drawback of Ceylon, as understood by senior figures such as Nigel de Grey and Alastair Denniston, was that it might not prove safe. The idea of east Africa was mooted yet further, with discussions about the transportation of technical coding material, such as the Hollerith machines – card-operated behemoths ordinarily used for simple accounting and calculations which had a use in terms of processing encoded letters. But time ran out and the Singapore staff were posted – in the nick of time – to the naval base just south of Colombo known as HMS *Anderson*.

Most of the staff evacuated from Singapore immediately; a few stayed behind in order to 'assist Army and Special Air Intelligence'. At the same time, Bletchley Park's special liaison contingent also left: among them was Arthur Cooper, the brother of senior Bletchley codebreaker Josh Cooper. The departure of such personnel from Singapore was vital on two levels: to keep the flow of decrypts moving smoothly; and to prevent such people falling into the hands of the enemy. If interrogated, they would have a wealth of secret information to disclose under torture. As one veteran has already noted, capture in these circumstances would have meant the life of a wireless operator would no longer be worth living; and death would be both terrible and slow.

There followed weeks of ferocious fighting. On 7 February, General Percival announced that Singapore would stand to the last man, as the Japanese guns were turned on the city. Come 15 February, Singapore surrendered and over 60,000 soldiers were taken prisoner.

To this day, the fall of Singapore is an episode of Second World War history that causes many to shake their heads. We were 'looking the wrong way'; the disgrace that was brought upon the British was almighty; and the suffering caused to so many thousands of soldiers by their Japanese captors still evokes horror.

Yet amid the carnage, the Y Service and the codebreakers, removed to Colombo, returned to work with remarkable speed; the ferocity of the Japanese onslaught appeared to have the effect of stimulating fresh, successful efforts to pierce the Japanese codes. The Far East Combined Bureau massed itself a little outside Colombo; its staff now included thirty-eight Wrens trained in Japanese wireless transmission. By March, the Bureau had managed to intercept and unscramble more Japanese signals, and its efforts were shared this time with the Americans.

And as time went on, it became apparent that as a posting, there were many worse places than HMS *Anderson* to be sent; indeed, a number of the young people who sailed halfway across the world to reach those shores found instantly that there was something quite enchanting about them. This was especially the case in an age of rationing.

'HMS *Anderson* was well off the road,' says Victor Newman, who arrived in Colombo some time after Singapore's fall having beforehand rarely left his native Weybridge. 'Every day, there was a lorry called the Liberty Boat that would take people down into Colombo. But rather than going into town, I used to enjoy going to a spot called Mount Lavinia. It was a place where you could go swimming.

'You would see local ladies there,' Mr Newman continues, with a note of wistfulness. 'They would have baskets on their heads that were full of pineapples. Imagine having all that delicious pineapple juice running down your face . . . and then washing it off with a swim. It was a beautiful spot.'

There was also the eye-popping nature of the local wildlife. On the night train from the harbour at Trinacomalee, says Mr Newman, 'I saw fireflies out the window. Millions upon millions of fireflies. I had never seen anything like that before.'

Unlike many of the Wrens who were about to arrive, Mr Newman was not keen on the lively Colombo nightlife – the local fauna once again being part of the reason: 'You only went to the cinema in Colombo if you didn't mind getting insect bites. After the film, you'd get up and find the underside of your legs had bites all over.' As for other exotic sightings, 'There was the occasional snake – I saw one on a football pitch. Then there was a large reptile like an iguana one day, which some of the locals were chasing – presumably,' he adds with a laugh, 'to eat it.'

Mr Newman was also – given his technical position as a wireless interceptor – suspicious of being made to take part in any form of barracks-confined military activity. 'HMS *Anderson* was quite a big station – two huts on the side, canteen and the mess. They brought in a small squad of marines – and this resulted in paper raids, Sunday divisions. Our work took precedence over parades. And we could sometimes bunk off them too. They were building a new mess hall at that time and when parades came round, some of us could go in there and hide ourselves. That worked until one Sunday when we were hiding in these cupboards and got caught. We weren't allowed to go into town for a week after that. Not,' he adds, 'that that was any great hardship.'

And while the Wrens in Colombo lived in rather less regimented accommodation, the men of HMS *Anderson* were very much enclosed within barracks. 'Accommodation was camp beds, with mosquito nets over them. We had the blankets that we had been issued with but quite often you didn't need them at all. When you were working, you wore shorts and short-sleeved shirts. And the mosquitoes were not a worry because down that end of the country, they were not malaria carrying. More uncomfortable for the RAF, who had to wear long-sleeved shirts and long trousers.'

Victor Newman – who, just weeks beforehand, had been working in the Home Counties countryside, in a tiny office attached to an oil-seed mill – took to his new life of colour and intensity with a readiness that older people might not have been able to match. And he was by no means alone. It would not be too long before fresh female recruits were to discover that, alongside the gruelling work, there was something magical about this part of the world that they might otherwise never have seen.

8 Feuds, Farce and Panic

The secret listeners were young, and very often they were women. But back in Britain, an honourable role was carved out for middle-aged and older men too – without any intended disrespect, a sort of *Dad's Army* branch of the Y Services, as Ted Mitchell recalls.

Mr Mitchell's father was sought out for his radio skills in the early stages of the war. Slightly too old to fight with the regulars, he none the less had a huge amount to contribute, and he did so in circumstances that were occasionally very funny and rather surreal.

'As a teenager during the Great War,' says Mr Mitchell now of his father, 'he went straight from school to Leith Wireless College. After graduation, he joined Marconi as a Wireless Operator and thereafter was assigned to a series of merchant ships during and after the war – torpedoed once!

'He left the service on marriage in 1926 to embark on a career in the fledgling electrical sector.' Like everyone from Richard Gambier-Parry to Ray Fautley, Mitchell senior ploughed himself into what would prove to be one of the most crucial of the new industries. And like those others, he clearly had an abiding love and fascination for what he did. As Voluntary Interceptor Ray

Fautley has wisely observed, for those who were fortunate enough to pursue radio and make a living from it, 'it hardly felt like work.'

'With the looming prospect of another war,' says Mr Mitchell, '[my father] volunteered initially with the Merchant Navy Reserve which led to his joining the Voluntary Interceptors.' Indeed, among his father's papers is a letter from Lord Sandwich, chief of the Radio Security Service, welcoming him into the fold with words of encouragement and warning:

> Valuable results have already been achieved by Voluntary Interceptors. And the very nature of our work must mean that in many cases, watch may be maintained for weeks without apparent result. Do not let this discourage you; the fact that there has been no illicit transmission does not mean that there will not be and we must be ready and watching to catch it when it happens. Finally, I cannot impress too strongly upon you the need for silence and discretion. Great care is taken in the selection of Voluntary Interceptors and equal care should be taken by them to ensure that this trust is not abused.

But that was only the beginning. A little later on, Mitchell senior found himself being drafted into rather more hands-on activities. 'My father was called up to full-time duties with the Radio Security Service,' says Mr Mitchell. 'He was provided with an Army uniform badged as Royal Signals and he was sent to Penzance, Cornwall. There he was billeted in a guest house with two similar recruits, all of whom would be stationed at the newly built receiver at St Erth. There they met up with all the other operators, who were aged between forty and seventy plus.'

Mitchell senior was introduced to this new life by means of another Radio Security Service letter, which read: 'For reasons of security and discipline, personnel who are employed by RSS will be enlisted as serving soldiers.' But, it added, a 'special form of enlistment is used whereby the soldier is bound only to serve in

RSS. Should his engagement in RSS be terminated, he becomes automatically entitled to a free discharge from the Army and return to civilian life.'

'Definite discipline' was a given; and yet, as the letter intriguingly added, 'the whole organisation is run in accordance with modern ideas which are very different from traditional notions of Army discipline.'

Perhaps so; the area of Cornwall to which Mitchell was being sent was remote – far from parade grounds – and St Erth was the highest point. It had fine strategic value, and these gentlemen of a certain age were doing vital work. 'They were organised into teams working in shifts covering twenty-four hours, monitoring German signals from occupied France as well as from U-boats in the eastern Atlantic,' says Mr Mitchell.

Of course, having such a 'phantom' company of soldiers did result in strange encounters – embarrassing at the time but amusing in retrospect. On one occasion they met some regular Royal Signals personnel at a pub and had to be rather evasive in response to queries – so much so that the regular soldiers officially reported that they had met suspected spies masquerading in Army uniform.

'On another occasion, the Army Command suddenly heard of the existence of this squad of Royal Signals which apparently had no documentation. Command therefore sent a drill sergeant to Cornwall to discover more,' says Mr Mitchell. The notion of 'modern ideas of discipline' was pushed to one side as the fearsome sergeant caught up with this incongruous and mature platoon. 'The drill sergeant planned to start by giving them all a good dose of PT but when he saw them all lined up, he was aghast and decided to substitute this with a walk instead.'

Even that was to little avail. 'During this "walk",' continues Mr Mitchell, 'several of the men collapsed and had to be revived with cups of tea from local householders. The drill sergeant heard those householders muttering things like: "Poor old men – it's dreadful that they have to put them in the Army at their age."'

At their age, it must have been flattering nonetheless to be regarded as skilled operators. And the Radio Security Service was most insistent on the precise levels of those skills. To make Grade A – and thus be in line for the sum of £7 a week – you had to have a 'speed of 23 words per minute' when transcribing signals, 'as well as an ability to read weak signals through jamming and a general aptitude for wireless interception work.' Incidentally, if £7 a week now sounds an absurdly paltry amount, it might be worth bearing in mind that many of the younger codebreakers at Bletchley Park – flat out, day and night, in the intricacies of Enigma – were often on £4 a week. From this we might gather that wireless interceptors were appreciated.

Even on Grade C – '18 words per minute or less where the applicant shows definite promise and aptitude for wireless interception work' – the operator could expect to make £5 a week. For the older recruits, such as Mr Mitchell's father, this might not have seemed much, but for some of the younger men, it was quite a sum.

Grading was carried out after an exam – 'practical and oral'. Even the Grade C test was tough; if they wanted to make Grade A, the wireless operators were required to take down '69 groups of 5 letter cypher in three minutes making not more than 8 mistakes'. The reward, other than the money, was the prospect of cosy quarters – 'they will consist of well-built brick huts with proper heating, etc' stated an RSS memo, adding: 'Those huts although built for 40 men will be used to accommodate only 20. Each hut will be partitioned into 10 divisions . . . Each division . . . will accommodate two men with a view to providing a degree of privacy.'

Compared to the bustling conditions encountered by ordinary soldiers, these premises have a touch of luxury about them. But in other ways, the Radio Security Service was very far from a cushy number. Given the almost preternatural concentration that the job required, a comfortable bed after eight hours' listening and noting weak signals throughout a black night was hardly too much to ask.

In wider terms, the organisation was deemed such a success that it became, in 1941, the subject of a jealous government departmental tug of love: which part of Whitehall should take control of it? The Radio Security Service was subsumed into MI6 that year, and came under the control of Lieutenant-Colonel E.L. Maltby (with the ever-genial Brigadier Gambier-Parry taking a wider overview of all branches of the Y Service). Not everyone was thrilled. In the upheaval, Captain Trevor-Roper's old boss Walter Gill was demoted and Trevor-Roper's own job was recalibrated. According to Richard Davenport-Hines, editor of Trevor-Roper's wartime diaries, he was now chief of the intelligence sub-section to be known as the Radio Analysis Bureau. He had new bosses: Felix Cowgill, head of the MI6 counter-espionage unit, and MI6's deputy, Valentine Vivian. For both of these men, Trevor-Roper apparently felt 'mutinous contempt'. His wider opinion of the secret services was extremely low, and his periodic spasms of rage would soon find creative outlet in some venomously furious private poetry.

Despite the inability of various parties in MI6 and MI5 to contain their mutual disdain, the wireless operation was working, and giving Bletchley Park invaluable material. In terms of interception, the RSS's main radio masts were now to be found at Hanslope Park, not far from Bletchley Park. This allowed the RSS to monitor the Abwehr around the clock, which was later to give piercing insights into German operations not merely in Europe and the Mediterranean but also around the world. It has been estimated that half the staff of the RSS had been huge radio enthusiasts in their civilian lives. Every hobby has its practical uses in the end.

Elsewhere, despite the nerve-jangling nature of the work, life at Beaumanor Hall was settling down into a pattern of quirks and small eccentricities that mirrored the anarchy of Bletchley Park. Again, this seemed partly to do with the volatile mix of civilians and military personnel (the latter chiefly in the form of ATS girls). The staff magazine, for instance – assembled by committee and laid out with surprising skill with plenty of illustrations – ran, almost from the start, regular 'gossip' items concerning the latest parties and romances. There were limerick competitions, in which readers were invited to complete the following from opening lines such as 'A wheezy young lady of Rye . . .', 'The curious habits of men . . .' or 'A frivolous filly of Bicester. . .', the whole being accompanied by little dustings of mildly saucy, lightly racist jokes:

> An ARP warden spotting a light showing through a crack in the door, knocked and said to the woman inside: 'I have just seen a chink coming through your door.' The woman exclaimed: 'The *******! He told me he was a Polish airman!'

Those who had been transferred from RAF Chicksands to Beaumanor were addressed with an especially lively editorial: 'We say farewell CHICKSANDS and HOLD TIGHT Leicester! Pigs, billets, free buses, wonderful canteen, plenty of smokes? Here, have all . . . we may, we hope, look forward to happier, freer and smokier days!'

There were other, less openly discussed concerns, such as romance. Many cartoons in the Beaumanor staff magazine involve Wrens and soldiers, with the soldiers apparently the focus of all the Wrens' attentions. Then there was the equally cartoon-like gossip around the establishment. Repeated with delight was the instance of a young female wireless operator who had been celebrating her twenty-second birthday. A male colleague told her that if he had known what the day was, he would have taken her out 'on the razzle'. She replied: 'I didn't know you had a razzle.'

The magazine gleefully noted elsewhere that one of the young female 'runners' – the messengers – reported being 'chased by a small man while on Night Duty'. 'We have long felt,' commented the magazine, 'that there is still too much wishful thinking in the country.'

The make-up of the place, says Beaumanor veteran Chris Barnes, was 'ATS women, civilian men. And I suppose there were occasional get-togethers in the canteen, and so on. But a number of people I know who formed lasting partnerships there are very small indeed. We didn't work in the same huts, by the way, men and women worked in quite different huts.' Although less a separation by gender than one of ATS (military) and civilian, perhaps this explains why, according to Mr Barnes's observations, there was a great deal less romance than one might have expected. 'Interestingly, I don't remember very many people getting married,' he continues. 'There weren't very many romances. In the staff magazines, you come across some, but those entries are mainly written by women.'

Beaumanor sometimes received distinguished visitors, from important politicians to top brass. Wren Ollie Pearce noted such special guests in a few sardonic lines of verse – as ever, these fragments illustrate conditions much more colourfully than their writers ever intended:

> I glance up as some strangers enter
> And hear a voice proclaim 'Nerve Centre'
> With vacant stares they gaze about
> In wonderment, without a doubt
> Regarding me as people do
> Uncommon species at a zoo.

A little later, a fresh influx of female recruits prompted Pearce to new heights of lyricism:

> Due to the recent innovation
> Of female scribes now at our station
> Life's taken on a different hue
> And interest has been born anew.

The effect of female colleagues on the menfolk was described thus:

Vocabularies have grown quite small
Some words are never heard at all! . . .
In answer to 'How does she shape?'
Some fellow, grinning like an ape
Will wave his two hands in the air
Describing curves beyond compare . . .

There was little time for such cheerful sexism in other listening establishments, chiefly because women had a more dominant role. Throughout the many coastal listening stations, ever greater numbers of Wrens were being trained. But this is not to say that life by the sea was smooth-going; rather, as at Chicksands, the intensity of the work – and the tight shift system – led to outbreaks of conflict. Elizabeth Mashall wrote:

Watchkeeping was one area where discipline was always maintained. Once a watchlist had been posted, changes could not be made except for sickness or going on leave – and in the latter case, only if there were enough operators to cover the period without causing undue strain.

I had to postpone my own leave once or twice because of this but there were two very traumatic incidents when I delayed the leave of two others. Neither of these incidents could have been foreseen, but that did not prevent the intense resentment that followed as a result. The first was at North Foreland when, to cover watches, I delayed the leave of a Wren for a few days. Her husband, who had been in England, was unexpectedly and at very short notice posted overseas and she missed seeing him before he went. The other incident . . . was really very tragic as when a Wren arrived a few days later than was originally intended, and was greeted with the news that her airforce husband had been killed the previous night.[1]

Mistakes were made too; how could they not be? There was often an inherent ambiguity in the very nature of call signs and messages – not just the heavily encoded material, but also in even the low-level code words used by pilots when communicating over the radio – and those who were listening could not always be expected to interpret correctly what they heard. The consequences of each and every failure, though, were tragic; and the authorities tried to keep up the pressure on the listening stations to achieve 100 per cent accuracy. In May 1942, Arthur Bonsall, who had done so much to establish the station at RAF Cheadle, was looking into a night of losses. During a Lancaster bomber raid on Augsburg, German fighter pilots had materialised without warning and shot four of the planes down. Was this because of faulty intelligence? And could the system be tightened up? 'Our aim is to discover . . . whether we can augment in any way the information we pass to RAF Kingsdown,' wrote Bonsall, 'so that in the future even more operational intelligence can be extracted by them from the R/T intercepts.'

Bomber Command claimed that the Kingsdown listeners 'were not able to supply them with details of where the bombers were intercepted and by whom'. 'It is not suggested that Kingsdown missed an obvious tie-up,' the memo continued. 'The intercepts in question were taken by Beachy Head and were very restrained.' But somewhere along the line, the German fighters had been detected by their messages, and yet two and two had not been added together when it came to their targets. 'This instance does tend to show that the art of correctly melding relevant intercepts is by no means an elementary one.'

It was not a blame game; nonetheless, the pressure under which the wireless interceptors operated was perhaps occasionally greater than that endured by the Bletchley codebreakers. The results of their work were immediate and concrete: unlike the mathematical abstraction of cracking a cipher, the women and men in headsets, taking down those messages, were also in some cases hearing a moment-by-moment commentary – real, live pilots' voices, not staccato dots and dashes – on the deadly manoeuvres being executed in distant skies. The lives of Lancaster crews were often in their hands.

The conflict was of course every bit as grave in the Middle East; but those posted to Cairo continued to find – even as Rommel and his forces made their seemingly unstoppable progress east – that the city had its own curiously detached atmosphere. Harold Everett was now 'attached to one of those mysterious units whose function was to provide information to HQ about enemy communications and to provide replacements for the intercept units in the desert'. They were, Everett wrote, 'a special wireless group and covered everything from Panzer Armee Afrika to – it was said – Balkan Tramways'.

Everett was conscious of being the new boy; also there when he arrived were veterans from desert units: 'To a newcomer like myself, everyone seemed so "dug in". They knew the best restaurants and cafes in Cairo, they knew when free concerts were to be given . . . and above all, they knew where not to go for fear of risk to life, limb or wallet.'

Nor was Everett especially charmed by the workplace that had entranced Aileen Clayton and Barbara Skelton – the old museum at Heliopolis: 'Both its exterior and its interior were ornately decorated in oriental style and the absence of glass in the window openings kept the place cool. Opposite our museum was a strangely elaborate carved tower said to house a collection of pornographic paintings belonging to King Farouk. Unfortunately, it was kept locked.'

This was not the only setback:

Our camp was in the museum grounds. It was a miserable place. Unbearably hot in the afternoons, when we did not work, and with practically no amenities to enliven the evenings or other time off. The food was atrocious and was served in a scruffy cookhouse thoughtfully sited next to the latrines. There were flies everywhere and 'Gyppy tummy' was prevalent.[2]

Despite this, the community was close, even in the face of the ongoing feud between the military and the cryptographers – the latter led by Major Freddie Jacob, Director of the Combined Middle East Bureau. In late 1941, Lieutenant-Colonel Scott of the military fired off another scorching memo to his superiors in London concerning what he considered to be the Bureau's shortcomings. 'You are aware that it has always been difficult to work with Director CMEB,' he wrote. 'Cryptographic institutions are curious things. We have always made allowances for this, and put up with many things for the sake of "Y" as a whole. Records of the correspondence between this HQ and Heliopolis show this clearly enough . . .'

Scott went on to quote from Heliopolis memos that complained of lack of staff, as well as about having to provide 'cryptographic personnel to work with sections in the Western Desert'. The cryptographers' position was that 'all ciphers should be solved at the School [Heliopolis], and that partially readable low grade ciphers should be handed to officers who have been trained at the School to handle and exploit traffic passing in such ciphers. These officers can then be sent to the forward sections, and not cryptographers on the School's establishment.'

Scott was beside himself over the 'flagrantly dishonest' position taken by Heliopolis; his view was that barely a handful of its cryptographers had been sent to the Western Desert. On top of this, it was his opinion that Major Jacob . . .

lives in a curious world of unreality in which he sees himself as the emperor of all the 'Y' services . . .

The present state of affairs should not be allowed to continue. The military 'Y' organisation here is strained to its utmost and the friction and opposition that we meet with from Heliopolis in our efforts to improve and expand use up time and energy which should be devoted to beating the enemy.

This was followed by a smoother, more darkly treacly memo, copied and distributed more widely among a few other officers, quietly and calmly explaining that the Director of the Combined Middle East Bureau was 'a representative' of the Government Code and Cypher School, 'consulted on all matters concerning our own ciphers and those of our allies' and steeped in all manner of hidden responsibilities that gave him a wide purview over the needs of the services when it came to interception and codebreaking. He proceeded to list – with a feast of acronyms – the exact functions of each and every branch of the Y Service in the Middle East, and concluded that 'we are all here to serve' and that 'our links with the "Y" organisation in the UK are purely technical ones.'[3]

There is no secret about communications in war; all combatants understand that the enemy will be listening, and at all times. We have only to think of the young Luftwaffe pilot who addressed his jovial remarks directly to the young women he knew would be monitoring his transmissions in the coastal stations. But for the Army in the Middle East, there was a point when the workings of the Y Service seemed to become opaque; it was to this that Lieutenant-Colonel Scott objected so vociferously. How could it be that the listeners seemed beyond the control of the military? Furthermore, how could it be that in Heliopolis, they appeared to be running an autonomous and independent operation, answering apparently only to an even more clandestine hierarchy?

But the fact was that the Cairo listeners and the cryptographers were largely under the aegis of MI8, and of Bletchley Park too. This was not just a matter of concealing from the enemy that you had tapped into his radio signals, for he would assume that you had done so. It was a matter of concealing the fact that you had then either decrypted his messages on site in Cairo, or sent those messages, in their impenetrable codes, back to Bletchley Park, where they had been unlocked. For any commander to act on information gained thereby, the source obviously had to be concealed, or faked.

Internal tension was therefore inevitable. There were occasions when the military accused the codebreakers of 'holding back' vital information concerning German tanks; the Heliopolis station vehemently denied doing any such thing. Then there were the unsubtle accusations that the station personnel were behaving almost like spoiled children. 'I have had a series of periodic wails about a shortage of staff . . .' declared one military memo. 'It is difficult to be moved by the story of the hard work being done at Heliopolis. Other "Y" troops are working just as hard in the field, and under most uncomfortable conditions. Heliopolis still finds time for its vague and long letters.' The memo concluded saltily: 'If Jacob would stick to co-ordinating the crypto work of the three Sections and leave it at that, things would be easier. No-one questions his crypto ability.'

But then one day in 1942 came the panic-stricken evacuation of the British operatives from Cairo to Palestine, and it was noted that, for those who had been in the city for any length of time, news of the move – caused by Rommel's seemingly ineluctable progress – came as a heavy blow. The day became known as 'Ash Wednesday', when, in the face of the Afrika Korps' advance, GHQ in Cairo burnt all vital documentation and the ashes of so many secret documents formed billowing clouds in the air. Harold Everett's wry observations turn a scene of undignified panic into something closer to Keystone Kop comedy:

Ash Wednesday – the famous day on which the British Embassy burnt its secret papers and showered ashes on Cairo is well known, but running the embassy burnings a close second was the incineration that took place at the School [Heliopolis]. Every piece of paper on which there were any indications that intercept was the School's 'business' was to be burned. I was one of a group of NCOs entrusted with this task. I burned paper until I was up to my ankles in ash and had succeeded in burning my mini-puttees. Others armed with india-rubber were ordered to erase all call-signs or other revealing graffiti that was written on walls, tables or chairs. An unfortunate few were detailed to the latrines to remove, if necessary, any secret waste which, contrary to standing orders, had been used as toilet paper.

We were somewhat cheered up in our task by a rumour that the electrically obsessed captain had given himself a shock trying to dismantle some of the wiring which had so fascinated him. Every sign of our existence was to be expunged. Like Baloutha the walls were to be left desolate.[4]

According to another Cairo officer, Lieutenant-Colonel Sayer, who later that year wrote a long letter – now held in the National Archives – on the subject, it was quite an achievement to keep the Y Service properly operational during the crisis. 'The "flap" was terrific, with "evacuation" the slogan,' he wrote, adding sardonically:

> Many an awkward file must have disappeared in the holocaust, which became one of the jokes of Cairo. Our plan was simple. To get away as much of our 'Y' resources as we could, so that we could build up and start again somewhere else. While order followed order, we quietly slipped across the Canal . . . B sections, a large part of the Special Wireless Group . . . this lot made me feel that, if the worst came to the worst, we could get going again in Syria or Iraq in next to no time.

The subsequent embarrassing evacuation of Cairo – embassy staff, refugees, escaped politicians from Greece – sounds, from Harold Everett's account, extraordinarily chaotic. There were scenes of confusion and distress at the railway station as a disparate population of expats were corralled on to trains for destinations such as Gaza in Palestine. Sayer, in an informal dispatch sent back to London, subsequently contrived to see the lighter side of it:

> Sarafand [in Palestine] was standing room only. Most of 5 IS got parked in the camp of a Weapon Training School, where they ate the bread of idleness for many days. Then the O.C. School decided that it would be good for them to have some training in bayonet fighting. And they had to do it. This was one of the more humorous incidents.

He was also robustly rude about a couple of the female Y Service operatives, who 'have an enormous sense of their own importance, although they haven't produced anything worth fourpence since east Africa. Well, they were told one morning that all women employed by the Army were to be temporarily enrolled in the ATS in order to facilitate control during evacuation . . .' But these women, according to Sayer, had their own condition to lay down: that they be enrolled automatically as captains. 'Imagine it, mon cher . . .' wrote Sayer to his unnamed correspondent. 'Rommel bowling gaily towards Alex[andria]; the smoke of the burning GHQ papers clouding the sky . . . and these two damn women arguing that their positions in 5 IS would be jeopardised if they were evacuated as privates ATS and not officers.'

Having been informed by the First Secretary at the Embassy that her association with King Farouk was unsuitable, 'cipherine' Barbara Skelton herself left Egypt, and found herself in Jerusalem. 'After buying some Syrian silk stockings,' she wrote of her introduction to the city, 'I boarded a car loaded with Wrens who never stopped chattering about their mothers' dogs, other Wrens' young men or dances. The driver and I exchanged desperate glances.'

But she took to the city, and to Palestine, very quickly. Indeed, it seemed to come as something of a relief to her sensibilities. She admired the strong-looking women with baskets of fruit on their heads, and even the healthy-looking donkeys, which she compared favourably to their 'wiry' Cairo counterparts. Overall, she found much more colour here, even in the occasional bad meal, with fish that tasted 'like drains'. The idyll was not to last; a matter of weeks later, while she was sunbathing in Haifa, a 'very dilapidated' bus with the word ENSA stencilled on it drew up; the drivers assumed that she was an ENSA girl and as a result, they drove her all the way back to Cairo.

Even in the aftermath of the chaos, there were more uplifting moments in Cairo; one such was the trapping of a German spy, who had been operating with an illicit aerial, some poor counterfeit currency, and codes deriving from Daphne Du Maurier's *Rebecca*. Wireless intercept operators were able to pick up the spy's lame transmissions and in the end, he was cornered on a boat by a British major. The spy tried to escape by throwing a 'grenade' which turned out to be a pair of rolled-up socks. Sometimes it is difficult to know with the Abwehr whether such gambits were purposely bathetic.

In terms of security, British communications back home appeared to be reasonably watertight, though there were doubts, precisely because of the intense secrecy, that the military top brass in the desert were getting the full benefit. Because the work of Bletchley was known only to a very few in Whitehall, Ultra information had to be parcelled out in ways that obscured its source. In mid-1942, Churchill himself instructed the head of MI6 to make sure that the full text of two German situation reports was sent to General Auchinleck, so that he could be in no doubt that he had access to genuine intelligence, as opposed to what he might have seen as suppositions from various agents. Bletchley Park until that point had been careful to paraphrase such information to muddy the source; after this, according to the Bletchley official history, they were more relaxed about sending precise messages – though in the summer of 1942, as Rommel's eastwards rampage continued, these were of limited value.

The difficulty was that although the messages were being decrypted, interpreting them was another matter; and Rommel was adept at disguising his plans and misdirecting his enemies. Thus, just before the Battle of Gazala in May 1942, even though his forces – the artillery, the tanks, the divisions – could be heard massing via the build-up of radio traffic, no one among the British could work out how these were to be deployed. Rommel's messages were so carefully couched that even once the code was broken, the terms he used remained elliptical – a challenge that no codebreaker can surmount without direct access to the relevant glossary of code terms – and his plans could not be immediately divined.

Rommel had one other hugely useful secret weapon at his disposal; the Germans were in receipt of decrypted messages sent from the US military attaché in Cairo back to Washington DC. As a result, during the Battle of Gazala, the Germans were rather better informed than the British. The British fought back fiercely, forcing the Germans on to the defensive for a time, with heavy losses on both sides; but Rommel counter-attacked, and the British were forced on to the back foot and ultimately had to retreat from Gazala. And now Rommel's forces advanced inexorably upon the Allied positions at Tobruk, creating carnage. Here, however, Bletchley Park and the Y units were able to provide a constant stream of Enigma decrypts; possibly thanks to these, the British Eighth Army retreated in time. Nonetheless, Tobruk surrendered. Rommel was made a field marshal. Allied anxiety was profound: were Rommel's seemingly unstoppable forces on the edge of seizing Egypt? In June, the British had created a new line at El Alamein; Rommel's intention was to smash right through it.

However, in one of those smoke-and-mirrors reverses that seem to characterise the intelligence world of Bletchley and the Y Services, the intercepts eventually picked up messages showing that Rommel had been reading the US military attaché's reports.

One particular dispatch stated that the British were pretty much beaten; this in turn led Rommel to believe that now was the right time to take the Nile Delta. It is thanks to decrypts from the Y Services at Heliopolis and Bletchley that the British, in turn, were able to note Rommel's plans and predict the date of his assaults.

In fact, the interception services were getting sharper; it also helped tremendously that in August, Rommel's field Signal Intelligence Unit was captured, leaving his forces a little vulnerable. The exhausted General Auchinleck was replaced by the then Lieutenant-General Bernard Montgomery, and just days after he took command, a crucial Enigma message was decoded; it was, broadly, an outline of Rommel's attack plans. The line at El Alamein was strengthened, while Montgomery encouraged even greater fluidity in the flow of Y intercepts and Bletchley intelligence to the front, asking that reports be shorn of jargon so that they could be understood by all those who needed to see them.

Thanks to these decrypts and interceptions, Montgomery was able to build up a brilliantly accurate picture not merely of Rommel's land forces, but also of the air power being mustered between the Germans and the Italians. When at the end of August Rommel's fresh advance was launched, the British forces knew exactly what to expect, and countered it expertly. 'During Rommel's attack in August, we had him "taped" the whole time,' wrote Lieutenant-Colonel Sayer in a letter back to London in November. 'The El Alamein line gave us our first chance to use Loop D/F.' Direction finding with a loop aerial was to prove especially effective at picking up the sources of enemy transmissions. 'It was immensely valuable.'

The Germans drew back; and at this point, the desert war started to turn decisively. Decrypts and intercepted messages showed within a couple of days that Rommel was concerned about his lines of supply, and about the transport losses the Afrika Korps had suffered before its retreat. This intelligence allowed Montgomery the breathing space he needed to put his forces through ever more intensive training. The work of Heliopolis and Cairo had given Montgomery the opportunity to plan with much greater effectiveness, even in the face of pleas from Whitehall that he should go on the offensive before Rommel had the chance to summon stronger defences. The Second Battle of El Alamein would come just a few weeks later – a battle in which the Y Service was to operate at the very peak of its power.

As the USA finally entered the war in December 1941, with her forces materialising throughout 1942, the question of just how much the British could share of the secrets of Bletchley Park was raised. It was not merely a matter of pooled intelligence; there was again the altogether more vital question of security. Even by this point, very few people outside Bletchley Park knew the extent to which the codebreakers had been taking the Enigma codes apart. And no matter how staunch an ally the US was, there was an understable initial hesitancy when it came to sharing their deepest confidences.

But from the start, Bletchley's relations with their counterparts in the US military were friendly, and there was a great deal of mutual respect; respect that was not often mirrored in political circles. And as a small party of Americans were inducted into the secrets of Alan Turing's bombe machines – the advanced electrical contraptions, standing eight feet tall, at Bletchley and its associated out-stations, that crunched through potential Enigma permutations at industrial speed – so too was US command taking a strong interest in the way that the British had organised its Y Service. And much as the military forces were fighting side by side, there was interest in setting up American Y bases on English soil. Early in 1942, the Y Committee invited Captain Brown of the US Army Signals Corps to take an overview of the entire operation, from Hampshire all the way to Mombasa. His subsequent report, lodged in the archives, makes for fascinating reading – he was especially impressed with the thoroughness of the training that each of the new recruits was put through. 'At the conclusion . . . the students are given a practical exercise,' he wrote. 'Linguists, log readers and check clerks' would be assembled:

> [Then the] background of a certain military situation is explained to all concerned and the exercise begins. From messages intercepted on the headphones and operation orders delivered by 'dispatch riders', the syndicates are expected to deduce the enemy intentions and report them to the instructing officer . . . Misleading and irrelevant messages are interposed between those containing valuable information and this information is in turn given sometimes in terms which should be obvious to the dullest intellect and sometimes in a more subtle or indirect form. 'Noises off' such as of dive bombing and shell fire are introduced into the microphone in an attempt to simulate active service conditions as closely as possible.[5]

What impressed Captain Brown particularly was the care with which each recruit was selected and graded before being assigned to particular Y Service duties; from dexterity with complex messages, to the ability, in battle situations, to screen out the tumult and focus in the face of disorientation and danger, on the signals coming through. All this required both special techniques and special character.

It should be remembered that the US military at that time lacked the breadth of experience in wireless interception that the British had gained. And so Captain Brown concluded by recommending that 'the American Signal Intelligence Service maintain the closest contact and co-ordination with the British Y Service to the end that our units may be quickly trained to penetrate the complexities of the German system'.

But there were still delicate security considerations – and matters of diplomacy – for the Y Committee to debate. Any American listening base established in Britain would be passing its material both to Bletchley Park and to US headquarters in London. The Americans wanted a prime site at which to train their own secret listeners; the Y Committee felt that the base already established at Trowbridge in Wiltshire might be ideal. In the archival memos of the Y Committee, we see a fascinating – and fleeting – deference shown towards the British. The Americans were happy to tug at the sleeve of MI8 to ask advice on such matters as the security implications of sending raw material via teleprinter. And MI8 was also on hand to help out with 'suitable lists' of call signs and frequencies.

In fact, the amount of hand-holding that went on in the early stages now makes for charming reading; just as Y Service operatives such as Pat Sinclair and Marjorie Gerken were later to be amused by the influx of American personnel, with their hilariously direct ways, so the British authorities were pleasantly helpful, especially when it came to smoothing ruffled feathers. One such case involved the proposed US listening site in Trowbridge; in order for them to move in, the British company already there, headed by Colonel de Cros, would have to be shunted out. The Americans were anxious that MI8 do the talking to de Cros; they thought it would sound better coming from them. The British were happy to oblige.

A few weeks later, though, it turned out that, for technical reasons, Trowbridge was not what the Americans were after. Could they instead move to another base they had had their eye on – Tidworth? Again, the Y Committee was pleased to be of service. But the novice Americans were in turn anxious not to cause offence. Pleased with British offers that training officers be sent out to the US to bring operatives there up to speed, they were equally keen not to cause diplomatic strains regarding the destination of their intercepted signals; the Americans' Colonel Bicher informed the Y Committee that of course all traffic should be sent through to Bletchley Park, and that everything would be done to ensure that the Americans and the British did not simply end up duplicating each other's work. It was the start of a beautiful friendship; one which, in the aftermath of the war, would become uneven and strained.

At roughly the same time, security considerations of quite a different order of magnitude were arising – with the Russians. In September 1942, Major Edward Crankshaw was in Moscow, reporting back to the Y Committee. By this stage, the Soviets were already deep in the unimaginably bloody struggle with the Germans that would claim the lives of countless civilians and lay waste much of eastern Europe. Acutely aware of the difficulties in dealing with Stalin and his brutalised, terrorised underlings, Crankshaw was in the Russian capital to try and reach an agreement about the sharing of certain intercept information. 'Y service evidently wanted to co-operate owing to value of our offerings and initial meeting went well,' he wrote in a communication marked 'Most Secret', adding tartly: 'This was followed by comatose dry-up. I was not even given chance to hand over material badly needed by Red Army.'[6]

Even now, the extent to which the alliance between the British and the Soviets in the war allowed the Russians in on vital secrets is ambiguous. Certainly there was no intention that Stalin should be vouchsafed the greatest secret of all – the continuing decoding triumphs of Bletchley Park. None the less, Churchill was swift to understand the value of passing on choice Ultra decrypts, with their true source suitably obscured. In the case of wireless interception, the field was more open, in the sense that the Russians and the British each knew that the other was doing their best to listen in and could in certain cases help each other out with particular intercepted signals or messages. But – perhaps based on a justifiable suspicion that the British were monitoring the Soviets as well as the Nazis – there was clearly an initial sense either of reluctance or distrust on the Soviet side. Major Crankshaw, together with senior military figures in the Moscow mission, had clearly had to push hard for a deal to be made.

'Impression is that [Soviet] Y people were warned off by higher authority,' wrote Crankshaw of the delicate negotiations for the sharing of Y information. As a result, British higher authorities were themselves invoked, and wrote strong notes to Russian military figures concerning discourtesy and a failure to fulfil promises. This seemed to cause the Soviets to shift a little. Crankshaw wrote:

> This meeting highly successful. [Senior officer] Tulbovitch less nervous and more confident than ever before and obviously relieved to have comprehensive directive behind him at last. Through him Soviet High Command formally reaffirmed their intention to play square with us and agreed to my proposals. My reproaches were met with unprecedented apologies . . . My main request was for access to senior 'Y' officer to discuss policy matters.

Even then, it was an exhausting process. But one which opens an intriguing window on the levels of co-operation – and more vitally, perhaps, of mutual trust – attained. 'My telegrams will have conveyed the general atmosphere here . . .' wrote Major Crankshaw just a few days later from the British Military Mission in Moscow, 'in spite of the keenness of the [Soviet] Y people to get hold of my material, the first three weeks were one sustained crisis. This crisis has now resolved itself, and we have started work.'

In a curious mirroring of the relationship with the US, it seemed that the intercept teams got on better than their superiors; Crankshaw related how the Soviet Y team were making efforts to outmanoeuvre the official liaison department that oversaw all operations. 'It will not be the fault of Y if after a month or two we don't have a good routine running,' he wrote. 'I have handed over Col Tiltman's Japanese material, and this is being digested. It has been agreed in principle to give me the traffic I have asked for and very soon I hope to have a special meeting about this.'

In return for this valuable information, the Russians were handing over German identifications, and other vital ways into German radio signals. And there was more. 'Cryptography, as expected, is a delicate subject,' ran the memo, 'but I also hope for progress here. I think they may ask for someone like . . . [Bletchley codebreaker Henry] Dryden to come out and visit their cryptographers for a few weeks.' It was clearly possible to do this without letting on about the cracking of Enigma; there were other coding systems in use in the field, such as Double Playfair, a manual encryption system using square grids, which the British and the Soviets could quite safely discuss. A few days later, and the two teams appeared to be co-operating with much greater ease and fluidity.

'I have so far given Red Army Col Tiltman's material, the Bird Book, the Fag System, D/F safety service, ground station call signs and some oddments. The Russians are now setting the pace . . .'Again, in return, the British were benefiting by means of more German material captured by the Russians, 'the low-down on Russian cryptographic situation' and 'full details of Army network and traffic in front of Armies, with serials, frequencies, identifications etc, present and future'. A little later, an even more significant concession was made: Russian naval officers came to Britain to see the workings of several Y establishments, and all the technology of interception – though one site they were not allowed anywhere near was Bletchley Park. According to the official history, the British also proved to the Russians that the Soviet cipher systems were hopelessly insecure, and that the Russians could not expect to receive any more helpful messages from Bletchley until this security had been tightened up. For if the Russians were to blunder while handling information from Britain, German intelligence would correctly deduce that the British had broken their code systems, with potentially catastrophic results.

All of which makes for very striking reading now. Just three years after that memo was sent, the British listeners were focusing their clandestine attentions on the very Soviets into whose infrastructure they had been permitted to look. Nevertheless, as allies, it was thanks to the work of the Bletchley codebreakers that – to give one striking example – the Russians were supplied with vital information about German tanks, which enabled them to win the 1943 Battle of Kursk; and in turn, it was the Y Service that ensured that such information was expedited.

Quite apart from the sensitivity of international relations, there was continuing ill will within British cryptography circles, tension and jealousy between the different departments of intelligence. There was a particular distrust and dislike among some for the operatives of MI6. In 1942, Captain Trevor-Roper, now working for the Radio Analysis Bureau at Arkley View, and having great success with Abwehr codes and communications, confessed to his diary his opinions of 'the Secret Service' – a 'colony of coots in an unventilated backwater of bureaucracy', a 'bunch of dependent bumsuckers held together by neglect, like a cluster of bats in an unswept barn', 'high-priests of effete religion', mandarins with 'Chinese ideograms' and 'green ink' and 'Palace eunuchs in the Great Within'.

On another occasion, and without explanation, he wrote: 'I am sick of them, sick to death of them, that nest of timid and corrupt incompetents . . . I would rather grill in the desert with unambitious idealists who have something to sacrifice . . . than sit here in the shade and watch the endless, meaningless, purposeless ritual of these Roman augurs.'[7]

In contrast to Trevor-Roper's citric views about the workings and personnel of MI5 and MI6, there was a sense of smooth, assured expertise about the Y Service; an expertise acknowledged by admiring Americans. It has been suggested that around the Special Relationship, there was nevertheless a continual element of unease to do with security, and that as few American top brass were apprised of the Bletchley triumphs as possible. This, some say, is why the Federal Bureau of Investigation's efforts during the war were directed by Washington more towards South America than Europe; pressure to have FBI work deflected elsewhere came from the British, who were anxious about sensitive information being given to the FBI, a young organisation with plenty of potential for leaks. And so it was that, despite the atmosphere of co-operation between US signals personal and the Y Service, many American commanders and operatives could only shake their heads with admiration at the quality of intelligence that the British were obtaining, without having the faintest idea about its provenance.

9 Wilder Shores and Secret Missions

The war in the Far East and the Indian Ocean created its own specialised demands upon Bletchley Park; not least of which was the need for some young recruits to be given swift, intense courses in rudimentary Japanese. Moreover, the codebreaking and interception stations in Asia were, in the 1940s, a truly vast distance away from home; this was a consideration that was certainly to skitter through the minds of some of the younger people sent out there.

The other aspect of life during those years – taken for granted then, but increasingly alien now – was the fact that these out-stations were located in countries that were still part of the British Empire, even if that empire was nearing the edge of disintegration: India, Ceylon . . . And so it was that those who sailed out to these parts, like those posted to Egypt, had their eyes opened to a way of life that no one would see again.

In 1942, Hugh Denham, a nineteen-year-old undergraduate from Jesus College, Cambridge, received his summons to Bletchley Park. Within a few short weeks, his horizon was to be widened considerably. The station at Kilindini in Kenya let the Bletchley authorities know that they wanted three new operatives. Denham, together with fellow youngsters Jon Cohen and Wynn Davies, had been trained to work on Japanese codes. Now they were transferred on to the payroll of the Foreign Office. Denham got a letter from Permanent Under-Secretary Sir Alexander Cadogan, summoning the young man to see him at Downing Street, and thence the ostentatious splendour of the Foreign Office – rather in the manner of one of William le Queux's fictional Edwardian heroes. Denham's orders were that he and his colleagues were to be posted with all speed – and travelling across Africa for seven weeks – to their new home in Mombasa.

That home – in common with other Bletchley naval out-stations – was referred to in seafaring terms: in this case, as HMS *Alidina*. It was, Denham recalled, based in a 'requisitioned Indian school' (which is where its name came from) on a 'rocky northern shore'. In architectural terms, it was stunningly ornate; not merely redolent of the grand nineteenth-century colonial era, but fantastically decorated on the exterior with intricate rococo touches.

Manning the base were two senior Japanese translators who were naval men, alongside several career diplomats who had previously been interned by the Japanese. On top of this was a contingent of about thirty specially trained Wrens. 'The "front line" of the unit was the wireless operators, who intercepted the enemy messages,' wrote Denham.[1] Highly meticulous and scrupulous these operators were too; at the end of each working day, as Denham recalled, they would go out to the back of the building and carefully monitor the burning of all the top secret waste paper that had been produced.

There was a tropical echo of the cerebral atmosphere of Bletchley. Denham and his colleagues made full use of the large and airy former school rooms; they pushed big laboratory tables together and used them to lay out their complex decryption spreadsheets. In the meantime, as Denham noted, the Wrens 'did a superb job. They were young, usually well educated, away from home probably for the first time, living under tight discipline on low pay in austere accommodation and engaged in routine work of an opaque nature. They did it all accurately, conscientiously and cheerfully.' And though the hours were uniformly long – seven-day weeks were quite common, with the occasional half-day off – there were extraordinary bonuses. One such was that some members of staff were permitted a little extra free time to climb Mount Kilimanjaro, 'just over the border in Tanganyika'. Today's celebrity charity ordeal was yesterday's ideal recreational pick-me-up.

A year earlier, intercept stations had been expanding throughout India. Captain Frank Dickinson of the Royal Signals – a physicist by training – was posted to Delhi, and to a station in the south of that city:

> It was a former private school situated on the top of a rocky hill with excellent buildings but a very poor site for radio reception. It was a fully integrated Intelligence station incorporating radio intercept and indentification, codebreaking . . . and comprehensive communications. On arrival at the 'Hill of Happiness', one walked up to an open gateway to a large, bare quadrangle, surrounded by solid-looking buildings . . . Many of the officers were volunteers who had been living in India or further east – as civil servants or in business – and . . . they wore the most extraordinary jumble of uniforms and badges.

After some unhappy experiences with a martinet officer called Pyster, who once threatened some of the operatives with a court-martial simply for taking time out to perform in a male voice choir for All India Radio, Dickinson requested a transfer, and soon found himself travelling across the country to Abbottabad, in the Khyber province of northern India (the city is now part of Pakistan). This involved gruelling train journeys, and frightening river crossings made by dilapidated ferry in remote regions. But life at the Abbottabad intercept station was lively and a great deal more colourful than anything he would have found back in England.

At Christmas, we despatched signalmen Howden and Russell (a couple of cockney wideboys) and signalman Joseph (their Madrassi equivalent) to the nearby Naga village where they successfully bargained for a pig. This was successfully dispatched and dismembered by Waters, who had almost completed his apprenticeship to the trade in his father's butcher's shop and provided a superb Christmas dinner for the entire section.

Another course of the dinner involved 'a pound and a half of rice on a banana leaf, surrounded by ten heaps of various curries and dahls, every one calculated to make steam come out of our ears'.[2]

There were moments of high comedy too; while British soldiers were on the move through the Kabaw valley, it was necessary, in their absence, for the interceptors to double up and carry out guard duties for the camp, which was set up in a teak forest and surrounded with a barbed wire fence. It was all apparently too much for an operator nicknamed Tug:

Guard duties had placed a lot of strain on operators and 'I corps' but produced one humorous incident when an elephant . . . walked into a booby trap (a hand grenade on a piece of string between two trees) and set up an awful screaming dance crashing through the trees. The noise was quickly increased when 'Tug' leaped out of bed and dashed around the camp in his pyjama trousers yelling: 'Man the defences!' The scene returns to me whenever I see Corporal Jones on 'Dad's Army'.

Section VIII operative Bill Miller – who had been dealing with ciphers and radio work covertly out of Spain in the early years of the war – found in 1942 that he had to leave, and quite hurriedly.

The Spanish government had registered that large numbers of ambiguous figures were working in embassies. And so the authorities caught up with Miller; when he asked permission to extend his stay in the country, that permission was abruptly denied. This might not have been too heavy a blow. Although Spain was neutral, Miller had sharply noted the pro-German propaganda everywhere, from the faintly gloating coverage of the Dunkirk withdrawal that played in the cinemas a couple of years back to the latest headlines in the local newspapers.

During a brief stopover in Lisbon, Miller was informed by his superiors of his next posting: this was to be Tangier, in the international zone of Morocco. Despite the place's neutrality, General Franco had sent Spanish troops in. Even with this Spanish presence, the city remained genuinely international in feel and – more importantly – was to become one of the world's leading nerve centres of espionage. Our images of the region in this era have been coloured immortally by the film *Casablanca*; there are those who would affirm that the film was not so very far from the truth. Tangier was a city swarming with spies, and electric with intrigue.

Immediately upon arriving, Miller reported to the grand British consulate, and to the Consulate-General Colonel Ellis, who also happened to be SIS head for the region. Miller was given a cover: he was to become press attaché to the consulate. His real role, however, was to work directly to MI6 as a cipher operator, dealing with encoded traffic between embassies while ensuring the security of British encrypted communications. According to Geoffrey Pidgeon, the city had the faintly disorientating quality of a looking-glass world; the enemies – British, Italians, Germans – sat in their legations not far apart, each pretending that their own business was wholly above board. Miller told Pidgeon that there was something especially jarring about walking through the Tangier streets and suddenly seeing the swastika fluttering in the warm breeze; the flag hung from the German legation, which was close to the main marketplace.

It was not too long, says Geoffrey Pidgeon, before Miller's wireless duties expanded to taking on board other forms of espionage. He was required, for instance, to maintain contact with a wireless operator in Casablanca who was monitoring a strategically important French battleship – keeping constant tabs on its position in Casablanca harbour, watching for signs that its fifteen guns were being made ready to engage in combat. Intriguingly, the battleship's position changed whenever it was not being observed, surely a sign that there was covert activity afoot. The looking-glass element was to the fore again: the watchers and the watched, perfectly aware of one another, playing their pre-assigned roles while at times neatly reversing them. This was a city in which German and British intelligence operatives would sit at adjacent tables, failing to acknowledge one another but at the same time piercingly aware of each other's presence.

Another of Miller's roles was to train secret agents in the use of transmitters small enough to be carried in suitcases. There were agents from all backgrounds, including a French Moroccan and a Spaniard. He was also quietly involved in what Pidgeon refers to as 'boat operations': nocturnal manoeuvres at sea, intended to transport secret equipment – and, on some occasions, refugees – between Tangier and the British fastness of Gibraltar. The vessel used was an ordinary fishing boat; perfect cover although vulnerable, especially in stormy weather. It says something for the sturdiness of British wireless receivers that when one such article was accidentally pitched over the side of the boat during a storm – and, miraculously, retrieved swiftly afterwards – the equipment had only to dry out before working perfectly again.

Not so far away across the Mediterranean, the strategically important island of Malta had been heroically holding out against Italian and German onslaughts. Some codebreakers and wireless operators posted to Heliopolis now found themselves being redirected to Malta; what was more, they discovered that they were to complete part of the journey by submarine. It was not an attractive prospect. But the experience, as Y Service veteran John Boylan found, had a quality of fascination, not to say novelty, amid the trepidation and claustrophobia.

'All submarines going to Malta carried the maximum quantity of stores in short supply on the island,' he recalled. That was on top of transporting himself and several other Y Service colleagues. 'We were soon given a welcome on board by the Captain over the loud hailer, who told us we were in for a fairly uncomfortable journey owing to the limited accommodation . . . The first order was for us to replace our army boots with gym shoes and vest – our clothing for the next 8 days.' Day and night were turned upside down: some of the submarine's crew operated nocturnally, when the vessel would surface for a short time and messages were swiftly transmitted; by day, the vessel would dive once more to the depths. Boylan and his Y Service colleagues had barely enough room to sleep: the submariners naturally had the bunks, the wireless men had to bed down 'in the sitting position'.

'We had limited water for ablutions and drinking,' recalled Boylan, 'although the taste of the tepid water didn't encourage over-indulgence . . . One soon lost all sense of taste and this remained for days, even after the completion of the journey. It was . . . like the taste from sucking pennies.' But the relief on finally reaching his destination was great; Boylan recalled the 'fresh air, brilliant sunshine, blue sea'. In Malta, the Y Service operatives were based in St Paul's Bay; it was pleasingly cool by comparison to Heliopolis, though during the winter rains, 'the station was in the middle of a sea of mud.'[3]

Boylan and his male colleagues made the transfer to Malta with some ease; this was not the case for Cairo WAAF operative Aileen Clayton. She had been telling her commanding officer that she felt she could make a valuable contribution on the island, which thanks to its strategic significance was acutely vulnerable to German aggression. Clayton argued that her experience, acquired both in

Egypt and beforehand back in England, would be valuable. But as one would expect for the time, her sex counted against her. Malta was clearly considered too dangerous to be a suitable posting for a young woman. Clayton wrote:

> I made up my mind that this was something I had to do. Rowley [her superior] on his return, did not think much of the idea and suggested that we send someone from Suez Road. I was furious at his decision. Here was the first opportunity since my arrival in the Middle East to put into practice the lessons that I had learned and the experience I had gained at Kingsdown.
>
> It hit me forcibly that this was a foretaste of what I would be up against unless I took, there and then, a firm stand. Had I been a man, there would have been no question of my going, but merely because I was a woman, I was not eligible for work in which I was much better qualified and experienced than any of the men whom they proposed sending to Malta . . . I went on arguing [with Rowley] but it was to no avail.
>
> Finally, choking with rage and frustration, I picked up my heavy German dictionary and hurled it at him. It missed, and that only made me more angry . . . I walked down to the YWCA at Dharbanga House and found a quiet corner of the courtyard of the old Arab palace to sit and think about what to do next. The sun was filtering through the fretted 'musharabiya' screens, making patterns of light on the floor.[4]

But the dictionary had hit its metaphorical target. Her superior eventually relented; and Clayton was flown to the Y station in Malta (this is in contrast to Boylan's submarine voyage – 1940s feminism had its limits. Indeed, it is only very recently that women have been granted the right to sail in such British vessels). Not long after she arrived, the nature of the day-to-day jeopardy became all too clear:

I was returning one evening to my hotel with an airman from the radar site, when we saw a single fighter coming in very low over the water. 'He's low,' I remarked. 'I hope he hasn't been shot up. If he doesn't pull up a bit, I doubt if he'll make Ta'Qali.' Suddenly there was the chatter of machine-gun fire. 'Christ!' yelled the airman. 'He's a bloody Hun!' We smartly threw ourselves flat behind one of the stone walls enclosing the field. Having missed us, the ME 109 . . . went on its way to beat up the airfield. 'Phew, that was a close one, the f—ing bastard,' the airman exclaimed. 'Are you all right, ma'am?' 'No, dammit, I'm not,' I replied. 'I've wrecked my stockings, and I've only got one more pair with me.' The airman roared with laughter. 'You're great!' The only reply I could make was to comment: 'Well, after all one must have a sense of proportion. You can't have an improperly dressed WAAF running around.'

Prior to the siege of Malta in 1942, further practical difficulties were thrown up by the bombing raids, as John Boylan recalled. 'The . . . raids increased in frequency and intensity . . . and the island was under a state of almost continuous red alert . . . If you were on duty, work continued as normal as possible but when the bombs were dropping in the vicinity, the noise blotted out the signals in your headphones. With the screaming bombs, you certainly couldn't take the Morse through the noise.' Those working on messages and codes managed to use their rest periods to watch Hurricanes and Spitfires 'get stuck into the bombers, even through the heavy barrages'. Aside from these spectacular pyrotechnics, though, operatives began to notice how the rations had started to go into a 'gradual decline', at first not especially noticeable, but then sharply conspicuous. For the interceptors, it must have been a strange and alienating period; at an extraordinarily tense moment of the conflict, they had found themselves bearing witness to the action while being right at its centre.

10 This is No Holiday Camp

Wireless operatives who worked in far-off countries had the curious solace of jeopardy. Even though their work could be mind-numbingly tedious, it was carried out in exotic, alien conditions that at any point might erupt in anarchy, or worse. The precious knowledge that they carried, plus the imperative never to be captured, gave a biting edge to their experiences. From Singapore to Colombo, from Cairo to Malta, the listeners were part of a company; a direct boon to the troops with whom they worked so closely. These listeners could see, on some level, the results of the good work they were doing.

For those back in England, it was not always so simple. And by 1942, in RAF Chicksands, morale was plummeting fast. The authorities were not merely chastened but also startlingly sympathetic to female operatives who lashed out.

At the beginning of that year, pressure on the Chicksands personnel had started to increase sharply as the Luftwaffe took some unwelcome security precautions. The official history of Chicksands in the National Archives points out:

On January 1st 1942, the German Air Force introduced a variety of new keys . . . this made a great increase in the number of [receiving] sets required and forced us to devise new methods of obtaining the maximum interception from the sets available. The difficulties were overcome to a large extent by increasing the Search teams at Chicksands and Harpenden . . .

But where were all the extra recruits to come from; and would all of them prove suitable to the demanding nature of the work? A few months later, an ominous internal memo began to tell of developing staff difficulties, to do both with the hours and the deadening lack of recreational possibilities in the vicinity. There was, the memo stated, an 'increasing sense of injustice among the personnel concerned, which is already threatening to lower the standard of efficiency'.

Days afterwards, it was noted at Chicksands that '77 WAAF ops arrived – bolshie for lack of leave.' The unremitting pressure, and the never-ending nature of the task – combined with the need to keep such WAAF operatives effectively in the dark about the nature of the information they were receiving – was stoking resentment.

By 13 June 1942, things were so bad among the operatives that the authorities proposed in a further internal memo that the station be visited by a psychologist – one 'Mr Chambers'. He was to be asked to 'look into cases of neuroses among the WAAFs'. The memo went on:

Very recently, [a senior officer] told me that Chicksands WAAFs . . . could only cope with a 6-hour day, and on checking with the other Y services, I found that their experience was the same. Cheadle, on the contrary, still manage to get their people to do an 8 hour day, but ask that the WAAF may be reinforced considerably above the usual four watch basis so as to give them additional rest periods.

Chambers the psychologist did indeed visit Chicksands; and by July, he had filed part of a report that caused the authorities a great deal of annoyance – not because it pointed out awkward truths about the wellbeing of staff, but because it put forward no obvious solutions. When WAAFs had nowhere to go and relax, when their accommodation was uncomfortable, when their spare hours away from the grinding work were still dreary and depressing, what precisely could the authorities at Chicksands do about it?

'I have seen the extract from Mr Chambers's report affecting Chicksands and do not find it very helpful,' wrote Commander Ellingworth. 'He has tabulated all the difficulties inherent in the place which we told him, without offering any constructive criticisms. Incidentally, his criticism of me as a "regular service officer" and his remarks that my subordinates do not see eye to eye with me I resent very much indeed from many points of view.' He concluded, with a magnificent flush of anger: 'Quite apart from anything else, my Squadron Officer and Squadron Leaders DO see eye to eye with me – and the rest better had.' (Indeed, when Commander Ellingworth was a little later transferred to the Y establishment at Beaumanor, veteran Chris Barnes remembers that his attitude was always rough-edged and autocratic. Not that this was necessarily a bad thing; 'I think he was respected if sometimes feared,' says Mr Barnes.)

None of this helped at Chicksands, though; and neither did a report the following month from a 'senior medical officer' in response to rising sickness rates at the establishment. It listed the main difficulties as 'Shortage of personnel. Half-completed camp. Long distance from civilian amusements.' Again, a 'batch of discontented WAAFs' were noted. 'Not every operator . . . suitable for the work', it stated. There was a 'lack of facilities during short leaves for people who live at a distance'.

Then there were the technical difficulties. Too much respon-sibility was placed on the administration staff, alongside a lack of 'runners', or messengers; this meant that wireless operators not only had to take down messages with pristine accuracy, they then also had to hare around the station to give them to the right people for transmission to Bletchley Park. The authorities at this stage were trying to set up a system of pneumatic tubes in order to remove this chore; but the tubes themselves were too slow.

Drawing comparison with Chicksands' sister RAF station at West Kingsdown, the medical officer's report was damning:

> This is a bad station. The work is similar to that at West Kingsdown but instead of listening to intelligible radio trans-missions, the operators listen to and note cypher signals in Morse. There is little or nothing in their work to hold their interest.
>
> The men work an eight hour watch and the women a six hour watch. There is somewhat more regularity of life than at W Kingsdown but this is paid for by rather fewer days off . . . Living conditions are in a state of flux. At present, the women are rather uncomfortably housed in a camp; the men are in billets. Civilian and recreational facilities are scanty, but improving . . .

Intriguingly, the medical officer also noted that 'operators come from a less privileged strata of society' than at West Kingsdown. Not only did they have less rewarding work, he suggested, Chicksands recruits were more likely to come from working-class backgrounds and were less likely to have received further education than those at West Kingsdown. And this – as far as he could see – was an important contributory factor towards their unhappiness. 'There is . . . a much stronger leave fixation and a very real urge towards posting or remustering. There have been,' he added ominously, 'indications of the possible imminence of a sudden breakdown.' For the women stationed here, the 'only emotional satisfaction is in leaving the station.'

If changes were not made, the officer concluded, 'I feel it is my duty to warn that there is likely to be a progressive deterioration in morale, a strong possibility amounting to almost a probability of sudden collapse, and a high probability of an increase in the sick-rate.' And there was the hint of a further comment about the issue of social class in his conclusion that 'there is little to be said . . . for [wireless] operators doing such work as cooking and general cleaning of the camp, particularly if undertaking such work means, as it does at RAF Chicksands, that time off duty and days off have to be reduced.'

The authorities did have one idea for improving morale, expressed in yet another memo: 'Need for "privilege" or some form of "glamourising" of operator's trade', it stated. 'What can you tell the operator without breach of security?'

This was the core of the issue. The nobility of the war effort was one thing – everyone was familiar with Gracie Fields' song about 'The girl that made the thingummybob' (a paean to the heroic yet unsung factory girls whose dedicated labour in producing small components for planes and weapons was proving immeasurably valuable); but these women at Chicksands, at all hours, were expected to take down an abstract collection of seemingly random signals, with no sense of where the results were being sent, or how they were helping. Unlike the factory girls, they had no tangible idea of the value of their work. Certainly they could use their imaginations; but even the most colourful daydreams would pall after a few nights spent in the darkness at 2 a.m. noting down interminable series of dots and dashes.

Who could fail to side with the operators? At Bletchley Park, there was a full team of support staff and most codebreakers had comfortable billets; in contrast, the WAAF operatives at Chicksands were not only required to live in spartan camp conditions, but were also responsible for maintaining that camp on top of all their other work.

This perhaps contributed to a surprising physical assault against an officer, quietly referred to in a memo in the archives dated a few weeks later. 'There had been grave concern as to the state of discipline and morale at Chicksands,' it stated. 'It will be recollected that the discontent culminated in an act of violence against the C.O. by a member of the WAAF.'

In general terms, however, the consequences were more empathetic than punitive. 'Subsequently, the Commanding Officer was changed, a new padre has been installed and the hours of work for WAAF reduced. The root of the trouble, however, was the fact that the Commanding Officer and staff were trying to meet operational requirements with an inadequate staff and, in consequence, over-working the personnel.' Over-working seems to be putting it mildly; a round-the-clock interception rota, combined with drudgery, and in a location with scarcely the entertainment of a village hop, must have seemed to the women who worked there a kind of grey purgatory.

Yet, not too many miles away at Beaumanor Hall, the War Office Y Service seemed by 1942 to be a remarkably smooth, even happy operation. In that year, the station's numbers had been greatly expanded with the arrival of the ATS women; their presence was to make an already congenial atmosphere even more lively and amusing, especially for the civilian male Experimental Wireless Assistants.

One cartoon, drawn for the in-house magazine, depicts a fellow, sitting in a comfy armchair, twiddling a wireless knob while arrayed around him are three attractive young women: one bringing him tea, another massaging his shoulders, and the third sitting on his knee. The caption to this drawing: 'My job – As seen by my wife.'

Elsewhere in this notably irreverent and good-humoured staff magazine was a decidedly ungallant comic poem inspired directly by the influx of female company:

> Now females thin, and fat, and old
> and females young and vital

> Are toiling in our midst, 'tis time
> Someone gave them a title
> Whatever she's been – a debutante
> or humble 'char' or waitress
> She wouldn't care for anyone
> To call her OPERATRESS.

There was also a joke concerning one such young lady who, on overhearing talk of 'jamming', exclaimed: 'I can't understand where they get all the sugar from.'

Even the personnel complaints at Beaumanor seemed to be better natured than elsewhere. One such complaint concerned the perennial lack of chips in the canteen, and yet how, poetically, somehow their aroma continued to haunt the place. Poignantly, even in 1942, there was an awareness that the secrecy of the work – and its quiet nature – would make for some awkward conversations after the war had ended. One waggish poet dramatised this in a comic poem concerning a little boy badgering his father for details of what his war work had involved:

> Oh! I was an EWA my laddie
> My part I most nobly did play
> And although I ain't got any medals
> I sure took my part in the fray.

But the boy is sceptical – if he wasn't a soldier or a sailor or a pilot, what exactly did he do? Daddy, of course, is not permitted to say. All he can show for his war are ten pairs of trousers kept in the chest upstairs. There the boy would find:

> a record of service unstintingly given
> I completely wore out each 'behind'.

It has been noted that the social mix at Beaumanor was more

varied than at other stations. It was a blend that seemed equally at home in the local pubs and at organised activities such as the Beaumanor Choir, which rehearsed in the Quorn Church Room and offered, as bonuses, 'Dancing, games', 'entertainments' and 'light refreshments'. This heterodox mix of people may have contributed to an atmosphere that seemed rather more forgiving of the authorities' shortcomings.

Furthermore – and this is not something you often hear of either Leicester or Loughborough these days – both towns seemed to be oases of pleasure, easily reached by bus after long hard shifts at the radio receivers. The range of cinemas were a particular blessing, and it is ineffably sweet to read Beaumanor magazine's very own guide to 'What Was On': from dreadful forgotten turkeys such as *Black Dragons*, a thriller starring Bela Lugosi as a Nazi scientist using plastic surgery to transform Japanese agents into replicants of American politicians, to reissues of hugely popular hits such as 1939's *Gone With The Wind*, 'presented in Technicolor'. Of course, colour cinema was still a luxurious novelty then; and in purely visual terms, it is quite easy to imagine the escape that the operators enjoyed as they left their drab desks in drab rooms and made their way through black soggy nights to the sudden rich burst of gold, red, green and blue on the cinema screen.

Beaumanor's resident film critic, Dudley Truin, offered his own views on every one of the offerings, from *In Which We Serve* – 'British films before the war were a subject for derision, and justifiably so but since 1939, in spite of immense difficulties, they have gone from strength to strength' – to *The Ghost of Frankenstein* – 'Lon Chaney Jr has in my opinion more than lived up to the high standard of acting set by his father'. The latter, incidentally, was an opinion held by very few others.

Just a few miles away, at Whaddon Hall, fourteen-year-old Geoffrey Pidgeon had had his earlier wish granted; although a bright lad, he was not remotely engaged with his school work at Wolverton

Grammar, and so he was able to join his father, and indeed a growing number of family associates, in the highly secure wireless section. Geoffrey was obviously to start not in uniform, but working on the manufacture of specialised sets, some of which were destined for secret use out in the field. He very quickly developed a feel for the work – the complexities of coils and wiring, the fascinating new possibilities that rapid technological change was throwing up.

A close analogy for the workshops of Whaddon Hall might be inventor Q's laboratories from the James Bond films; there was that blend of labyrinthine wiring and machinery, combined with improvisational genius and the sense that, underneath the chaos, this was a secret powerhouse of invention and technology. And though young Geoffrey Pidgeon's very first job might have involved the unglamorous process of engraving Bakelite, he knew that he had a privileged insight.

'So how on earth did I get into Whaddon?' says Mr Pidgeon now with a laugh. 'I knew I was skilful with my hands. I had always made models. I painted things. We all had to have hobbies at school, and had hobby contests. I made some very good models of HMS *Renown* [a nineteenth-century gunship]. The guns moved. And I made a model of a Messerschmitt 110. This was on a base of the sea, all in colour, with a destroyer running alongside.

'My father was so thrilled with this model that he took it up to show it off at Whaddon Hall. Percy Cooper, Royal Navy, who was in charge of the workshops saw it, and he said, "Your lad seems to be talented. We're looking for people with an aptitude for wiring. Do you think he would like a job?"'

Pidgeon's father suggested that Geoffrey was unlikely to progress very far scholastically and asked his son if he would like to think about it. 'So I said yes. I went up to Whaddon Hall, and saw this great man in an office – I had no idea what I was doing – and he asked if I would like a job there.'

Pidgeon asked what work he would be expected to do. 'And he said, "Well, you've been making models – it's something similar to that." So then we had to go back and see my headmaster Mr Morgan, who said something to the effect that "this boy's wasting his time here – he's not going to get anywhere". I was brilliant at several subjects, but that didn't carry the whole lot.'

As it turned out, young Geoffrey Pidgeon was more than happy with the way his career had found this early shape. In the months and years to come, he would find himself bobbing around in the Solent helping to oversee trials of revolutionary remote-controlled radio apparatus housed in sleek missile-like tubes. And he was to be sent up in aeroplanes for tests of top secret equipment such as a device that would enable pilots to get precise fixings on radio receivers on the ground. This was an invaluable tool for spies: rather than having to spend agonising minutes transmitting so that their headquarters could get a fix on their position, in order to keep track of their movements – minutes in which the Germans could also lock on to them with ease – the new technology would enable them to be detected before the enemy even realised that they were there.

Many of his classmates, back in those soporific schoolrooms in Wolverton, poring over Latin and maths and chemistry, would have been sick with envy if only Geoffrey Pidgeon could have told them anything. But of course he couldn't: even at fourteen years of age, the Official Secrets Act applied.

Some of the later young recruits to the Y Service found themselves in incongruously festive surroundings at the start of their training. Victor Newman, having been called up at the age of eighteen and opting for wireless telegraphy, found himself packed off to the Yorkshire seaside resort of Skegness – and more particularly, to a 'Billy Butlin's Holiday Camp' requisitioned by the Royal Navy.

'There were all the huts still there, which had been built for family accommodation,' says Mr Newman with a laugh. 'And because they were family accommodation [each chalet] had single and double beds in which all the recruits had to sleep. The double beds had a board down the middle. Not that this is something that we had ever heard about before, but the board was to prevent men getting at each other.' The idea of such a precaution makes some other recruits to Skegness laugh to this day. One veteran recalls that he and another recruit removed the board in direct contravention of the rules, simply because their chalet was so bitterly freezing that they needed the shared warmth.

The whole holiday camp had been taken over by the Navy – it was hardly as if there was any civilian demand for it at that time – and so in these invigorating seaside surroundings, Mr Newman and his comrades were put through 'parade drills and learning to tie knots' as well as being inducted into the mysteries of Morse messaging.

Some female recruits recall being packed off to other branches of Butlins on the south coast where the fresh air also seemed to inspire officers into notions of parades and drills. Great numbers of WAAF personnel, meanwhile, were sent to the wireless training centre established on the Isle of Man. Here there was a focus on physical, as well as Morse, training. And perhaps the aforementioned rarity of travel goes some way to explaining the curious atmosphere – part hilarity, part resistance – that was to be found on the island.

It was certainly a different world from the wartime mainland. As well as the often fine weather, the Isle of Man's shops and grocery stores were – for those rationing-straitened times – extraordinarily abundant in produce. 'The shops on the Isle of Man were full of things that you couldn't get at home,' says Jay McDonald, who had been brought up in quite another island community, that of Mull. 'All sorts of stuff that wasn't available – the war had been on some time and there was generally so little that you could buy. Even a comb for your hair could be hard to come by.' Not in Douglas, though, where the emporia overflowed. 'I presume there was an abundance in Douglas because of all the holidaymakers who had never come because of the war.'

There was one other terrific boon too, especially for sharp young appetites: 'The food was also very good in Douglas, there was an

century Beaumanor Hall, in Leicestershire, where the Army Y Service was based, and
als were intercepted in huts like those in Bletchley Park. There was a vast and incongruous
rehead of Admiral Cornwallis in the courtyard. *English Heritage*

main house at Bletchley Park, regarded by some codebreakers as a 'Victorian monstrosity'.
Images

Base of the RAF Y Service, Chicksands Priory
in Bedfordshire was reputedly haunted by nuns.
Priceless medieval stained glass was removed for
the duration of the war.

A wry cartoon – one of a great many – from
Beaumanor's amusing quarterly staff magazine.

From Beaumanor Staff Magazine

Hanslope Park, Buckinghamshire, HQ of
Intelligence wireless operations, later the workplace
of Alan Turing, and still a restricted security site.
IWM HU 68039

"BUT I KEEP TELLING YOU THAT NO-ONE FROM BEAU-MAN
LIVES HERE!!"

The early wartime scale of the Bletchley Park estate, as seen from above – the yew maze is still there prior to being uprooted to make more space. *English Heritage*

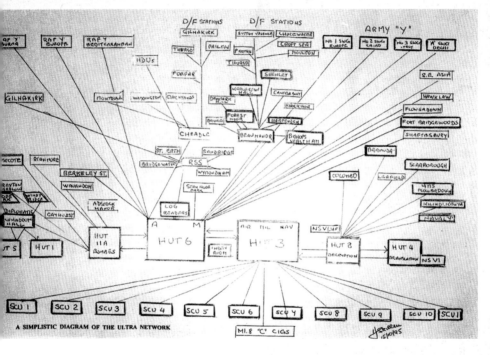

A SIMPLISTIC DIAGRAM OF THE ULTRA NETWORK

...ontemporaneous diagram of the maze of ...erations, and to which parts of Bletchley ... the encoded interceptions were sent.

Major Hugh Trevor-Roper, who brilliantly intercepted and analysed Abwehr traffic. He was later assigned to investigate Hitler's ...eath in the bunker. He aimed his sharp wit at ...telligence figures for whom he had little time.

Total focus: Wrens taking down encoded Morse in the Mombasa station. Some used their leave climb Mount Kilimanjaro.

below: In training: young recruits absorbing the complexity of the work. Total accuracy was demanded at all times – it could mean the difference between life and death. *IWM A 004769*

left: An illustration of interception equipment. The Brit favoured the American HRO radio receivers, prized for their delicacy of tuning. HRO was said to stand for: 'Helluva rush on!' *Lt. Cdr. W. E. Legg RN (RTD)*

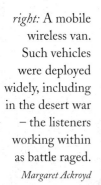

right: A mobile wireless van. Such vehicles were deployed widely, including in the desert war – the listeners working within as battle raged.
Margaret Ackroyd

The Singapore station was evacuated just a matter of hours before the Japanese invasion. Because of sensitive coding knowledge, it was vital that Y Service operatives should escape enemy capture.
IWM IND 4817

he Bletchley out-station Colombo, Ceylon, was source of wonder to the ung recruits sent there – m the exotic food to the minous insects at night.
IWM ART LD 5765

w: Wrens serving Colombo threw mselves both into the k and the glamour he local night-life.
A A 24959

Intensive training was carried out on the Isle of Man, which Wren Jay MacDonald also remembers for its abundance of fresh food and glorious bathing opportunities. *Getty Images*

Many Wrens on the Isle of Man also recalled the rigour of military training, and occasionally giving the slip to watchful officers. *IWM A 10029*

The island of Malta, subjected to a terrible siege by Axis forces, and on which Y personnel were witness to increasing desperation. *IWM GM 1430*

ne rather stark telephone exchange equipment on Malta. Y operatives called how the shortages extended om food to official stationary. *Alamy*

w: Greenock signal city – this so how the shifts were operated IMS *Flowerdown*, with Wrens sailors working side by side. The It was a great deal of romance and eed many marriages. *IWM A 13707*

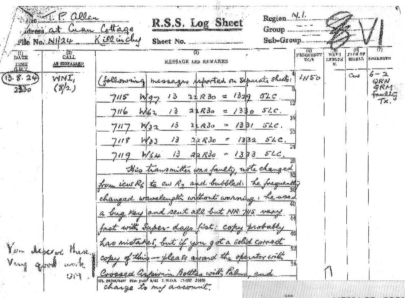

A Radio
Security Ser·
log sheet, as
distributed t·
the Voluntar·
Interceptors ·
civilians who
would monit·
Abwehr
transmission·
on a nightly
basis from th·
homes. *Courte·*
Ray Fautley

right: Voluntary Interceptors were told to
send their intercepted message forms to
the mysterious address 'PO Box 25, Barnet'
and were provided with special labels. The
address was that of the Radio Security
Service at Arkley View in North London.

Courtesy of Ray Fautley

below: The Enigma encrypted messages
– all those seemingly random letters –
were sent in groups of four or five in Morse.
Some young Y service operatives could
translate Morse at astonishing speeds.

Courtesy of Ray Fautley

ve left: Monitoring Morse transmissions in tropical climates such as Mombasa could be made ɪcult and painful by tropical storms, which reverberated and crackled in the headphones.

ve right: Young Voluntary Interceptor Ray Fautley, who diligently – and successfully – monitored wehr messages from his parents' front room in south London aged 17. *Courtesy of Ray Fautley*

w left: Plotting signals and their locations. The Y Service had a world-wide range. Operatives e also trained in Direction Finding, particularly vital in the race to track down lethal U-Boats. *1 A 21440*

w right: A code and cypher room in Algiers – where the conditions were pretty severe and tere for the women, as well as the men. *IWM CAN 4164*

Y service operative Peter Budd – 19 years old and standing on
the beautiful Cocos Islands, where he was based for 18 months.
Courtesy of Peter Budd

Peter Budd, a little later in the war, intercepting enemy messages and codes. *Courtesy of Peter Budd*

below: Commuting in the Cocos Islands! Peter Budd and his young colleagues enjoy a warm sea filled with manta rays. Mr Budd describes his time spent serving there as completely unique.
Courtesy of Peter Budd

The crew at the Mombasa out-station in 1942, enjoying the sort of delicacy that was pretty much impossible to find back home.

A touch less exotic, yet just as much camaraderie: Y Service operatives enjoy a break from wo in Ventnor on the Isle of Wight.

woven palm-leaf constructions at HMS *Anderson* in Colombo meant that women on night
s were constantly assailed by flying tropical insects that would get through the slats.

rvice operatives enjoying a rare break in Colombo. Veterans recall the luxury of the oceans
indeed the local swimming pools.

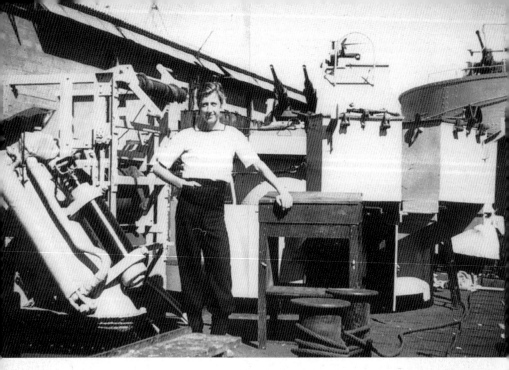

Homeward bound: after his spells in the Cocos Islands and Karachi in the then north of Indi the war ended and Peter Budd was eventually demobbed. *Courtesy of Peter Budd*

below left: When he got back to England, young Peter Budd found the grey austerity rather t sharp a contrast with the amazing and hazardous world he had seen. *Courtesy of Peter Budd*

below right: Peter Budd today. Before the war, he says, even the idea of a trip to Calais seeme exotic. His experiences changed his entire approach to life. *Courtesy of Peter Budd*

Above: The English countryside in wartime featured many aerial 'stonehenges' – beautiful but also conspicuous to overhead bombers. Efforts were made in many places to disguise them.

© Crown Copyright English Heritage

The modern-day establishment of GCHQ in Cheltenham. Morse has been consigned to history, save as an amateur enthusiasm; now the secret world of interception is all digital and even more complex. *Alamy*

Although perhaps less well known than the codebreakers of Bletchley Park, the Y service operatives deserve all the recognition they can get. Without their dedication and ingenuity, Bletchley would have had no material to work on at all.
Philip Nixon © Copyright National Memorial Arboretum, 2012

Having broken Japanese codes in Colombo as an 18-year-old girl, as well as operated Turing Bombe machines, veteran Jean Valentine is hugely in demand for talks at Bletchley Park and elsewhere. *Bletchley Park Trust*

abundance that we didn't have at all on the mainland. Eggs were in good supply, for instance. They may have been getting extra food from Ireland, which was not playing a part in the war. There were fresh kippers you could get in Douglas, and you could arrange to have them specially boxed and packed and sent on. I had kippers sent back home to my mother in Tobermory, who then distributed them among people.'

As well as Morse, there was instruction in radio technology. But the hours, Miss McDonald recalls, were not especially onerous. 'When we got time off, we went to the pictures, dances, went for swims in the sea. All the usual things that teenagers did.'

Indeed, for some male wireless trainees in the Signals Corps, the ratio of male to female recruits on the Isle of Man was the stuff of daydreams. Romance, though, could prove rather more elusive, as Dennis Underwood said: 'We were on one duty or another almost every night, guard duty, fire piquet, kitchen fatigues, et cetera. So when the occasional night off came we were too exhausted to take advantage of the opportunities!'

For Jay McDonald, this was a jolly time: she could only ever see the town of Douglas as a seaside resort, rather than the site of her training as a Special Wireless Operator. Even the most sonorous lectures on the mechanics of wireless transmission were tinged with the promise of constant fresh sea air: 'And of course, after the work was done, all we had to do was cross the road and there was the sea. I was there in the high summer, which also made a big difference. We could swim in the sea or walk along the promenade. The atmosphere was very nice.'

For ATS volunteer Cynthia Grossman, however, the Isle brought back shuddering memories, not least of which was the crossing that she and her fellow girls had to endure:

We embarked on a sorry-looking ship to cross the Irish Sea. Most of the Isle of Man ships had been lost or battered in the Dunkirk evacuation. The skies that had been blue in the early morning had our spirits high, and we were hustled on board with wishes of good luck and gifts of chocolate bars (rationed at the time), from the WVS and the Salvation Army. We were soon to regret gobbling this delicious chocolate, for the skies turned grey, and the waves tumultuous. Cheerful excited chatter turned to whimpers and moans of 'I want to die' as uniformed girls gave up their chocolate whilst clinging to the rails of the ship.[1]

After this unpromising start, the young women arrived at Douglas after a tortuously long voyage:

Seven hours later, instead of the usual four, a bedraggled squad of girls from various training camps in the UK, trailed not marched along Douglas Promenade to the requisitioned hotels and boarding houses that were to be our homes and classrooms.

Soon we were into a routine of breakfast, morning parade, and into classrooms by 9 a.m., to learn the Morse code alphabet, the Q code, and to me the dullness of lectures on magnetism and electricity.

The lectures involved talks on atmospherics, how radio waves worked in certain conditions and how they could be affected by natural phenomena. In other words, they were not everyone's choice of intellectual stimulation.

This went on till 5 p.m., with a brief break for lunch. We had no idea what this learning was for, and the drill parades and physical training periods were welcome activities. At some point we learnt we were to intercept German messages that would be in code, and on no account were we to speak of this to anyone, not even our nearest and dearest.

The girls' ability to keep a secret was eventually put to a formidable test:

> We were to be inspected by an important visitor, the Princess Royal, sister of King George VI. She proceeded slowly down the line, and stopped in front of me. 'What do you do Private?' she asked. I floundered, saying in my mind 'You can't tell her' – 'We march and play games, Ma'am,' I said. She must have thought I was a waste of space, not knowing that the game was a form of bingo, the letters on our cards being sent in Morse.

Wherever the station, another crucial aspect of life for so many recruits remained their youth; as in the early years of the war, many were teenagers who had barely ventured outside their own home towns, let alone been called upon to engage in vital work. One such lad, and something of a prodigy, was Dafydd Williams. He had just taken his A levels and there was, as he recalled, talk of him being sent to Canada to work on a secret project involving physics (it was only many years later that he realised that the project actually concerned early atomic weapons research). In the wake of his exams, Williams went to a party; one of his fellow guests that evening was apparently a 'wing commander' who worked at Bletchley Park. As seemed so frequently the case, an ostensibly casual conversation led to recruitment. But Williams was not being drafted into the codebreaking operation; he was being drawn into the world of secret diplomatic communications. Interviewed by the staff of Bedford Museum for their website, Mr Williams said:

> I was sent up to the main Station at Whaddon Hall in Buckinghamshire which was responsible for secret com- munications between England and the various Embassies throughout the world and also the main Commanders in the Field. It was Section 8 of the Secret Intelligence Service

and I was at Whaddon Hall for four to five months as it was suggested I would go on various jobs from there. I went into digs in Bletchley. A station wagon used to pick us up every day. And the thing which I remember – remember I was only 18 at the time – I was given a salary of £7 0s 0d a week! £7 0s 0d a week, free of income tax! Plus keep, plus my accommodation.

Really this was a very big salary at that date for an 18 year old. At that time I was working shift operations, the Station was open for 24 hours a day . . . Basically it was sending and receiving coded traffic to Embassies and the Army Command in North Africa and in Cairo. I was supposed to go to North Africa and that fell through. I was supposed to go to Spitzbergen and that fell through and then eventually I found myself sent to Madrid in Spain.[2]

But for other youngsters, even when the work did not involve the heady excitement of foreign locations – indeed, even if it was focused on one little town – the high spirits of youth were difficult to quell. 'We had a lovely time,' recalled one ATS recruit of her posting to Scarborough. 'We were working with sailors – ask no more. There were dances at the hotel and we put on a little show. A marvellous time we had.' One of her colleagues recalled her landlady with immense fondness: 'Mrs Craig's cooking was . . . well, we put on weight!' And when not eating, they were able to find other amusements. 'In our breaks, we'd go to the pictures and Chapel on Sundays – a great big central hall, like Westminster Hall, with tip-up seats.' Among the Scarborough girls, there would be the occasional outbreak of one eternal preoccupation of the young: seances. Several ATS operatives recalled what would happen after coming off shifts late at night. 'We were not ready for sleep at midnight. We would have many a discussion – on politics, how our parents made a mess of things. We even dabbled with a ouija board.'

After her blissful training period on the Isle of Man, Jay McDonald found herself posted to Harrogate, and the exposed and wuthering listening station located on Forest Moor. She remembers her time in Yorkshire with deep affection, and has been back there for several reunions in the intervening years. One of the aspects of life that appealed very strongly to her was the chance to meet girls from all over the country, and from all sorts of different backgrounds: her home community on the Isle of Mull was close but also perhaps a little limited in terms of variety. In any case, even the rigours of her duties at Forest Moor now bring back fond memories.

We were taken from Harrogate to Forest Moor on these troop carriers. It was cold on the Yorkshire moors, even though we were well clad. For a reunion not long ago, on the way there, we were singing the songs that we used to sing on those carriers. Everyone sang those wartime songs. We worked a shift system, three rotas. You did all the shifts, and then you would get thirty-six hours off to recover.

The night shift was always a bit of a bind. There were all the usual difficulties. Trying to sleep when everyone else was getting up, trying to sleep in the daylight (even though we had blackout). But we were living in Queen Ethelburga's, a requisitioned school, which was great. Outside the room I slept in was a cherry tree. There was parquet flooring. So only the night shifts spoiled things a bit . . .

The work was very focused – but then, you could also sit there for seven hours, and the station you were listening for just wouldn't come up. So either that or you could be very busy, the messages all coming through at once. But in any night shift, there were always two of you there. A partner, in a sense. The two of you would be doing the same job. So one might be busy and one not, and one would be there really to help the other stay awake. You might have had some nights when you were idle; but you couldn't read a book, you couldn't write, you couldn't knit, you had to sit there. So when the other person wasn't busy, you would make conversation.

And this is how you got to meet girls from all sorts of different backgrounds that you would never have met before. I got to know girls from London, they got to know me. I would tell them about the Isle of Mull and they would ask if there were trains there. When I'd explain there were no trains on the isle, they would be taken aback. Some would ask about the Gaelic language – others would never have heard of it.

And they would show you photographs of boyfriends, mothers and fathers. You really got to know people, you really liked them.

On the south coast, meanwhile, Wrens on the windy clifftop stations overlooking the Channel found inventive means of entertaining themselves. Miggs Ackroyd recalled the most unlikely amusements: 'While sitting in a wireless van on the end of Portland Bill before the Americans came into the war, we used to pick up the Boston police cars "calling all cars" and listen to the American Ham operators operating on the Skip distance. They had funny call signs. "TWV – Tiny White Violets" or "GYD – Granny's Yellow Drawers".'[3]

There was also, she recalled, the task of making sure that the radio sets on board the flotilla of destroyers were working satisfactorily, which entailed getting into boats and sailing out into the Solent – and working not only with British vessels, but also a couple of Norwegian ships and even a Free French vessel.

'I got the delightful job of going to sea on trials with them to see if their sets were behaving properly,' she wrote. 'The French, of course, served excellent French wine in their ward room. They used to say the Free French Naval HQ existed solely for the purpose of providing it. They were vereeee French!' There was also the simple exhilaration of being out on the waves. 'Out manoeuvring with the British ships in the Solent was a riot. I found myself trying to help a harassed British liaison officer on the bridge converting flag signals . . . into English and then into French.'

For Vivienne Alford, the time she spent at the out-station at Hartland Point, north Devon, could be quiet to the point of being idyllic. 'The Hartland period was sheer delight . . .' she wrote, 'peering into pools, swimming in the bays, sunbathing on the rocks (with the RAF flying low) and cadging clotted cream. Watches were not eventful . . . One summer night . . . I sat on a cliff watching the sun go down, making a golden path across the sea.'[4]

Social engagements on the coast could be variable in quality, Elizabeth Mashall recalled:

We fared much better at North Foreland than at Portland Bill. To begin with, we got the usual invitations for 'a party of Wrens', usually to a beery, smoke-filled hall but our luck changed when I actually knew one or two officers of a Hampshire regiment that came to the area. My stock rose and we were invited to some better organised dances. I have very pleasant recollections of dancing an extremely energetic 'Bumps-A-Daisy' at one of these events.

Dancing was one of the key amusements of that era; not merely during the war, but for some time before it too. Women and men alike were apparently addicted; the romantic side of these occasions was obviously important, but so too, it, was the energy of the dance itself. One beguiling image we have of the Wrens – right the way across the world, from remote corners of Yorkshire to the shores of Ceylon – is of young women who, having worked hard, then went out in determined fashion to dance hard too. In the more exotic climes, it was one of the ways in which these young women managed to adapt to their new lives.

One unprecedented aspect of the conflict was the numbers of young women who voyaged around the world to be near or at its heart, and the almost casual courage echoing through so many different accounts seems extraordinary now. By 1942 and 1943, Wrens were being dispatched in greater numbers to theatres of war such as north Africa. But the stories that we hear from Cairo, Tangier, and indeed the Western Desert, are vivid illustrations of how women were starting to negotiate a form of new settlement for themselves. In some cases, they were to volunteer themselves determinedly for duty in hazardous arenas which were then considered suitable only for men – just at the point when the fortunes of war in north Africa were begin to turn.

11 Storms in the Desert

Wren Rosemary Norton was based in and around Plymouth, listening to U-boats, when she heard that there might be opportunities for overseas service coming up. Those with a working knowledge of Italian, she recalled, were particularly sought after. Her own grasp of Italian appeared to be at best sketchy – but, showing admirable verve, she rushed out and acquired a text book of Italian grammar, along with any other volumes that might help familiarise her with the language. She had the necessary wireless qualifications and so – as far as she could see – the language itself was the only hurdle. A brief though intense period of cramming followed. She applied to go abroad and was accepted. There was, she recalled, fortunately no test of fluency in Italian.

Was the adventure quite what she had expected? Having sailed out on a troopship, she arrived in Algiers on her twenty-first birthday. 'My first impressions of north Africa were the smell and the flies,' she wrote. 'The smell one got used to, but the flies were a bore.' From here they were flown to Bone, in a troop-carrying plane that sounds terrifyingly antediluvian. She recalled that it had 'small open port-holes', so that 'one could put one's hand out and feel the wind rushing past.' This was clearly not a supersonic aircraft.

On arrival in Bone, she and her Wren colleagues were stationed on the top floor of a hotel in a village called Bugeaud, which lay above the port. The ratio of men to women was, as one would expect, extremely high and as a result of this, she recalled, 'we led a very social life.' 'The views over parched brown hills, cork forests and eucalyptus trees to the blue Mediterranean were spectacular,' she wrote. 'Marvellous bathing and sailing and expeditions by mule down the mountainside.'[1]

Paradise had its practical setbacks, though. 'Every drop of water for drinking, washing, cooking etc had to be fetched in four-gallon petrol cans and carried up to our top storey quarters.' Moreover, much of the cooking was done on the roof of the hotel, with wood dragged up from the groves below. Yet it is easy to see how even these conditions had their own sort of poetry; and how they lent an intensity to life that could hardly be forgotten years afterwards.

A chief Wren who had helped make even these rackety arrangements possible had been there some weeks before. Beatrice Bochman had previously run a mobile listening unit near Portsmouth, in a small coastal village where the greatest hazard had been coming off the night shift and trying, without a torch on a moonless night, to negotiate a field of cows and a clifftop path. She too had applied for an overseas posting; and when the summons came, she responded with alacrity. 'After some hectic shopping for tropical kit, I found myself . . . on a troopship bound for Algiers.' At that stage, it was considered that the port of Bone was uncomfortably too close to the actual conflict for women. So, for a while, Bochman and her colleagues were set to work on deciphering captured coded Italian documents. The working space was spectacular: 'An exotic turreted castle at Dravia which housed a large RAF "Y" unit, six Psychological Warfare civilians from Bletchley and a few peripatetic naval "Y" officers.'

A few weeks later, Bochman and her colleagues scouted out the hotel at Bone and set about making the most of the charmingly vintage facilities. But for all the brilliance of the high vantage point, the conflict against Italy was constantly moving on and there was a fast-decreasing amount of traffic for the station to deal with. So while it was decided where best to dispatch three dozen or so Wrens, they were moved from the hotel to a rather striking villa. Again, their experiences there were the sort to sear themselves on to the memory. Mrs Bochman wrote:

> Our 'Villa Lavie' looked very Algerian. Castellated white walls with a coloured frieze and a cupola from which we flew a flag. Every day a number of Italian Prisoners of War were brought to work for us. Some made miles of pasta which they dried on washing lines around the galley (by morning, some had fallen down and crunched when you walked on it); others made pretty patterns with shells round the flower beds and all sang 'Santa Lucia' as though they were in the chorus at La Scala.

Not all such adventures were so picturesque. Across the Mediterranean a few months previously, Aileen Clayton – who had volunteered for Y Service duties on beleaguered Malta – found that life had an increasingly pyrotechnic edge. One night, in the confusion and alarm of a German bombing raid, she had been attempting to board an Alexandria-bound plane on the military runway while bearing an attaché case filled with classified documents. But one explosion caused a horrific chain reaction:

> Without any warning, there was suddenly the sound of a terrible crash. Another aircraft taking off on the runway had smashed into our guide and immediately the two aeroplanes were engulfed in flames . . . The pilot yelled: 'For Chrissakes, get the hell out of here. There are mines on board that kite!' There was no time to put down the ladder, so we dropped straight to the ground. I was clutching for dear life my precious briefcase which was filled with secret documents. The heat

was intense . . . Then there was an enormous explosion. The mines on board one of the aircraft had blown up. My companion flung me to the ground ramming my briefcase, which I was still clutching, on to the back of my head.

He did it only just in time. A splinter slithered across the case, jamming my face down into the mud, and scarring the leather – and incidentally, breaking my jaw, though I did not realise this at the time . . .

After this catastrophe, there was nothing for it but to head back for cover. Departure from Malta that night was obviously impossible. 'Eventually we found our way back to the underground control room,' she wrote, then recalling how she exclaimed: '"What a way for a girl to spend her birthday," I grimaced . . . I was just 24 years old.'[2]

Clayton was not alone in finding the Malta posting wearing, both physically and mentally. For the people of the island, the situation was dire; food supplies were diminishing, and luxuries such as tobacco becoming scarcer by the day. Lieutenant Eric Wilkes, who was later to return to the academe from which he had been pulled, was posted to the island's tiny Y Service unit from the Middle East. His first few hours on the island, having arrived by night, told him almost all that he needed to know. 'An army car took me to my overnight lodging at Valetta – a lovely spacious bedroom,' he wrote. 'I think it was in or near the Castille. In the morning, I realised why I had been warned not to walk around in the dark. The building had been partially bombed and various surviving doors opened into thin air.' He also recalled how, that bright morning, an air raid started and he witnessed a priest 'sending children flying' in his anxiety to get to the bomb shelter.

The shelters were in constant use; and according to Wilkes, they could be smelled from fifty yards away. The officers already manning the Y unit were upright military men, not apparently very keen on the 'untidy graduates' being sent their way; young cerebral types like Wilkes had very little interest in drill or weapons maintenance, and there was not much that his comrades could do about it. The wireless station was on the seashore, with minimal facilities such as an adjacent cookhouse.

Yet even in the midst of the grimness of Malta – the ever-sparser rations, social hours restricted to a local inn called the Lord Nelson, which specialised in cheap grog – there were odd moments of Ealing-style comedy. One concerned the use of the military phrase 'Most Immediate'; owing to an overabundance of pads stamped with the phrase at the top of every page, there were rumbles of irritation back in Cairo, and indeed Bletchley Park, when requests for simple equipment replacements appeared to be couched in terms of the utmost urgency.

The work being done on Malta was still extremely important; during the German bombing raids late in the year, it was Bletchley Park's success in penetrating the Luftwaffe codes – with all of the pilots' messages assiduously sent on thereafter – that enabled the British to shoot down so many German planes, thus preventing more wholesale destruction.

Aileen Clayton soon found herself transferred back to the Middle East. Her first posting was to Cairo, where, after all the adrenalin and fear of Malta, her role was rather calmer and more considered. As well as Y Service work, there was a more therapeutic role: to be a friendly face to some of the younger officers who were pouring into Cairo on leave after harrowing ordeals in the desert, and who knew nothing of the city, merely that they wanted to lose themselves in it briefly. There were dinner invitations, and Clayton recalled how these were regarded as part of one's duty; if one was not available, one would ring around one's friends to see who was. Then the young lads would be dragged into Cairo's social whirl, and taken to parties and dances.

Poignantly, Clayton recalled one flight commander who had been through a great deal and simply wanted to come round to her place and drink tea out of a china cup, with the tea things on a tray; in other words, the marks of normality, the metonyms of calm domesticity. The tea clearly made a tremendous impression upon the airman: when he was finally shot down over Sicily, his parents wrote to Clayton, both to tell her and also to thank her.

The extraordinary atmosphere of Cairo was also maintained for Hermione, Countess of Ranfurly, despite the news that her husband Dan had been taken prisoner in Italy. Working for General 'Jumbo' Maitland Wilson, later to become Supreme Allied Commander in the Mediterranean, she established her office next to the Map Room – 'an Aladdin's Cave of immense interest if only one had time to devour all its information,' she wrote. After a sojourn in Baghdad, the Countess and her colleagues had returned with a parrot that she called 'Coco':

> He had a very small cage so . . . I went in search of something better. In a slum shop filled with snakes, pigeons, guinea pigs and finches, I found one and after much bargaining, bought it. The shopkeeper gave me a present: a white mouse with pink eyes called Faud, which he put in my pocket . . . later, when people came to see the General and Faud was running around on the floor, some would say 'Oh – is that your mascot?' Others saw him but didn't comment. We suspect they think he is part of a Cairo hangover.[3]

The very idea that there was such a phenomenon as a 'Cairo hangover' tells us much; but there is also a defiantly quirky and eccentric sense of humour, the notion that the dignity of a hugely important general's quarters would not be decreased by being shared with a parrot and a white mouse.

Incidentally, the story did not end happily for Faud the mouse; one day, he was accidentally squashed flat under a falling filing cabinet. For weeks, even figures such as Lord Gort would ask of the creature's whereabouts, only to be told the news. Again, we see an irrepressible compulsion towards irony, which perhaps had the effect of blocking out the real horrors of the conflict in the desert.

That war was still considered no place for a woman; but Aileen Clayton persisted in getting closer than most. As she said of the role of the interceptors in the desert: 'The Y Officer's function was to keep the controller informed of all intercepted information which was of immediate operational use, and to assess, by co-ordinating this information with data from all available sources, the extent of enemy air activity. In this way, Operations could be given at any time a complete picture of the opposing airforce, its organisation and its methods.'

It hardly needs to be added that Clayton, by now a senior Y operative, regarded herself as an ideal candidate for such a role. Perhaps surprisingly, the moment at which such a chance materialised was conflated in her memoirs with a moment in her romantic life:

Wing Commander Morgan came over from Algiers to discuss the future of Y in the Mediterranean and indicated that he wanted me to join his staff there . . . On top of this, I was on the verge of becoming engaged, but I had seen too many of my friends widowed within months of marriage and I wrote to my mother explaining that 'my job means so much to me, I couldn't have it ruined by constant worry over a mere man. I just cannot let my private life seriously affect my interest in winning the war – that would be too unpatriotic.'

To today's reader, for a 24 year old to make such a dispassionate decision must sound incredibly pompous and jingoistic. But it must be remembered that, young though we were, we had a dedication that is perhaps incomprehensible in the climate of today.[4]

Dedication such as Clayton's was soon to be rewarded, for after months of bloody conflict in the desert, the Allies were preparing in the latter part of 1942 to finally drive the Germans back.

Mobile Y units had a vital role to play in this gambit, and some months beforehand, specially trained men had been deployed from Bletchley Park. One was Noel Currer-Briggs, who had been given codebreaking tutorials in the directorate of Bletchley by the veteran cryptographic expert Colonel Tiltman. After he and his colleagues had passed gruelling initial tests, they were set to work on Afrika Korps codes; their speed at unravelling the messages ensured that they were later sent off to join the Allied forces which were to land in Tunisia. Lieutenant-Colonel Sayer wrote a memo concerning another highly skilled Y service operative:

> One of the most cheering things that's happened this year is the collection of undoubted evidence that our new Signal Procedure has badly upset the enemy 'Y' service. They don't like it at all, and from the documents we collected, it was evident that they were floundering badly. Most of the credit for this goes to Bill Tozer . . . Bill has since had a personal letter of thanks from General Auchinleck. Richly deserved.[5]

Y operatives such as Currer-Briggs spent their time in cramped, hot mobile units reading encoded German traffic at great speed; once again, the traffic was bound for Bletchley Park. Very great care was taken to ensure that no mention – in memos or even by telephone – of intelligence from such messages was obscured.

And now, the British interceptors were being joined by their American counterparts; there were differences in skills, as well as cultures. 'In the field, [Y operators] had to write with one hand keeping the other on the tuning knob, as the set would drift off frequency, so that the operator had to retune slightly to hear the answering station,' wrote Hugh Skillen. 'Very good British operators could handle two sets at once, double-banked. The American officers could type very fast, in capitals, and the Commanding Officer himself could read semi-automatic Morse like most of them.' There was apparently some confusion when the Americans hand-wrote 'S' like 'Z' and vice versa, and there were a few tutorial sessions on such matters with diagrams drawn on blackboards. But the operation, as the Allies prepared to consolidate north Africa, was notably slicker than at any other time.

As preparations continued, recalled Hugh Skillen, 'Bletchley Park sent out rapid information on how to decode certain Army and German Air Force codes.' Even though the Heliopolis school had contained within itself a sort of miniature Bletchley Park, with Major Jacob's recruits working on certain ciphers, the bulk of work on the ever-changing codes was being done at Bletchley. According to Skillen, even as this supremely confidential information was being carefully parcelled out to certain chosen military units, the British were still taking extreme care not to bandy it around with their American friends; a little later, General Patton himself could not be entirely sure of the provenance of the codebreaking triumphs. Although dissatisfied with the performance of many other military units, Patton was, apparently, thrilled with the Y Service. On one occasion during the push through the desert, after a successful skirmish following the receipt of a decrypted enemy signal, Patton apparently exclaimed: 'I want to give two medals: one to the G.I. who took that message – and one to the British soldier who decoded it.'

Patton was not to know that both interception and decryption involved the expertise of a wider range of people than this. Nonetheless, the citation was requested. A few months later, it is rumoured that Patton owed his success at El Guettar in Tunisia in 1943 – when the Americans managed for the first time to overcome German tank units – entirely to a single decrypt involving Axis attack plans and timing.

But before all this, and set against such instances of harmony and praise, was the discordant noise of internecine sniping on the British side via means of memos and letters. Lieutenant-Colonel Sayer, writing to London in 1942, once again took the opportunity to review the shortcomings and deficiencies of 5 IS: 'This institution has cost me more fret and worry than anything else in "Y" put together . . .' he wrote, 'from the 5 I.S. correspondence you saw what intolerable behaviour I had put up with in the interests of smooth working.' The source of this behaviour was Major Wallace, who had himself been firing off incendiary memos concerning unsatisfactory colleagues and maddening working practices. '[Major] Jacob refused to consider giving up Wallace,' wrote Sayer. 'Then the latter took a piece of particularly high-handed action which left no alternative but that he should go, or I would have to.' He never stipulated quite what this action was, but added that the 'whole air of intrigue and mystery is to me nauseating'.

Reshuffles were made within the Y Service, and both Jacob and Wallace were moved to other sections. Sayer wrote:

> Now that Wallace has gone, there is a marked improvement in the atmosphere at Helio[polis]. Wallace was an odd fish, extremely pleasant socially; but he did a great deal of harm. The atmosphere at Helio was most unpleasant, and he fostered in the 5 I.S. personnel a feeling of spite against all the rest of 'Y', with myself as Public Enemy number 1. The officers in the field loathe the very name of 5 I.S., which is a good pointer as to how things were.

Indeed, in his view the impact of the work of 5 I.S. was almost negligible at times: 'After the East African campaign, 5 I.S. subsided into a state of lethargy. They did little or nothing to prepare for the German problem, about which they were defeatist.' Sayer added that it had actually been a plucky 'amateur in the western desert' who had broken one particular German communications link that was now a valuable source, 'after material had been coming back and lying untouched in Helio for a month'. He went on to state that the group appeared to know nothing and care less about wireless transmission intelligence.

'Things like this, I think, made Wallace feel that he was behind the times and had no grasp of the situation, which was perfectly true. And being a jealous man he disliked us because we were organising the expansion and improvement which he had failed to do. Added to all this,' Sayer concluded magnificently, 'Wallace was not a normal character.'

There is something appealing about the fact that such a letter – filled with the minutiae of inter-office rivalry – could be written amidst the intensity of the desert conflict. Sayer referred obliquely to the savage realities of those battles – and the casualties – as he recalled arriving at Ma'aten Bagush, a base on the Egyptian coast several hundred miles west of Alexandria, some months previously, facing the Germans square on. 'Rommel walked around 10 Corps,' he wrote (10 Corps being a formation attached to the Eighth Army). 'Some got away and some didn't. Most of the B section didn't. It was a sad loss, because half the operators were old hands from Sarafand, first class at Italian and German. A fine old vintage which takes years to mature.'

Y Service operator Corporal Harold Everett, who had been working in Cairo, had vivid memories of that time spent in the desert:

> I was already desert worthy, in that my digestive system and bowels had more or less adapted themselves to a perpetual admixture of sand with their normal intake. Daily life was like life with any Army unit in the Western Desert. Great heat by day and intense cold at night, sand in everything, millions of flies that materialised from nowhere, a perpetual shortage of water, and the occasional attack of 'the trots'.

These, naturally, were not the full extent of the trials that Corporal Everett wrily recalled. There was also 'the horror of a young lieutenant, fresh from Cairo, at finding that our only latrine was the desert itself ("I shall only go after dark"), the sight of three officers, in the middle of nowhere, solemnly sitting apart from the men, being waited on by a batman at a table made of a plank of wood resting on empty petrol cans; our abortive attempts to train a chameleon to catch flies in the "I" van . . .'[6]

Even at the relative stability of the Kafr-El-Farouk RAF listening base outside Cairo, established in 1942, desert life brought on other trials for the wireless interceptors. 'Several cases of dysentery occurred, indicating necessity for improved sanitation,' ran one internal RAF memo about the base, dating from April 1942. 'Adjutant approached Works Directorate, stressing urgency of completion of ablution blocks and latrines.'

As the weeks wore on and the conflict intensified, so conditions deteriorated in this interception base established on sand. As much as the troops on the front line faced harrowing conditions, it was also difficult for those in necessarily sedentary work to maintain wellbeing. One memo ran:

> [There] has been the unfortunate epidemic of streptococcal sore throats. This in turn has raised the problem of accommodation and hygiene as the medical officer considers that the spread of the epidemic is largely attributable to the general lack of physical stamina, which has been undermined by the inability of personnel engaged on night duties to get proper sleep in the daytime under tentage from which flies cannot be excluded.

The knock-on effects were serious; the intelligence being provided was vital and any decrease in man (or woman) power would take its toll on the quality of the work. Nor were these any old sore throats: a few cases developed into scarlet fever, others into diphtheria. There was also the threat of quinsy, a complaint little heard of nowadays involving abscesses in the throat that can lead to a blockage of airways. This, combined with the unaccustomed dry, dusty air of the desert, must have been torment.

'Gargling prior to going on watch was ordered . . . and has been maintained since,' declared a Kafr-El-Farouk RAF memorandum from October 1942. 'All personnel were inspected by the medical officer before going on duty. Several throats were caught in the early infection stage . . . the NAAFI was closed, all lectures, concerts and dances were banned.'

Given the otherwise sparse opportunities for entertainment, it is as well that this plague soon began to abate. Even more drastic measures were considered by the authorities but quietly dismissed. 'Surgical masks for personnel were suggested but not used because 1) they would have to be worn for six hours at a stretch; 2) they would interfere with smoking which is the only relaxation possible in a Wireless Transmission room where constant watch is maintained . . .'

What is interesting through all these archival memos and carefully kept records is that among the military personnel were not merely civilian experts (some in uniform, as noted) but also a number of women recruits, who were coping admirably with the unpredictable pressures and strains of being right at the edge of the combat zone. And at Kafr-El-Farouk, the sickness rate rose and fell insidiously. 'Heretofore sickness incidence among airmen has remained steady at 2% . . . The breakdown has now occurred and it has risen sharply to 4%', noted one internal memo. As for the WAAF operatives, they suffered 'lack of sleep, irregular eating and irregular habits. As a result of this, the morale of the WAAF officers was low, their percentage of sickness incidence was more than 50% greater than that of the airmen.' And the answer? 'Working hours to be made more regular by adopting definite day and night duty, alternating from one to the other,' was one suggestion. This helped, as did more regular leave.

In the earliest days of this station, the influx of civilian recruits, with their minimum of military training, caused some raising of eyebrows on the part of the squadron leader, who duly recorded in the official journal:

Although the number of personnel despatched to this station was satisfactory, an initial test revealed that a large percentage of these tradesmen were very far from the standard to be expected from their classification.

Only 6% of the wireless operators tested at 20 words per minute were able to complete the test satisfactorily. Many of the test papers had so many errors that it was impossible to mark them, and up to 70 errors in 40 groups was not unusual. From questions put to the airmen it would appear that the majority have been misemployed for considerable periods and no arrangements made to allow them to keep in practice with simple buzzer and key arrangements during this period . . .

With hindsight, it is possible to see that the operatives concerned were simply a little rusty. As the weeks progressed and the work intensified, such complaints were to thin out considerably.

One other intriguing aspect of life in such a desert base was how the men and women commingled, if at all. The authorities had seen to it at first that, especially in their leisure time, there was a strict separation between the genders almost like that of medieval monks and nuns. But was this wise? 'There was some question raised by higher authority of the desirability of the partition of the present combined WAAF and RAF officers mess,' wrote one squadron leader. 'Although there was much to be said in favour of such division, there were difficulties in connection with the structural alterations of the mess . . .' But there were difficulties of an emotional nature too. 'Also it was felt that the RAF officers stood in some degree in loco parentis to the WAAF officers.'

Fortunes in those sandy wastes were turning decisively; and codebreaker Henry Dryden later gave a concise account of one of the crucial military engagements of the war, and of the vital role played by the Y Service:

Before the El Alamein battle started, I was in quick succession promoted to the rank of Major, transferred to 5 IS . . . and shortly afterwards appointed Commanding Officer of the unit. The first major decision I had to take concerned the deployment of 5 IS personnel. Until then, my predecessor had maintained the principle of retaining all cryptanalysts at Heliopolis, with only occasional exceptions, such as the 7th Armoured Division Unit. Now, with a campaign designed to end the war in Africa imminent, and the need for an all-out Y effort pre-eminent, it seemed essential to jettison the principle. Accordingly, I sent nearly all the younger members of both the German and the Italian sections up to 8th Army, for further deployment as required.[7]

In August 1942, the secret listeners in Egypt had perhaps their finest hour. Feeling himself to be firmly in command of the Western Desert, Rommel decided to launch the attack that was supposed to lead to the German conquest of Cairo. However, he was completely unaware that the British knew – down to the finest detail – exactly what he had planned. The intercept stations and the codebreakers had noted and unravelled not merely German Enigma messages but also messages on the Italian system; in essence the British had almost a full itinerary of the ships and cargoes that were to bring in the vital supplies for Rommel's forces.

And even as Rommel was preparing, the pre-emptive fightback was beginning; the very ships carrying the supplies were being sunk by the British on the back of such intelligence. Within two days, Rommel's supplies of fuel were being strangled and at last, the Germans were forced to pull back from the Al Haifa ridge near El Alamein. When at last the Battle of El Alamein began, there could be no question of the courage of the troops and the pilots fighting; nor of the effectiveness of General Montgomery's military tactics. The fact remains, though, that this was also a terrific triumph for signals intelligence.

According to many, it was Rommel's attack on 28 October that proved the decisive moment in the battle; after days of increasingly heavy losses among Axis troops and tanks around the El Alamein line, and with supplies increasingly precarious, Rommel's forces launched another assault on the Allied positions. But thanks to Bletchley, Montgomery knew how desperate Rommel's situation was: he was given a Panzer decrypt which read that the situation was 'grave in the extreme'. Indeed, German and Italian troops were exhausted. Montgomery feinted that he was planning to move his forces north; and thanks to Y Service intercepts, he knew almost at once that his ruse had worked. Several days later, the 21st Panzer Division received orders over the radio waves to attack. So too did the British field Y Station, which was in a position to relay those orders instantly; Rommel's tank gambit was – after an intense clash – thwarted. With this, the remainder of his Panzer divisions were ordered to pull out, forced into full retreat.

Despite the triumph, the repercussions of the conflict could be felt throughout Cairo. In November 1942, the Countess of Ranfurly wrote:

> Surely this must be the beginning of the end of the war in north Africa . . . So the days begin – on peaks of optimism. But as the hours wear on and I visit the Cairo hospitals, I sink back into chasms of gloom. The price of this news is so terrible . . . you see it in the long wards where the burn cases lie so still – sometimes even their eyes are bandaged; it glares at you from screened off beds where people are dying. You put on your gayest frock, paint your face, collect sweets and magazines and determine to be cheerful. Then at the hospital, the smell of rotting flesh meets you in the long dark corridors and you begin thinking again . . .[8]

Operation Torch, launched on 8 November 1942, was 'the largest amphibious invasion force thus far in the history of warfare:

300 warships, 370 merchant ships, 107,000 men', all landing on the beaches of French North Africa: Algiers, Oran and Casablanca. And to enable this mighty Allied push, the American commanders were relying upon decrypts of Luftwaffe Enigma messages, supplied to them by the Y Service and by Bletchley Park. Within weeks, the British Eighth Army was pushing the Afrika Korps ever further back; in the German efforts to hang on to Tunisia, Luftwaffe air power was diverted all the way from Russia. This in turn had the consequence of weakening the Germans on the eastern front. Meanwhile, in London, all significant German Enigma messages, having been decrypted, were read by Churchill himself; which is how he could inject so much confidence into his assertion that this turn in the course of the war marked, at the least, 'the end of the beginning'.

Churchill's sense of relief at the news from the Middle East was shared throughout the country. Back at Beaumanor, resident magazine poet Ollie Pearce felt moved to contribute an illustrated ode to the efforts of the Eighth Army:

> Reversals too they suffered but their spirit still remained
> For every inch of ground they lost a dozen more were gained
> Against a highly organised, well-trained and ruthless foe
> This novice army battled and returned each stinging blow . . .
>
> On to Tunisia they went and with their comrades won
> The victory of Africa which saved it from the Hun.
> The failures of Norway, of France and Greece are past
> The Army's prestige is restored, Dunkirk avenged at last.

In the wet and the rain of the Leicestershire countryside, life off duty at Beaumanor had settled into almost hyperreal normality. As the recorder of the table tennis club noted of his society's success: 'We have now passed successfully through the initial stages of awkward adolescence, and the club is going ahead well . . . At the Club, besides Table Tennis, we have the use of a billiards table and darts board; space is somewhat limited but we have managed, so far, to get by.' Elsewhere, the local football league was also continuing apace: 'Dickenson had the misfortune to break a collar bone in the match against Brush Apprentices,' noted A.H. Appleton, the Hon Sec of the Football Society. 'This was the result of an awkward fall.'

So what of the experimental wireless operators who, listening and transcribing in their stuffy Leicestershire huts, began to wonder what their wars would seem like in comparison to that of the Eighth Army? How might those back on home ground, following – headphones firmly clamped over their ears – the exploits of Montgomery's troops, see their own role? There is no suggestion that their contributions were somehow of a lesser kind; but it is interesting nonetheless to glimpse what the Beaumanor listening crew thought of themselves. Through another wry little poem, this one from a man calling himself simply 'Nosweh', we begin to hear a sort of answer.

Here he is writing as though his future self is looking back at his wartime experiences:

> Our work was arduous, none could know
> our untold misery and woe . . .
> We toiled while watching daylight fade
> And even as the dawn came creeping
> And birds and beasts alike were sleeping
> Still we sat and laboured on
> Tired and weary every one.

You hear a double defensiveness here; for these men and women knew at the time that their contribution to the war effort would go coldly unacknowledged, simply as a result of secrecy and security. They knew when the troops finally returned home and were enjoying their victory parades, that the Experimental Wireless Assistants would be left instead with silence. So it is unsurprising that those working through the night, taking down those signals, might find their thoughts heading in the direction of melancholy.

It needs to be reiterated that wherever they were being worked – from Devon to Cairo – night shifts could be almost hallucinatory in their tedium. For the first few minutes, one could perhaps listen to the stream of Morse and conjure vivid images of the skirmishes, the battles, the raids. But after an hour, two hours, three, of simply sitting there, concentrating furiously, the brain in the middle of the night would shift into a new and wholly unfamiliar gear. 'Not all the time was melancholy,' noted 'Nosweh' in his verse:

> At times, nay frequently, 'twas jolly
> We had our football, cricket, dancing
> Beery hope and much romancing . . .

But those night shifts were surely an exception.

For the listeners there was also an element of brooding on the 'what ifs'; especially for the men, following the exploits of General Montgomery, there must surely have been a stab of curious envy. The Eighth Army were rightly lauded; would the men and women who manned the headphones themselves receive any sort of appreciation, even tacit? In the end, it was all a question of duty, rather than glory; but in Ollie Pearce's tribute to the Eighth Army, it is nevertheless possible to hear that twinge.

12 Rommel and the Art of Dirty Tricks

In the Middle East, the harrying of Rommel's forces continued into 1943, as the Allies pushed into Libya and Tunisia. Owing apparently to tight security, there was some difficulty in getting a full quota of Enigma messages into and out of Tunisia. Meanwhile, the Y Service in the field lost none of its vigilance; but when Rommel attempted a counter-attack at the Kassarine Pass in Algeria, the American forces were taken by surprise, and in the most demoralising way; under attack from artillery, troops scattered. 'The British Y station attached to the US 11th Corps [was] able to provide some warning that Rommel was continuing his attack,' states the official Bletchley Park history. But there had been earlier confusion concerning interpretation, with some senior commanders convinced that Rommel simply intended to try a feint while General Von Arnim's forces struck from the north. In the wake of this, General Eisenhower dismissed one of his commanders for favouring only one sort of intelligence – that is, the results of Enigma decrypts – while ignoring the even more valuable intelligence being produced by the local Y stations.

As it happened, the Y section in question was headed by

Captain Hugh Skillen. And as he recalled, a recurring problem faced by operators was the tangle of bureaucracy, and the way that top secret information was quietly parcelled out. 'Although the Y officers in the field did not know that Enigma was being systematically broken and distributed to commands in the field,' he wrote, 'in fact . . . Bletchley Park was receiving thousands of Enigma messages through . . . Cheadle . . . Chicksands . . . and Beaumanor.' On top of this, there was also of course the 'mini Bletchley Park' established in Heliopolis. But the eternal problem was: how could the secret intelligence be distributed in such a way as not to alert the enemy as to its source?

'To receive the high-grade intelligence Ultra,' wrote Skillen, 'it was necessary to provide ultra-safe Special Liaison Units (SLUs) which decoded the Ultra sent out by BP . . . The Army provided a number of Special Wireless Sections for this purpose.' But, he added, 'at no time was the American 11 US Army corps a recipient.'[1] So really the Kasserine debacle had a very simple cause: Rommel and Von Arnim had been planning an attack elsewhere, all of which had been correctly monitored and logged by Bletchley Park's cryptographers. And it was this that the military had planned for. The difficulty was that the Germans had changed their plans, and had done so in such a secure way that no indications came through. Save, that is, for the fragments picked up by Captain Skillen's Y unit.

Rommel's offensive at the Kasserine Pass eventually lost momentum. Instead his forces focused on building the strength of the Mareth Line in Tunisia, and on launching a surprise attack on the Eighth Army, which was struggling to keep a supply line going along the single coastal road back to Tripoli, 200 miles away.

As the Bletchley official history points out, though, in many defensive skirmishes, such intelligence could only be of limited use. The need to protect the Enigma secret meant that any counter-strategies would have to have a further layer of misdirection thrown in, so that Rommel would not suspect that Montgomery had such an advantage.

Another example of this disguising of the Enigma secret came shortly afterwards. Having been promoted, Rommel now succumbed to illness and was forced to leave Tunisia. Every step of his departure was noted in Enigma decrypts. Yet Montgomery and the British had to behave – and communicate – as though they had no idea that this was the case.

The Bletchley official history also notes the occasion when General Patton made a terrible slip-up with Enigma; one that he apparently learned from very quickly. Advancing on the Mareth Line, the general was informed that the 10th Panzer Division was about to attack. The official history notes that Patton was not on the distribution list for Enigma intelligence, and it is not clear whether the information came from Bletchley or from the British Y Service in the field – nevertheless, he declared on the radio to his commanders in II Corps: 'Sure source informs me . . .' This, in turn, was picked up by the German Y service and as a result, there was an instantaneous tightening of security around Army Enigma signals. But this was in fact to prove a relatively minor setback: at the time, the airwaves were filled with noise, and there was never any shortage of material for the British Y Service to intercept. It also left General Patton with an enhanced sense of respect for such intelligence-gathering skills.

For WAAF officer Aileen Clayton, who had, after some official resistance, received her posting closer to the heart of the action, the prospect of the desert was daunting but thrilling; the journey from Cairo to Benghazi, however, shook her high spirits a little:

I flew up in one of their Wellingtons to their new base at Benina, outside Benghazi . . . we had no navigator on board so we flew low over the desert, keeping beneath the haze, and I spent my time lying in the bomb aimer's position in the nose of the aircraft trying to pick up points of reference en route. After a while, my sense of balance began to object to the midday upcurrents, and I was not sorry when we finally touched down . . . The crew of the aircraft decently refrained from mentioning my lapse.

Yet there was a further outbreak of unpleasantness to come: and that was over what some in authority regarded as her incongruous figure. Upon arrival, she recalled, '[the naval Y officer] could not get over a woman being in the desert and he was still flabbergasted by the evening.'[2]

This, perhaps, is not an entirely unreasonable reaction, nor indeed an especially chauvinist one. It's tempting to judge the past by the mores of today; but the fact was that in 1943, the idea even of women in factories – let alone working among battle-hardened troops in the desert – was distinctly novel. Clayton seems amusingly breezy about it; the fact that she assumed a man's 'flabbergasted' reaction to be worthy of particular note tells us much about how formidable she was. And as we have seen in her recollections of Malta, she obviously commanded a great deal of respect wherever she was posted.

In a wider sense, though, she is also an illustration of how the Second World War pushed and stretched boundaries in terms of social and sexual assumptions. Just as the largely middle-class undergraduates recruited to Bletchley Park were later to become the dominant voices of the age in politics, science and the civil service, so women such as Aileen Clayton were forerunners of feminism; they demonstrated, quite unselfconsciously, that women were quite capable of undertaking work previously thought to be the sole domain of men. And incidentally, of the women back in Britain who took up all the factory positions once held by their husbands, many – even those in smelting works – felt the loss keenly when the war was over, the men returned, and they were compelled to return to the ordinary lives of housewives.

A little later on, Clayton flew on to Algiers, to continue with her interception and cipher work. Again, in the midst of the carnage of recent battle, she seemed more surprised by the implacability of the response to her presence:

It was a strange feeling finally to land at Castel Benito, on an airfield which had been in enemy hands for so long. The whole place was devastated. It was a mortuary of gutted hangars and derelict aircraft keeling over in grotesque angles . . . I had difficulty finding somewhere to sleep. The transit facilities were understandably still primitive but I was rather hurt when the officer-in-charge told me peremptorily that there was no accommodation for women. This was one of the very few occasions when I met with downright hostility towards a woman being in a forward area.

Again, though, one thinks of the officer-in-charge, and one can quite easily imagine that the idea of a young woman of twenty-four in a camp filled with Tommies would have been awkward.

Clayton's righteous indignation was extended to her female colleagues, who as 1943 unfolded began arriving in north Africa in greater numbers:

One of the first WAAF to arrive in North Africa had been Section Officer MK 'Rusty' Goff. But to her chagrin, when the unit [later] moved over to Sicily . . . she was not allowed to go with them. However, when the Italian naval vessels surrendered after the armistice, the energetic and irrepressible 'Rusty' flew over, first to Taranto, and then to Gibraltar, with our scientific officer . . . to act as his interpreter when he examined the radar equipment on board the Italian warships.

In the meantime, Clayton was getting on with the task in hand – which sometimes involved playing dirty tricks on the enemy:

There was a period . . . when the British Y-Service did its best, with malice aforethought, to help their German opposite numbers. When an RAF reconnaissance aircraft sent a signal back to its base in Malta giving details of an Axis convoy that it had spotted, this was usually intercepted by German Y. The message, re-enciphered, was then transmitted verbatim to the enemy convoy. Malta Y, of course, intercepted the German signal, and since they knew exactly the contents of the original reconnaissance message, they were then able to break the code for the day. As even the best of Y operators were not infallible, the German Horchdienst would occasionally miss a message, so 'pour encourager', Malta would re-transmit the original RAF message at high power, ostensibly to the Navy in Alexandria, thereby presenting the enemy with another opportunity to give us a lead into the current code.

Then there was the ongoing business of cracking the ever-shifting kaleidoscope of German codes. Also sent out to Algiers in 1943 was Patrick Wilkinson from Bletchley Park, who took with him several others including Sheridan Russell, described by Wilkinson as 'a first rate cellist (he had been spare man of the Lener String Quartet), no great cryptographer but a delightful, unusual personality of gypsy-like appearance – a genuine Bletchley Park eccentric'.

But before too long Wilkinson found himself tangled up in an imbroglio of embarrassment about codebreaking and the chain of command. Low-grade codes were one thing, but he and his team were soon required to work on higher-security messages:

I knew there was a long-standing tug-of-war between Bletchley Park and the Commands abroad, the former being worried lest the secret that we were reading the machine traffic should be compromised by multiplication and exposure of the stations where this was done, the latter anxious to avoid the delays inevitable in transmission via Bletchley. I was a civilian employed by Bletchley Park, and we [he and his team] were now being told to go beyond our brief.[3]

The situation was finessed to Wilkinson's satisfaction; unlike Captain Hugh Trevor-Roper, who had been roundly reprimanded for having quietly broken into the Abwehr code on his own account, Wilkinson and his civilian team – working under the auspices of the military – were given a free hand. He and the team were 'delighted that they were to be given this far more exciting and responsible work'.

Not everyone in Egypt was in a position to drink in the extraordinary atmosphere. Robert Hughes from Islington had been shipped out with other fellow Special Operators and pitched up in Alexandria; unfortunately, as he recalls, they were in a vast camp of about five or six thousand men with pretty ramshackle working, and indeed living, facilities. 'We had nowhere to go, as Y Service Special Operators, as a unit. We were just chucked into this melee of matelots,' says Mr Hughes. 'We were no different to anyone being dumped off a ship and waiting for the next job. We were all lumped in together. And every morning, we Special Operators used to be marched out of the camp to the wireless area.

'Now it was some time after that they had these areas purpose-built with facilities – in the meantime, the wireless areas were just simple slabs of concrete and four walls. Since we took two months to sail out there, you'd have thought there had been some pre-planning about this. They could have put three of these buildings up in a week.

'But instead,' Mr Hughes adds with a laugh, 'we were stuck in this camp. We did three eight-hour watches. Some of us went for the Italian signals, some of us went for German.'

So, a teeming mass of thousands of soldiers were thrown together in somewhat extemporised circumstances. And unlike Barbara Skelton and Cherrie Ballantine, the greenhorn Islingtonian Mr Hughes had no access to the extraordinary distractions that Egypt could offer. 'Time off?' he snorts. 'There wasn't a lot to do in Alex.' Even the films that were shipped out for troop entertainment, and passed up and down the lines of the Eighth Army, were notoriously terrible.

'People would ask "What's on?" and we would jokingly reply with the oldest film we could think of: the 1920s silent version of *Ben Hur*,' says Mr Hughes. 'But one night, that film *was* bloody on. They took these films to different units and – as a joke – they would cut frames out of them before passing them on, so when they were next shown, you'd watch a scene with a man singing, then suddenly he would be flat on his back, knocked out.'

Even the beach held out little promise, especially to a London-born non-swimmer: 'I nearly got killed swimming. We went in the water, and I thought I'd keep in my depth. But the water began to rise and rise . . . God it frightened me, that was a frightening experience.'

There was one sporting consolation. 'We did have a very good football team there. The Special Operators. I played for them. They were a particularly good side.' Indeed, a little later in the war, Mr Hughes's football skills were to land him in one of the most extraordinary and potentially lethal matches he was ever to play.

For other personnel, hazards could be found in the most unexpected places. In May 1943, for instance, the RAF listening station at Kafr-El-Farouk had been hit with a mysterious bout of typhoid fever. The authorities, naturally, were keen to find its source. A ban was placed on drinking tap water; boiled water was taken instead. However, there were several further outbreaks. Was this sabotage of some kind? In the event, the explanation was both sinister and everyday. A common factor was that the men and women afflicted had been served lemonade. After stringent tests, it was found that the lemonade itself was not the source of the outbreak; so what could it have been? It was eventually realised that the drinks had been served with ice, and that the probable source of the bug was the cooler in the WAAF mess. The story illustrates how, in such places, personnel could be struck down from the most unexpected angles; constant effort was required to resolve such intractable problems.

The arts of bamboozlement – the low tricks, tactics and covert operations employed in the Y Service – were very much in use in neutral countries too, which for some of the younger recruits could prove hugely exciting. Eighteen-year-old Dafydd Williams, having been trained in the arts of wireless work at Whaddon Hall, received his first foreign posting in February 1943. 'I was told that I was being sent to Madrid in Spain,' Mr Williams recalled. 'I remember I was given leave and a whole pile of clothing coupons to buy clothes. Yes, they told me to buy a couple of suits to fit in with the life there.'

The business of getting there, like the journeys undertaken by other recruits, throws interesting light on wartime travel. 'I flew from Bristol, Bristol to Lisbon and then by train from Lisbon to Madrid,' Mr Williams said. 'There was a section of the Dutch Airlines, KLM, that operated flights between Bristol and Lisbon throughout the war as both Spain and Portugal were neutral countries.'

For a teenager, such work – and his official attachment to the Intelligence Service – was obviously a formative experience, and later on in life, a source of some pride:

First of all because we were members of the Intelligence Service we were kept . . . separate from the main Embassy – and we operated from an out building in the Embassy compound. Of course I was a very junior person being the age of 18 – but the only people we came in contact with were people doing similar work. There was the Escape Organisation, MI9. This was for helping escaped Prisoners of War. Occasionally one was involved in passing messages for them. And one was aware also of the SOE people in the Embassy although we didn't have that much contact with them. Everything was done on a need to know basis.

Mr Williams was part of a small, almost hermetically sealed community, one in which the culture of secrecy was pervasive. 'I lived in a pension a couple of hundred yards from the Embassy . . . there were four of us – Intelligence people – living in the same pension. It was the Coding Section that I was with.' Even the technical aspects of Mr Williams's work slowly came to acquire a cloak-and-dagger glamour:

> The wireless set in the Embassy was fairly large, a non-portable set, for operating the main traffic. But after about a couple of months on the main traffic work from the Embassy I was kind of allocated the job of organising the [installation] of small suitcase radio sets in all the Consulates and a few private houses in the ports of Spain so that we could set up a network which would pass information on German or Italian shipping using Spanish ports.
>
> 'For about . . . seven or eight months I was engaged on that work. Putting sets in, doing tests and occasionally passing some information . . . Although one had a feeling that one was doing useful work.

Useful but uncomfortable: the Spanish authorities, noticeably less friendly to the British than to the Germans, were now enforcing increasingly strict rules about clandestine radio communications. The British, explained Mr Williams, could not afford to be caught out or make any false moves.

> The radio sets were sent out from London in the 'Diplomatic Bag'. The method we used to operate was that occasionally I would go under non Diplomatic cover, but on the whole one used to go under full Diplomatic cover with someone driving a Diplomatic car, so that it wouldn't be stopped carrying somewhat incriminating equipment.
>
> I left the equipment in different ports. In places the

equipment was just left there so that it was available if
something came up which required its use.

Later on, though, Mr Williams' war was to hot up considerably,
as the wireless work became direct and aggressive:

> On the German iron ore trade (out of Bilbao) there were
> three ships – the *Hocheimer*, the *Rastenburg* and *Barfels*. They
> were the names I was using in the telegrams. The idea was
> in fact to sink the ships or to destroy them using submarines
> based just outside the various harbours. And the first ship was
> the *Hocheimer* that was . . . sunk by the submarine HMS *Sceptre*
> just outside Bilbao harbour after I'd passed the information.
> Well, we'd been telling them: it's getting ready, getting steam
> up, it's actually going out of the harbour.

Mr Williams and his colleagues were of course placing themselves at serious risk by making such transmissions. And as a further
indication of where the Spanish authorities stood on the matter of
Germany, reports of the sinking of the *Hocheimer* were firmly kept
out of the local newspapers. About six weeks later, though, the Y
Service once more began transmitting to the nearby offshore submarine. The target ship this time was the *Rastenburg*. Mr Williams
recalled lightly:

> The ship was tied up to be loaded when she was struck by
> torpedoes from HMS *Sceptre* which caused somewhat of an
> incident. As it was in neutral territory – and I believe a couple
> of Spanish policemen were killed at the time – so that [made it
> into] the press. Anyhow one was aware of what had happened.
>   The third ship was the *Barfels* . . . I remember going in,
> in the evening to start sending the messages and I was met
> and they said, "No, don't come in. We mustn't do anything
> tonight."

Mr Williams's colleagues had received advance intelligence that their role in the sabotage had been noted, and might soon be brought to a swift, brutal end. It was imperative that they avoid their transmission station that night. Instead, remembered Mr Williams, 'we went round all the bars and pubs in Bilbao in the most populated places eventually getting to bed very early in the morning.'

It wasn't until forty years later that, through a pure coincidence, Mr Williams discovered quite how close to lethal danger he had been. For while abroad, engaged in telecommunications work, he had an extraordinary conversation one evening. 'There was a German who was working for the International Labour Organisation (ILO) and we got talking, got friendly and he said that he been in the German Intercept Service during the war.' The pair established that they had been in Spain, and at the same time too. 'And from that I said, "Had you ever heard me?" And then he said, "Well, where were you on the night of July 14th?" And he said that he had been part of a German team sent to assassinate me!'[4]

The use of embassies as cover for Y Service work spread to cities such as Istanbul. Illicit stations were particularly good at picking up short-range messages that might be missed at a greater distance. Moreover, as Bill Miller had found in Spain, those sending such messages might be so confident that no one was eavesdropping that they would not even bother to encode them. In 1943, in fact, Istanbul was considered such a prized hub that no fewer than thirty secret listeners – headed by a very senior intelligence officer, Captain Thomas Howat, who had been drafted from the station in Sarafand, Palestine – were operating out of the attic of the British consulate. Their presence was explained to the outside world as 'shipping clerks'.

In north Africa, the Italians and the Germans were being pushed back step by step – General Montgomery having declared his intention to 'drive the enemy into the sea' – and the work of the cryptographers played a crucial role in this ineluctable progress. Thanks to the decoding of one especially detailed Enigma message, the Navy hunted down and destroyed an Italian merchant ship that was sailing with vast amounts of fuel and military supplies as cargo. Elsewhere, the American air force tracked down another supply ship. Days later, the Allies took Tunisia, after determined and desperate fighting from the trapped and beleaguered Axis forces. As the German military in Tunisia surrendered unconditionally, the Luftwaffe made a hasty withdrawal to Sicily.

Yet in Tangier, Morocco, the proxy intelligence wireless war continued. For Y Service operative Bill Miller, this was to be one of the most significant times of his life; a colourful blur of excitement and, indeed, love.

One hot day, Miller and his colleague Roy 'were walking down to the Old City and had to cross the "Socco Grande",' recalls Geoffrey Pidgeon. The Socco Grande was a 'large open square where the market was held'. And it was very much the sort of market that would have attracted any English person; a cacophonous blend of local merchants, silks, spices and fruits, alongside diversions such as snake-charmers and storytellers. Also situated on the square was the German legation, with its swastika flag flying from the side of the building. As Pidgeon wrote:

> It was then that Bill glanced across to a cafe at the entrance to the market place, which had an adjoining tea room. Although [he and his colleague] knew most of the bars and cafes in Tangiers, they had never been in that one, one reason being that it was frequented with Germans from the legation opposite . . . It was at that moment that Bill was stopped in his tracks. He felt he had never seen such a beautiful girl as the one who was then glancing through the window . . .

Whatever scruples he may previously have had about taking refreshment with Nazis at the next-door table, Miller apparently swiftly abandoned them in the face of this extraordinary woman. '[They] went into the tea-rooms,' continued Pidgeon. 'Sure enough, there were a couple of Germans having coffee and cake. They looked at one another, each knowing who the other was, but then ignored each other. Bill's eyes and thoughts were on the girl. She was well-dressed and extremely beautiful . . .'[5]

Whatever the yearnings of the heart, there were other immediate and serious considerations. Men in the Y Service were constantly warned about women, and particularly about talking to strange women. And extra care was advised to be taken about talking to strange women in the marketplace of Tangier. The town was milling with spies and agents. Pidgeon concluded the story:

So [as] Bill and Roy sat in the tea-room they tried to make out her nationality. 'Whatever their nationality, people in Tangiers were either strongly pro-Allies or pro-German . . . Bill began going to the tea-rooms regularly, often with friends from the office. At various times they heard her speaking French, Spanish and Italian . . . Eventually he asked a friend who she was and was told "Oh, that's Ramona". She was Spanish and a member of the pro-Allies Spanish community. Bill asked to be introduced and to cut a long story short, eventually they married.

13 Not So Quiet on the Domestic Front

The amateurs in Britain had been silenced, their aerials long since taken down. At the very start of the war, it had been decreed that radio enthusiasts – no matter how patriotic and finely intentioned – would have to sacrifice their beloved hobby. The risk to national security was simply too great. If home-made aerials at the bottom of gardens were to remain commonplace, it would be a huge boost to enemy agents working on British soil; they would be able to make clandestine reports to their Nazi masters unnoticed by anyone in the neighbourhood.

As we have seen, the passion of the amateurs was instead channelled brilliantly into the Voluntary Interceptors movement, and indeed, these volunteers performed invaluable service. But the agents of the Radio Security Service were constantly alert to the possibility that more sinister forces were at work.

A few years ago, one former RSS agent, interviewed about his war years, told the BBC that when enemy messages from spies were transmitted and picked up by the RSS monitors, the agents would go out in cars with portable receivers in order to track down the exact source of these radio emissions. The image that comes to mind is that of an old TV detector van, the aerial on its roof. The truth was not so very different.

Illicit transmissions were not always directed towards the Germans, though. There were other clandestine interests. And a case of this kind from 1943 involving the RSS has links to one of Britain's longest-running spy controversies. It involved a woman spy called Ursula Beurton, resident in England throughout the war, whose remarkable career has long been a source of fascination to Chapman Pincher, the veteran hounder of Soviet moles. These days, Beurton is perhaps most notorious for having passed messages for Klaus Fuchs, the scientist who leaked to the Soviets the secrets of atomic weapons research. According to Pincher, though, her greatest coup was rather bigger: it directly involved the puzzling absence of the Radio Security Service.

By 1943, married to Leonard Beurton, Ursula (or, as she was later to be labelled, 'Red Sonya') was settled in a cottage in Kidlington, just outside Oxford. One night, according to Pincher, she opened up a cavity in the wall of the back garden, removed a hidden miniature radio transmitter, took it into the kitchen, and started transmitting in Morse. The nature of her intelligence was far from routine; indeed, according to Pincher, it was nothing less than the outline of the top secret Quebec Agreement between Roosevelt and Churchill – a pact in which the two leaders vowed to form an atomic military alliance, and also, vitally, to hide any suggestion of this alliance or the associated research from the Soviets. The agreement had been signed only two weeks beforehand: Pincher's theory is that Beurton could only have received this intelligence from someone in the highest ranks of MI5, a long-standing Soviet mole. And that she was used by this mole as the conduit to pass information back to Russia.

But given the illegal nature of the transmission – plus the fact that Beurton had a forbidden radio transmission aerial in her back garden – how exactly did she escape the normally hyper-efficient attentions of the Radio Security Service? Again, according to Pincher, in one sense she didn't: the fact that she was transmitting was noted and a Radio Security Service 'detector van' operating in Oxfordshire was sent to the Kidlington area. But a senior intelligence official supposedly advised the RSS not to pursue the case – Pincher's theory is that it was Roger Hollis, former head of MI5, long suspected of himself being a Soviet spy. And so 'Red Sonya' could keep transmitting – until, just after the war, she fled Britain for the sanctuary of Communist East Germany. In 2000, Russian president Vladimir Putin awarded her the comically distinguished title of 'Super Agent Of Military Intelligence'.

This story aside, there seemed throughout the war to be a great deal less domestic espionage activity than anyone had anticipated. Furthermore, thanks to the Radio Security Service and its assiduous monitoring of the Abwehr codes, it was usually known some way in advance when such agents or double agents would be arriving in Britain. From this point, there was either the opportunity of 'turning' agents, or indeed of ensuring that double agents obtained a stream of misinformation which they could dutifully feed back to their masters. (The most famous example, 'Agent Garbo', sent a great many detailed radio messages that were invaluable in deflecting attention away from the planned Operation Overlord, the Allied invasion of France.)

The intercept stations around Britain's coastline continued to foster their own small and often eccentric little communities. One such was in the Suffolk seaside town of Southwold. 'We lived and worked in a charming house, Stone House on Gun Hill,' wrote Wrens veteran Margaret Smee. This grassy area included 'a coastguard lookout' and also had 'a large gun trained out to sea'. Such weaponry was important; fittingly, given its name, Gun Hill had come under sporadic bombardment since the beginning of the war. And the German ships ploughing up and down the North Sea continued to pose a threat. In reading these Southwold accounts, one gets a strong sense of that juxtaposition of tea rooms, bathing huts, barbed wire and gun emplacements. 'Captain Clack, who was

in charge, had cleared some of the obstructions from the shore,'
wrote Margaret Smee. This meant that 'his men could bathe and
we were allowed to bathe here too.' But there was also a semblance
of military life. 'One of his officers instructed us in how to use a
rifle, which only got as far as lying on the dining room floor in the
correct position.'

Smee was promoted to Second Officer and a 'new watchroom
and tower' were built a short distance away from Stone House. No
matter how agreeable the town and the coastline, the work here as
elsewhere was never less than arduous and highly pressurised. 'We
took it in turns to do night duty and had a small summer house
to sleep in, before continuing up there until lunch-time next day.
This was fine in summer but in winter quite freezing. I never knew
before that it took so much snow to make a cup of tea!'[1]

Sybil Welch remembered the Southwold base as 'a pleasant,
rambling family house by the sea'. She wrote that it 'was a very nice
US Air Force major of our acquaintance who coined the phrase
"people in Stone Houses shouldn't throw glass".' And to make up
for the gruelling nature of the work, there were – occasionally –
extraordinary adventures. Welch recalled the night when a USAF
Flying Fortress flew in from a raid, 'crippled and on fire':

> Two of the crew baled out, their parachutes open, into the
> sea in front of us. The coast guards had been alerted but we
> were closer. Two of us set off down the beach – which was,
> incidentally, mined – and helped one of the airmen out of
> the water and into our kitchen. He was of course given the
> inevitable cups of tea and wrapped in a warm, fluffy dressing
> gown belonging to our cook, who was fortunately a lady of
> ample proportions.

A little way down the road was the Wrens listening station at the
port of Harwich, Suffolk, which according to veteran Joy Hale was
in many senses a terrific place to serve:

The work was much more exciting as we were next to the Ops room and could see what was going on, and the port was full of ships and sailors and naval officers. There were lots of dances and parties. The Free French came and any French-speaking Wrens were invited to their dances. The Czechs were there too. It was a frivolous happy-go-lucky time and we thought little about the seriousness and the reality of war.

Things were more serious further up the coast in Norfolk, remembered Hale. The station at Sheringham 'stood on Beeston Hump, the highest piece of cliff in the neighbourhood'. And, she continued, 'it was here for the first time I saw the whole intercept operation come together. We picked up E-Boat signals and identified the boats . . . we got a fix on them and quickly telephoned the information to the Intelligence Centre at Chatham.' Thus alerted, Chatham contacted Coastal Forces. For Joy Hale, there was the satisfaction of hearing gunfire; 'and going out on the cliffs,' she wrote, 'we saw the flashes of the "dust up" going on about four miles out . . . this was a textbook operation but it was only occasionally that everything worked out so precisely.'[2]

Incidentally, as I write, I have in front of me on my desk my late grandfather's wartime identity card. 'National Service Acts accepted for Royal Naval Service,' it reads. 'Registration number BKR1167, Mr Herbert Swindlehurst, R.N. W/T Station, Gun Hill, Southwold, July 1943.' Whatever the nature of the work he did there, he never told my mother, or indeed, as far as I can tell, my grandmother. A gentle man in the truest sense, he would have signed the Official Secrets Act, and would have had an acute sense of abiding by it. Born in 1901, as a young man my grandfather had found the science of wireless hypnotically fascinating; before the war he had travelled the world as the 'sparks' – the wireless operator – on various mighty ships and had seen and experienced very much more than even today's gap-year travellers. When war was declared, he was thirty-eight years old and by the time he arrived at Southwold, he was forty-two. According to veterans such as Bob Hughes, this would have meant that he was regarded by other operatives as 'old'; though having seen his Morse transcription skills in action in later life, I would like to think that he was still a great deal nimbler than most.

And with German vessels hurling various lethal weapons at the Gun Hill station, life in Southwold could hardly have been described as the quiet option. It was very much in Britain's front line: local troops destroyed the end of the pier in order to prevent Germans making a landing there. Low-flying German aircraft dropped enormous bombs. In 1943, a lone aircraft which, unlike the others, had managed to sweep in under the radar, unloaded a 1000 lb bomb which almost destroyed one street. At the start of the war, London evacuee children had been sent to Southwold; soon, they had to be evacuated out again. And the town was closed to holidaymakers. There were incendiary bombs and even, a little later, stray doodlebugs. So while being beside the coast had its aesthetic compensations, there was little in the way of tranquillity for the secret listeners.

Another lively – if remote – area to which to be posted was the far north coast of Scotland. 'My posting after training,' recalled one Y Service operative, 'was to Caithness . . . where the station spread out from a tiny village like an octopus – the control hut and five huts where enemy signals were intercepted 24 hours a day.' The freezing waters around Orkney and Shetland were seething with enemy vessels, and their transmissions were frequent; a vast amount of material to intercept, collate, and send on to Bletchley Park. Some of the wireless operators who found themselves dispatched to RAF Wick were taken aback both by the cold and by the astounding length of time it took to travel there, even from Inverness. But it was not all icy austerity; indeed, for a few, romance found a way, even in those slicing winds. 'I was a Wireless Operator, and worked in the Signals Section,' recalled Vi Mitchell, originally from Dundee, and so no stranger to such weather conditions:

This was quite a large building, housing the Wireless Section, the Teleprinter Section and Operations Room where they plotted the Aircraft, PBX (telephone exchange) and Met Office, so a large number of personnel worked there, right round the clock as it was manned 24 hours a day.

I met my husband at Wick. He came from Dundee like myself . . . he was a Teleprinter Operator.

The atmosphere did not seem immediately conducive to romance, though:

The WAAFs were in houses, which were called married quarters. There were three girls in the downstairs room, three upstairs and a Corporal or Sergeant in the small room. She was in charge of the girls, and had to report any misbehaviour. We shared a kitchen and bathroom, and had strict rotas. We got a ration of coal to put on a fire to heat water, so between seven girls it had to be rationed.

Social lives were further curtailed by other onerous demands placed upon these young women:

The billets had to be kept clean and we had a domestic night once a week, when all WAAFs were confined to camp to clean and polish. We had to polish our brass buttons and cap badge, and woe betide any WAAF who had dingy buttons, if an Officer spotted her. We had to salute all officers both WAAF and RAF either on the Station or outside in the town itself.

Despite that, she added,

I only remember the good times at Wick, I've forgotten all the cold dreary days when I wondered if I'd ever get home again. I remember the Pavilion Picture House, the Rifle Hall where we danced, the County Cafe and Mrs Lyall's Chip Shop where we enjoyed fish and chips, and the odd egg she put on our plate, when she had them.[3]

Equally warm memories were held by wireless operator Wilma Hall, who at least got to see a bit of action around the place. 'When I was there in 1943, there was a complete Operations Block among the main station buildings, and the school was then used for offices such as the Sports Office,' she recalled. 'The Operations Block, which is where I worked, contained the Operations Room, the Wireless Cabin...Meteorological Office, Intelligence Office, Signals Officer's Office, Teleprinter Room and Telephone Exchange.'

The work was relentless – partly owing to a relative scarcity of fully trained staff; the skills that Hall had acquired meant she was greatly in demand: 'Wireless operators were in very short supply at that time so we were kept very busy and worked hard seven days a week on a three-watch shift system. We never had a day off, but I loved my work and didn't mind the long and often unsociable hours.' But occasional distractions helped to give a little colour to the otherwise grinding routine:

During my time two squadrons of Beaufighters, numbers 144 and 404 (Canadian) were stationed on the airfield. When they flew on operations they used to take with them carrier pigeons and when the crews came to the Operations Block to get debriefed for their mission they would leave the pigeons in their little carrying boxes on our wireless tables while they received their orders. The birds would pop their heads out and coo to us! They usually had a name on their box – Margy or Betty or Mary or whatever – named after wives and girlfriends back home.

One can imagine that the wives and girlfriends would have been thrilled to hear this. 'There was even an airman on the camp who had the special job of Pigeon Keeper.'[4]

This being the far north of Scotland, entertainment could be hard to find, although that corner of the country has always produced enthusiastic dancers. But for a young woman on a military base in a small, chilly town, where in winter the sun would barely rise before it had started to set again, a certain kind of fibre was required. Presumably this was why so many recruits sent there originally hailed from the north of the country: they would know what to expect, and not go into shock at the prospect. Even so, the veterans' fond memories for even the most basic creature comforts have an element of bathos.

'Food in camp was not very palatable, so we spent most of our pay (three shillings and four pence a day) on eating out in the town, where food was fairly plentiful,' recalled Wilma Hall. 'There was a cafe in the Square where one could get tea and a big plate of scones with lashings of butter for nine pence [about 3½ new pence]. Other cafes were the Victory and the Bon Accord.' In such times, scones and butter and cheerful cosy cafés would have provided more solace than we can imagine.

After doing a short course in direction finding, Marjorie Gerken, who had been based at HMS *Flowerdown* amid the golden fields of Hampshire, was suddenly told that she was to be transferred somewhere 'between Wick and Thurso'. The journey by train from Winchester was something of an epic: 'First, all day up to Perth. Then all night up to Thurso. There, we had quarters in a big old house. There were dormitories. When I arrived, I slept solidly for about sixteen hours, and someone had to come and wake me.' And the immediate prospect when this girl – who originally hailed from south-west London – awoke in the far north was not immediately comforting: 'The base was little huts in the middle of a field.'

But the compensations of her new life became swiftly apparent. 'It was very bleak, the landscape – but on the other hand, the locals didn't really have much of an idea about rationing. You would get tea in these very welcoming farmhouses.'

'And there was a bit of a social life – I went to a dance with Air Sea Rescue at Wick. Then there was a weekend in the Orkneys to go to a dance there – we were allowed to stay overnight.' This interlude came to an end quite abruptly when Mrs Gerken's sister down south was diagnosed with TB; in order to be close by, Marjorie was allowed to transfer back to HMS *Flowerdown* – her great friend, Wren Pat Sinclair, found a replacement girl who was willing to go north in Marjorie's place.

In more general terms, at a time when opportunities for overseas travel were very rare other than for the rich, and even travel up and down the country was not all that common, this exchange of English and Scottish girls was a source of great interest among them all. For as Marjorie Gerken and others were transferred north, there were women making the journey to the altogether softer landscape around Winchester. 'We had a first consignment of Scottish girls come down to HMS *Flowerdown*,' says Pat Sinclair. 'On the same job. And of course, I'd never been to Scotland, never met a Scottish person in my life. I was a real Londoner, and they were the most lovely girls. I remember them with great affection – we just gelled. They could have been from outer space for all we knew about them, with their accents. But we made good friends.'

Meanwhile, in the pulsing heat of the Mediterranean, the oldest game – that of spy versus spy – continued with no let-up in intensity. Thanks in part to the various young men dispatched to places such as Madrid and Lisbon, there to observe on neutral territory the movements of the enemy, MI8 had built up a solid picture of the key players in the secret services, and their foibles and dispositions. Captain Hugh Trevor-Roper was instrumental in collating this information for circulation in London and Bletchley Park.

'The following is a note on recent developments in German Secret Service W/T communications in Spain and Portugal,' stated one memo sent in May 1943, by which time the Axis forces were starting to look less invincible. The Nazis, it seems, were taking greater advantage of the authorities in these apparently neutral countries:

> Aided by Spanish and Portuguese co-operation, and diplomat-
> ic cover, [these stations] have hitherto controlled almost all
> other W/T stations in the peninsula . . . By this system, all com-
> munications from stations in Spain and Portugal have been
> routed through Madrid and Lisbon, which alone have contact
> with Abwehr headquarters in Berlin . . . But this system de-
> pends for its safe and efficient working first on the benevolent
> attitude of the Spanish and Portuguese.

There had been one particularly fat black fly in the ointment for the Germans; Allied success in the region had enabled the Y Service to start exerting covert pressure on their Nazi counterparts: 'Diplomatic pressure from the Allies, combined with an appreciation of their military successes and the implications of these for the future, has led both the Spanish and Portuguese governments to move closer towards a policy of pure neutrality in their relations with the Abwehr.'[5] But MI8 was also keen to underline that the German Y service – far from withering – was bolstering itself against these and further setbacks using technology and a cunning new approach to recruitment. The memo added:

> They have taken the obvious precaution of adding to their
> supplies of technical equipment, and it may be some indication
> of the priority accorded to their plans by Abwehr headquarters
> that, in spite of the shortage of wireless transmission sets
> resulting from the bombing of the Stahnsdorf station
> near Berlin in January, they have been allotted a very large
> proportion of the sets for which they asked.

On top of this, the Abwehr was taking on Spanish and Portuguese personnel to 'replace the German operators'. The new influx, as well as being natives, were also former employees of specialised concerns like Marconi. Their work, obviously, was highly secret; yet one or two were arrested and unmasked. A great many others weren't. The balance of neutrality was continuing to tip away from the Allies, for all their recent triumphs in the region.

MI8 had also become extremely interested in Abwehr head Admiral Canaris, and the ferocious internal politicking that was taking place among the Nazis. Canaris was considered to be doing his best to maintain the independence of the Abwehr; trying indeed – it has been suggested – to ensure that it maintained a measure of distance from some of the atrocities being carried out. It was reasoned that the key way to do this would be to maintain its dominance of wireless intelligence; this made the already murky atmosphere of the Mediterranean even murkier. Another MI8 report, this time in June 1943, proclaimed:

> The keystone of the Abwehr reporting-system is the observa-
> tion of ships and aircraft in the Straits of Gibraltar. If this were
> disrupted, the Abwehr presentation of the enemy order of
> battle would be hopelessly incomplete and inaccurate; this ex-
> plains the extraordinary importance which Canaris attaches
> to his relations with highly-placed Spaniards and in particular
> with Vigon, Spanish Air Minister, and Martinez Campos, vice-
> chief of the Spanish General Staff. His Spanish connexions
> are indispensable to him, not only as a source of intelligence,
> but also because of their political support; the exceptional
> facilities which the Abwehr enjoys in Spain . . . must be pro-
> tected against diplomatic pressure . . .

Its intelligence-gathering capabilities were one thing; but according to the wireless spies, the Abwehr was largely useless in other directions. 'The sabotage and insurrection department of the Abwehr has been remarkably unsuccessful, and we have abundant evidence of its incompetence in western Europe,' the report stated. However, other Nazi agencies were rising to fill this destructive vacuum and the report identified key figures – 'Dr Graeffe, for instance, directs subversive activity in Russia . . . In Morocco, Major Schultze foments sabotage and insurrection'. This was to say nothing of 'Franz Mayer's very ambitious insurrectionary organisation in Persia'.

Fascinatingly, Captain Trevor-Roper's unit was also monitoring Nazi wireless intelligence yet further east: beyond Turkey, and into Afghanistan. Given present-day geopolitical tensions, it is extraordinary to see how this country was the focus of quite another conflict in 1943. 'The [Abwehr] in Afghanistan operates against both Russia and Great Britain,' stated an intelligence report in May 1943. 'Against the former, it conspires with the "Union of Young Turkestan" emigres from Russian Turkestan; against the latter, with the Faqir of Ipi and with Subhas Bose's Forward Block.'

It had 'a double courier system through Persia to Istanbul . . . we should be able to watch this,' stated the report. It also had 'W/T communication with Berlin. For this purpose the Abwehr, as elsewhere, borrows the wireless transmission and cypher facilities of the German legation.'

More sinisterly from the British point of view, there was direct communication 'from Berlin to the dissident elements in India with whom the [Abwehr] in Kabul deals . . . made by means of code messages in the "Azad Hind" programmes from Zeesen. It is understood this material is taken and handled in India, and here its chief value will be in relation to the study of Axis broadcasts to other and uncontrolled places.'[6]

What surprises the reader now is the extent and the depth of Y Service intelligence, even down to the number of illicit wireless sets allocated to keep in secret contact with 'Delhi, Bajaur and the Faqir of Ipi'. Any suggestion of clandestine transmissions, and Radio Security Service India would be listening in and – as with all other communications – cracking the codes that the enemy considered unbreakable. Meanwhile, the ability to pinpoint individuals made the eavesdropping extremely effective. 'At Abwehr HQ [in Kabul], Dr Richter is in charge of anti-Russian activity and has appeared in Most Secret sources as controlling Abwehr parties destined for subversive activity in the South Caucasus', while 'Wendell . . . is directing anti-British activity in Persia.' Moreover, all these complexities had to be followed and filed and logged in such a way that even the most subtle and unexpected of connections could be made.

To this end, the work of Captain Trevor-Roper and his colleagues was strategically vital. This was not just about listening in to the enemy; it was also about the opportunity to disrupt the enemy's vital communications. For the Radio Analysis Bureau to have pinpointed with such accuracy the nerve centres of communications would mean that when the time was right, the SAS would be able to go in and carry out acts of sabotage: for instance, parachuting in near a wireless/teleprinter station, entering it and destroying the equipment. The destruction of teleprinters and local telephone lines would mean that the enemy would have to make all communications by radio – which in turn would be picked up by the Y Services, bringing in a crop of fresh intelligence.

Trevor-Roper's own war had been possibly more reflective and calm than most; when not working out of Arkley View in Barnet, with his witty colleagues, he was either pursuing his great love of hunting, or on leave back home in Northumberland, which always seemed to inspire him to heights of flowery prose. The two poles of his life were entangled in a dream which he committed to his diary. He wrote that he was in Bletchley Park, walking around the huts with 'hundreds of other human termites', when suddenly the entire place was invaded by a pack of hounds and a huntsmaster – the part of the dream that gave Trevor-Roper real pleasure.

The Park preyed upon him in other ways; for instance, he brooded about his perpetually fraught relationships with the Directorate. So much so that he was once moved to compose a poem about Bletchley's new director, Commander Edward Travis, and how he would eventually be compelled to leave the place like his predecessor, '[when] Denniston packed up and fled'.

At one point in 1943, he was on a yearned-for break in Northumberland when a letter arrived from his colleague Logan Pearsall Smith, acutely putting it to Trevor-Roper that he was considering his future and his fate, 'to decide what you want to make of your life . . .' This set Trevor-Roper brooding that perhaps he needed some 'sharp external blow to direct the aimless thoughts'. He considered asking to be sent to Yugoslavia, 'to live with the rebels there, in their woods and caves'.[7] He would join the SIS – and perhaps court death, or become a Byronic figure. Such musings were apparently extinguished when he got a phone call from Barnet asking him to go back to work. And it is just as well in some ways, for Trevor-Roper's later war was to take an extraordinary twist that would have repercussions throughout his life.

Back in Bletchley Park, the card-file index system – patiently built up over months and years by infinitely careful debutantes – gave an unparalleled advantage to codebreakers who could identify, for instance, the name of the son of Admiral Dönitz, which showed up in German naval reports and thus gave vital clues to the positions of certain destroyers. The various indexes had a global reach, with connections spanning continents.

Indeed, this steady accretion of information, allied with increasingly skilled methods of radio monitoring, contributed to the formation of what in the late 1940s would become GCHQ – an organisation in which Arthur Bonsall, the young civilian sent to RAF Cheadle, would eventually rise to become director.

The reading of Abwehr codes reached a euphoric peak in May 1943; for naval intelligence had pulled off the deception – now justly famous – called 'Operation Mincemeat'. This had involved the planting of the body of 'Major Martin', an important courier carrying vital intelligence, apparently downed in an air crash off

Spain. The body was found by a Spanish fisherman and handed over to the authorities. The authorities in turn alerted German agents, and the Abwehr eagerly passed the results of the find on to German High Command. Documentation found with the dead man included a letter addressed to General Alexander intimating that the Allies were about to launch an assault on Greece and Crete. 'Major Martin' was in fact a near anonymous body procured from a morgue; the stage dressings were the responsibility of Naval Intelligence; and, after Rommel had been sent by Hitler to take charge of the defence of Greece, thus confirming the staggering success of the bluff, the Allies were able to launch their long-planned assault upon Sicily. Even after the deception, the Y Service picked up Abwehr messages attempting to explain this disaster to High Command. They of course knew nothing of the highly classified deception, and indeed perhaps few of us might have done until recently were it not for Churchill repeating the story to his friend Duff Cooper; Cooper then used it in a post-war novel called *Operation Heartbreak*, which led in the 1950s to the non-fiction book and film *The Man Who Never Was*.

With Allied success in north Africa had come a reduction in the amount of wireless traffic emanating from Axis forces. As the assault on Sicily was undertaken and plans for Italy laid, there was anxiety in the service that back in Europe, much Axis traffic would be carried on telephone landlines instead of radios, and would thus be impossible to intercept. But as the German units arrived intent on defending Sicily, they persisted in communicating over the radio. The Y Service thus continued to pass invaluable information back to Bletchley Park; new codes, which were unlocked swiftly.

As well as instantly revealing German strategy with regard to Sicily – including details of the units drafted in from Russia – Abwehr messages revealed the full extent of the uncertainty in German High Command about the Mediterranean; Hitler and his generals had very little idea how or when the Allies would strike next. As Captain Trevor-Roper – who had been reading Abwehr messages throughout (and providing unsolicited interpretations for his various superiors thereof) – wrote a little later in an exultant memo marked 'top secret':

> The landings in SICILY were thus achieved without any apparent warning by the Abwehr; even after they had occurred, it was twice suggested that they were a feint for an operation elsewhere . . . a hitherto unregarded sub-agent in MELILLA had reported the departure from ALGIERS and TUNIS of an invasion fleet destined for the south-east corner of SICILY. The surprise which so accurate a forecast (though too late to be of any use) occasioned in the Abwehr is evidenced by the fact that Admiral Canaris himself sent a message enquiring what the sub-agent in MELILLA thought the Allies' next move would be. Evidently he thought him worth the whole of the rest of the Abwehr.

Perhaps the sub-agent was worth more. For, according to Trevor-Roper:

> [in] strategic matters, the Abwehr's record is one of failure. It failed to forecast the attack on MADAGASCAR; it failed over 'TORCH'; it failed over the Casablanca conference. Since then it has sought eagerly for intelligence of Allied plans for the Second Front, but it seems to have had difficulty distinguishing, among the spate of reports that it has received, between the good and the bad, the genuine and the tendentious . . . there has been in general a divergence between the copious and alarmist reports of Abwehr agents and the more critical attitude of the German Service Attaches, who work for the Abwehr.[8]

In terms of the Sicily operation, there were also indications beforehand from Italian naval messages that they had at least a shrewd idea of what was coming next; incidentally, these Italian Enigma codes, faithfully relayed back to Bletchley Park, had some time ago been cracked by cryptographers Dilly Knox and Mavis Lever.

As the invasion of Sicily was launched, an Army Y unit joined the Eighth Army for the landings; unfortunately, according to the official history, it was of little help in the field as the security of the German communications systems had been improved since the rout of Tunisia – the operators were more disciplined, less given to the lapses into laxity that would make their encryptions easier to break. Thankfully, Y units elsewhere were not short of material; messages flooding in from the Luftwaffe and the German navy were gathered in at lightning speed and relayed to Bletchley, which unscrambled the codes with equal speed, providing almost a form of commentary on the unfolding events.

And once again, women were finding ways to participate directly, as opposed to being distant witnesses. Aileen Clayton noted:

I met General Eisenhower for the first time soon after I started to work at Supreme Headquarters in Algiers. His suite of offices was on the same corridor as those of our own branch. 'Ike', as he was affectionately known to everybody, fascinated me by his almost computer-like memory. He seemed never to forget a fact or a face. I would take him a report on some subject, which he would read with incredible rapidity, and then he might say, 'I read something recently which ties up with that. Let me see, it is in a file on . . . about page 57, second paragraph from the bottom.' I would go back to my office, call for the file, and sure enough, he would be right.[9]

General Eisenhower was not the only notable American face. Serving time in the US ranks also happened to be one of the greatest playwrights and screen-writers of his age:

Thornton Wilder was with us at that time in the American Air Force, and he brought a breath of sanity into our otherwise somewhat unnatural military existence. It is interesting that he was so intrigued by the timelessness of the name of one of our prisoner-of-war interrogators – Antrobus – that he used it for the central character of the play 'The Skin of our Teeth' that he wrote after the war.

14 Life-Long Friendships Were Forged

Even before the declaration of war, a few girls knew exactly what role they wanted to play in the coming conflict. Intense patriotism was part of it, but there were other reasons too. It does these women no discredit to say that some sections of military life were deemed more glamorous than others, and that the Wrens were felt by many to have a special appeal. One such enthusiast was Pat Sinclair; born a cockney, within the sound of the old Bow Bells, she was living with her family in the semi-rural north London suburb of Southgate in 1939. When Mr Chamberlain's mournful broadcast was made on the Sunday morning of 3 September, Pat was too young to join up, even though she had put in an early request. Instead, in the interim, she went to work for her local electricity board, the North Metropolitan Power Company.

'I was a bit later going in to the Wrens than I would have liked,' she explains, adding: 'Why the Wrens? My brother was in the TAs as a young boy. The war started, he went to camp and didn't come back – he was already in the war, already a soldier. He said to me: "I don't want any sister of mine being in the ATS" – I think because they were mainly in the catering side of it. He said, "No – it's no life." He saw the rough end of the soldiers and the rough end of the girls.

'Actually, that didn't influence me. The Wrens was the smallest service and it was a senior service and they picked their recruits, so I aimed high and I went through all the categories. I could have been in the cookhouse, I could have been in an office, I could have been a lady's maid to one of the officers – stewards they were called.'

Obviously, none of those options would have been satisfactory. 'I thought, wireless telegraphy: wow. That was one of the highest categories.' Happily, Mrs Sinclair was able to do some preparation before she was called up. 'I got together with a girl at work and her father had a little [Morse] sending machine and I used to go round to her house to learn the alphabet. And she went in the Wrens ultimately. When I applied, I wrote these letters – to the Navy – and said I wanted to join the Wrens. And I told them I could do five words a minute.

'It was all a bit of a bluff. But anyway, they accepted me and the next thing, I was called up to Mill Hill.' Another suburb on the outskirts of north London, Mill Hill was where the initial stages of recruitment were carried out. 'We were there for two weeks. This is where they allocated what they were going to accept you for. That's how I found I was going to go on the wireless telegraphy course. And I got on it, because I had lied and said that I could do five words a minute intercepting – so I was put in the top class.'

This cheeky deception did not end in disaster, though, for it transpired that Mrs Sinclair had a genuine aptitude, as well as enthusiasm, for the work.

'Perhaps because I was so keen . . . it's like learning shorthand, you either take to it or you can't do it,' she says. 'And I took to it like a duck takes to water, I just loved it. It was the most glamorous group to go in and the job was quite high up. That's what spurred me on.'

Similarly spurred was Betty White, who found herself drafted into the Wrens and, like her friend-to-be Pat Sinclair, sent off to HMS *Flowerdown* in Hampshire. 'I was a bit late joining,' says Mrs White, although this was through no fault of her own; she had been working for the Public Trustee Office, a branch of the civil service that was reluctant to see her go. And even though the results of her IQ test, together with the fact that her older brother had already taught her Morse, ushered her quickly towards wireless telegraphy, she still had to face the initial shock of the Mill Hill training camp: 'Three weeks of scrubbing floors and cleaning windows,' she recalls ruefully. Then came further, and rather more technical training, at Soberton Towers, a requisitioned boys' boarding school in Hampshire.

Another friend Pat Sinclair was later to meet at HMS *Flowerdown* recalls a yen for the Wrens. Like Pat, Majorie Gerken had decided very quickly what sort of role she wanted to play. 'I had always been interested in the Navy,' she says. 'My uncle served in the Navy, and as a girl, I was in the Guides, and they had the Sea Rangers. This put me in a good position for later joining up.

'I got to the age of nineteen, going on twenty, and it was September 1942 when I was allowed to join. When applying to the Wrens, I had to write to an address at Queen Anne's Mansions. It was there that you went for your interview, and a medical, and they told you when you were required. I had a head start: we had been taught Morse in the Guides. Not to any kind of speed at all – but we had been taught it none the less, and so we knew what all the dots and dashes were.'

She continues, 'Even with this, though, there was a lot of training involved to become a wireless telegraphist. We did notice that in the first three months, we were taught nothing but receiving – there was nothing at all about transmitting. We did ask ourselves why. Were they going to concentrate purely on this? But at the end of three months, we were told about special duties.'

The first of Mrs Gerken's special duties took her down to Plymouth and in its own way had a frisson of genuine excitement.

'It was mine-watching at the Plymouth lighthouse. The Germans were dropping mines, and these were landing in the Sound. Our job was to plot their positions, and then teams could go out there and explode them safely.'

After this thrilling induction came the next step towards the Y Service. 'As to special duties, and the interception work: you had to sign the Official Secrets Act. There was super-secrecy,' says Mrs Gerken. 'So much so that we genuinely thought that if we breathed a word to anyone, we would be beheaded. It was very effective brainwashing. We really didn't say a word. The Y training was first at New College in London, then down in Doxford, near Petersfield. Throughout all of it, we never talked about it.

'My parents certainly never knew anything about it. But there was a certain amount that we knew. We intercepted shore stations in France, we'd know if they were seeking frequencies. There were tutors at *Flowerdown* who had been among the first intake of wireless telegraphists when the war broke out and in 1940, at around the time that the first codes were being broken. These older people might have told us what we were there to do. In terms of listening and Morse, we got up to very high speeds.'

And so it was, not too long after her introduction, that Majorie Gerken found herself being posted to Hampshire. Initially, she was rather peevish about this; she had instead wanted to go up to the station at Scarborough, chiefly because the idea of being beside the sea appealed. But once she had made friends – especially with Pat Sinclair – this new, rigorous, highly disciplined wartime life became, in many ways, very enjoyable. Certainly, her memories of the establishment are now extremely sunny (as indeed, curiously, are many of the photographs taken of the place, as though England in the early 1940s was basking in a perpetual summer).

'Really, though, we were lucky,' says Mrs Gerken. '*Flowerdown* had been a civilian station between the wars. And it had facilities, especially for games. There was football, hockey, tennis, squash. It had a special dance floor, and there was also a specially built lounge area. These were just brick-built buildings and Nissen huts. In some places, there were brick buildings like houses: we never went to these but I think that is where they housed families. Then there was a long brick building which had individual rooms, for single boys I think. We Wrens went into the Nissen huts. It was a very nice crowd of people. I made lifelong friends there.

'Our watch room was a long, low building, single storey. When you were on watch, you could never leave your radio set – in case. If you wanted to visit the loo, you had to put your hand up first and wait for someone to come and relieve you. But equally, there were times, if it was less busy, when you were allowed, after putting your hand up, to go and make a drink of some sort. This could be the case if you were listening in to stations on the French coast which would always be strict about the times that they transmitted.'

These little breaks highlighted one of the more free and easy aspects of the establishment: the casual commingling of servicemen and women. Somehow, if an institution is largely civilian (as in the case of Bletchley Park), then such an arrangement does not seem especially noteworthy; when the men and women are in uniform, however, it seems curiously modern. 'When it came to making those beverages,' continues Mrs Gerken, 'they would always pick a Wren and a sailor to go and do it together. Not two Wrens or two sailors but always a Wren and a sailor.' There were inevitable romantic consequences; lust simmering away over the beef tea. 'A great friend of mine there ended up marrying the sailor that she had made tea with,' says Mrs Gerken. 'I met my own husband at *Flowerdown*: it got a lot of sailors who were coming in, say, from the convoys, and who were there for what was termed rest and resuscitation.'

This was one of the elements that made the place so conducive to a certain light-heartedness. 'The lounge area – it was a beautiful building for us,' says Mrs Gerken. 'There was a canteen, which had a big piano. You could get a drink in there, nothing excessive, but I'm sure it was possible to get beer. We would sit in there to chat.

And if anyone was a pianist . . . Of course with the 24-hour watch there were very strict rotas. But when you got your time off . . .'

Love wasn't only brewing up in the tea-making areas. There was plenty of romance in all areas at *Flowerdown*. Having swiftly become firm friends, Pat and Marjorie were there to see each other through various scrapes and imbroglios. Pat, on one occasion, was in the awkward position of having met a soldier on a train down from London and agreeing to meet up with him for a date, without paying attention to his name. 'I said, "Would you like to come to one of our camp dances? On the Saturday? If I'm off duty?"' The man had eagerly assented. But as the Saturday in question drew closer, all Pat could recall was his first name. She told Marjorie all about it.

'I said, "Marjorie, I've done it again",' says Mrs Sinclair, laughing. Her companion, ever protective, asked, 'What have you been up to?'

'And I said, "Well, I've made a date with this soldier and I don't even know his name – only Peter. I can't remember what he looks like, even."'

Marjorie told her, 'Well, you'll have to go and meet him at the station.'

'I said, "Oh, he won't turn up", and she read me the Riot Act, she said at the very least I must go because it would be very unfair if I didn't.

'So, very reluctantly, I went on this hot Saturday afternoon – and Winchester then, the forces were there, lots of soldiers. The station was just outside the town, and there were not many cars, of course. I walked up the drive to the station and the train had gone, people had departed, and there were two soldiers. One was by the window, one was by the door, and I thought, I don't know which one it is. Fortunately, Peter came towards *me*, so that was that.'

Their first date was a dance: as it was 'on board' HMS *Flowerdown*, Pat had to make the official arrangements for her soldier suitor.

'You could only get on to the base with a pass. And you couldn't go just anywhere.

'But when I first put in a request to let this staff sergeant come on, I said to Marjorie, "I don't know what his name is, I'm going to have to put Sgt Peter Smith." And that was that.

'And I had to see him off the premises. So at the end of the dance, we got to the gate – Peter went to kiss me. I drew myself up to my five foot nine height and said: "But I hardly know you!" Can you imagine that today? I was such a prude!

'We laugh about that now. Then he just pursued me.'

With some success, as it happened. For Peter Sinclair and Pat are still married to this day, some seventy years after first meeting on that hot Saturday afternoon at Winchester station. Peter Sinclair's own story is remarkable; he was in fact German-born, and had come over with the *Kindertransport* in the 1930s.

But before Peter – and Marjorie's husband-to-be, Norman – materialised on the scene, Pat and Marjorie were throwing themselves with gusto into another celebrated aspect of wartime social life: fraternisation with the Americans. Though it should be swiftly pointed out that for them, these relationships were – by modern standards – extremely innocent. 'Pat and I had American boyfriends – who were friends – and we had a good time,' says Mrs Gerken. 'They would come on leave with us back to London. And indeed after the war, one of the Americans wrote to my mother every Christmas. They were nice boys, and after north Africa, where they had been through a lot, they were much more subdued.' This was in contrast to the often bombastic figures who had first arrived on British soil.

'There was always something going on at camp,' continues Mrs Gerken. 'Hockey. Very good amateur dramatics. Ballroom dancing was my thing.

'Now the Americans always had dances. And they would send a note out, saying that so many Wrens could come, and that those who wanted to should put their names down. Well, there was always a lot of competition. Although we had transport into town, the Americans were based a little out of the way, so they would come and fetch and carry us in their lorries, which is how we got to the dances in the blackout.

'One reason it was such an intense competition to get to these dances was that old – but very true – cliché. The Americans had all this food and all these supplies,' continues Mrs Gerken, laughing. 'They had tinned fruit and tinned ham. And chocolate. Our own ration was one tiny little bar a week.'

'And they had little guide-books to teach them how they were to speak to the English young ladies. How they were to behave . . .' adds Pat. Of the dances, she says, 'we were very chaperoned. I assure you, it was only cupboard love, because they would give us tins of peaches . . . a pair of silk stockings. They lavished us with all this stuff – but they were very nice lads.'

Chocolate and tinned peaches were one thing. But romance of a more lasting kind was to come to Mrs Gerken during the night shift at *Flowerdown*. 'The boys did a different watch system: we did four watches a day, they did three, so with all the changing rotas, it might be some time before you saw the same sailor again. One Christmas, my husband-to-be, Norman, was on watch with me. He was a Liverpudlian, though he didn't have much of a real Scouse accent. We couldn't talk because we were working. But at one point, he did manage to ask if I would go to the film show, and whether he could sit next to me? And when we did go, I did sit next to him.

'He walked me back to the huts. The officer of the watch came round but there was always a little time to be together. The second time we saw each other – well, we only knew each other's forenames so now we asked each other's surnames. He told me his: Gerken. I burst out laughing. In the end, he had to show me his paybook as proof.

'So we went ashore –' the constant use of naval terms was a source of good-humoured fun – 'we went to the cinema, we went walking – there was lovely country.'

Although Mrs Gerken is now sadly widowed, her marriage, like that of her friend Pat, was forged in this most apparently un-romantic of scenarios. But, as she says, there was quite a lot of it about. Betty White, who also met her husband, Charles, at HMS *Flowerdown*, naturally agrees. Indeed, the story of how Betty and Charles came to be an item illustrates perfectly how wartime romance had a certain sharpness to it, an edge borne out of proximity to danger.

They met at a time when Betty was starting to work on the complex Japanese codes. 'The petty officer told me that our section was taking two new sailors,' says Mrs White, 'and could I show them how everything worked and where everything was. One of these sailors asked for tea – and I explained that it was the sailors who made it. Then this man simply turned to me and said, "We will go out tonight."' The memory of this extraordinarily direct approach still makes Mrs White laugh fondly; and despite the abrupt chat-up line, they did indeed go out. 'We went to the cinema in Winchester,' she says. Because of the war, and their different duties, they were sundered for a while. But afterwards, when they both found themselves working in London's Square Mile, they caught up again with ease, married and enjoyed a great many decades together.

'As to romances generally? They were very easy,' says Marjorie Gerken. 'There were umpteen romances going on. Two great friends of ours, they married. But remember,' she adds insistently, 'we took it slow, even in wartime. There was no sleeping around. No fear. At that time, all we wanted was letters – it was all letters, that was the only way we could really communicate with each other. When I met Norman, I'd had different boyfriends and I was still writing to six. As with the Americans: all we really wanted to know is if they had got home all right.'

In a wider sense, that, of course, was the abiding undercurrent of the conflict: a pervasive dread and anxiety for all those men out there, the constant, desperate hope that they would 'get home all right'. This was particularly the case for men sailing with the Atlantic and Arctic convoys. There was the ever-present razor edge of jeopardy; the merciless German destroyers, the invisible U-boats in their wolf packs. And this was without mentioning the ordinary hazards of sailing in violent seas, in weather so cold that the eyes could freeze over. Those who went through such experiences found that the later reunions had a special resonance.

The Y Service operatives who worked from these vessels did an extraordinary job under unimaginably testing conditions. What can surprise now is the fact that some of their recollections are full of such good humour. Gordon Copson, writing in the Tel(s) magazine a few years ago, recalled his own time aboard HMS *Keppel*, an 'ageing destroyer, which had been converted into a destroyer escort vessel'. The working conditions were almost insanely claustrophobic. 'The Direction Finding office was little more than 4ft 6ins x 4ft 6ins and comprised of a shelf' for the wireless equipment. Every time a depth charge was fired, the fuses in the equipment would blow. Every time a 4.7 gun was fired, a 'tongue of flame' from the flashback would come down the corridor – and so the wireless operator learned to keep the door closed. There was so much surplus electrical equipment on board that on one occasion, in heavy seas, Mr Copson tripped over some loose wiring on the deck and almost went into the sea. Any time he attempted to fix the aerial near the rear funnel while the ship was steaming, he would come down looking like someone doing an 'Al Jolson impersonation'. Yet, as he concluded: 'Ah, happy days!!!'

There was little of this black humour for veteran Vic Stock of Chelmsford, working in the direction finding cabin of a vessel that was part of a group 'sweeping the sea areas south of Ireland' for German submarines. 'I only heard the din and had to guess the sight . . .' remembered Mr Stock, 'quite suddenly the ship started racing at full speed and in no time at all came a sickening crash, the ship coming to a sudden stop and listing to starboard.' Mr

Stock hurried out from his listening station to see what was going on and what greeted him was a scene of chaos and unforgettable horror. The ship had rammed into a surfacing submarine; 'flames were licking around the conning tower' and screams could be heard from within the vessel. 'But nobody was coming out,' wrote Mr Stock. 'They were jammed in for keeps.' Slowly the ship was disentangled from the submarine, and there was still no way out for the German submariners. Their vessel sank to the ocean floor, its crew helplessly trapped within.

The dangers of life in the middle of the rolling icy ocean were often utterly unpredictable. Y Service veteran Tom Goff, who was with HMS *Byron*, remembered that just after they had escorted a convoy to Murmansk, the ship's captain, who had been fighting illness but not admitting to it, suddenly collapsed – it was appendicitis. They were a vast distance out in the north Atlantic; the chances of getting him all the way back to land before the appendix exploded seemed remote. The only thing was to get a doctor out to the ship. Goff signalled to the escort group commander. But, as he wrote, it 'would soon be dark. Snow showers reduced visibility to a cable. There was heavy cloud. We were rolling like a pig . . . and there was said to be a shadowing U-boat reporting our position from astern of the convoy.' As the signals operative, Goff found himself co-ordinating an extraordinarily tricky operation, plotting the position of the boat carrying the doctor who had been sent across.

Even then, as the captain rolled in agony, in his efforts to board the ship in the swelling waves the doctor himself was swept overboard and almost keel-hauled; receiving a cracked skull, he fell profoundly unconscious. Goff, feeling increasingly helpless, realised that the only thing was to try and keep the captain's temperature monitored; he had heard that sudden fluctuations meant that the appendix was about to rupture. Somehow, with the aid of anti-inflammatory pills, the captain was kept as comfortable as possible; indeed, when the doctor eventually came round three days later, he pronounced the man out of danger before diagnosing himself and returning to his own sickbed.

Throughout the incident, and thanks in part to the menace of the shadowing U boat, Goff had to dutifully maintain a radio silence. When HMS *Byron* eventually came close to the Orkneys, he gratefully took to the airwaves again and by the time he was sailing past the Hebrides, he felt profound relief. The offending appendix was removed in Belfast.[1]

Back on land, Wrens such as Marjorie Gerken were keenly aware of what was happening out on the oceans, not least because some of the men who had sailed them spent short periods of recuperation at HMS *Flowerdown*. For this reason, Gerken had little sympathy with the Wrens at base who seemed to be constantly agitating for higher wages. 'There were a few girls there who were sometimes quite militant about money – "why shouldn't we get the same money as lots of others," they would say – but we didn't have to go on these terrible convoys,' says Mrs Gerken now, with some feeling. It wasn't just the sailors at *Flowerdown*; during her brief posting to the far north of Scotland, Marjorie had seen at first hand some of the survivors pulled from the dagger-cold seas after their ships had gone down. The sight evidently haunted her. For this reason, she and her great friend Pat were always grateful for the congenial nature of existence aboard HMS *Flowerdown*. They were fully cognisant of the fact that life out in the wider world could be brutal.

Their colleague Betty White was to know – a great deal better than most – just how brutal; her husband-to-be Charles had himself been a wireless operator on several convoys. The first, in 1942, had involved 100 ships, with just four escorts. The German U-boat wolf pack found them and, as Mrs White says now, out of all of them, 'there were just two ships left sailing.' Charles White was one of the lucky few to survive. When he eventually was sent to HMS *Flowerdown*, says Betty, 'it was almost as a rest thing. The sailors still worked, but it was intended as a sort of recuperation from the convoys.'

Invigorating as the off-duty atmosphere at HMS *Flowerdown* was, Pat Sinclair and Marjorie Gerken knew that they were here to give their fullest efforts to the tasks that they were faced with. Both of them now cite the advantage of youth. But one also had to have an aptitude, as demonstrated by Betty White. And both Pat and Marjorie were confident that they were very good at what they did.

'As to the work: we were extremely well trained,' says Mrs Gerken. 'But not everyone suited it. One girl really couldn't carry on. She was the first university-educated girl that I had ever met – back then, for so many girls, you might have been extremely bright but you wouldn't get to go to university. But with this work, she somehow just couldn't do it. Whether perhaps it was because her mind was so active . . . Morse – it's automatic. Yet by contrast I didn't ever find it boring. I found that the watches went by very quickly.'

There was also a clear sense of where the lines of authority had been drawn. 'With orders and hierarchy, I was always able to fit in, and do everything that we were told to do,' says Mrs Gerken. 'Pat was different – she would say why should we do this, why are they asking us to do that? – and I would just tell her, well, we've got to. You have to accept it.

'We did lack sleep,' she continues. 'If you went on at midnight, you were supposed to have a sleep beforehand. But if there was a dance or a film show and it happened to fall in that part of your rota – well, you couldn't go off camp, you did have to stay there, but you missed your sleep. Equally, with different shifts, you might try and get a sleep before midday, but that was difficult to do. I always found it difficult to go to sleep at those times. When we hitch-hiked back up to London, I'd catch up on my sleep there.'

Pat Sinclair too recalls that there were a few women who could not handle the intensity of the work. But she herself found it rather stimulating. 'We were given different frequencies. We were in front of a raised dais where two people sat and issued stuff to us. And also we had civilian chargehands. They supervised us and collected up our messages – we were given pads, and a pencil . . . so we sat there with our earphones on and you were told what frequency, and you had to try and find it. You twiddled the knobs and sometimes you'd get a clear signal, sometimes it was very difficult or it moved slightly.

'If you took down messages from one of the German naval establishments, they would send very, very fast.' But in the midst of that chilly, mechanistic efficiency, these operatives also found surprising shafts of humanity. Before the German sailors started transmitting the encrypted messages, the man going off shift would have a short conversation – also in code – with the man coming on; little more than light exchanges but all picked up perfectly by Pat Sinclair and her colleagues. 'They'd come in and you got so used to the sound of how they sent messages,' says Mrs Sinclair. 'They'd say, have you been busy, or what's the weather like? Some little chat. Then the person would get down to sending his messages.

'And somehow you felt that you knew them in a way because you got familiar with the sound of how they sent these communications. You could recognise the style.

'Once they started, you took it down, four letters, five letters. Then the watch charge hand would come round, and he would collect up the papers and take them off, and the only thing I knew was that they went to a place called Bletchley Park. I think they used to send them by motorbike. All you knew was where the messages were being sent from, that is what you were there for, to locate.

'There were rows and rows,' Mrs Sinclair continues. 'I don't know how many altogether but there must have been fifty or sixty – sailor/Wren, sailor/Wren. That's how we sat, mixed, all doing the same job. Then for a time I used to be on the dais myself, with a man called Dave Biggard. I suppose we were giving out new things as we were told to do, giving more paper, and generally overlooking and supplying.'

If you imagine an exam hall now, the conditions would not have been so very different. 'Because you didn't get up and walk about,' says Mrs Sinclair. 'You sat there. And no way could you ever miss a watch. Oh, it would be dire consequences. I only once missed a watch after I had been playing hockey with sailors – it was sailors against Wrens. This big fair-haired sailor hit the ball and it landed on my foot, and do you know, I still feel it. I just couldn't walk. So for two days, I was given permission not to come on watch. Otherwise you did not dare even to be late. Cold, flu, you just got on with it.'

And in keeping with other Y Service operatives, no matter what part of the world they happened to find themselves in, the nocturnal hours were the most gruelling. Pat Sinclair recalls that the routine took a little getting used to – especially the business of trying to catch a few hours' sleep in broad daylight before going on to a night shift. But, like so many of her colleagues, Pat was young and adaptable: 'You went on at 8 p.m. and you were there till 8 a.m. so that was twelve hours.' That is a long time to be sitting listening out for encrypted Morse messages.

'I never really found it difficult, can't recall any hassle. If you weren't all that busy in the middle of the night, you sat there. In the breaks, you'd have a sandwich and you'd gossip to your neighbour. You never wandered about. You stayed put. I'm afraid people smoked. I started to smoke.

'I came home on leave and my mother said to me, "Since you've joined the Wrens, you've changed – and I don't like the changes!" I was puffing away. I started just because there was nothing else to do in the middle of the night. I couldn't read a book, I couldn't take my knitting down to the watch room. I didn't even do knitting then, even if I could have taken it down.'

And if the work ever got too repetitive or tedious, the everyday dramas of life at *Flowerdown* occasionally proved spectacularly diverting. Even for a camp of that size, there was, it seems, an unusually rich diversity of life to be found there; sometimes of an almost transgressive nature.

'We did have one fellow, a sailor, a bit funny, I suppose,' says Mrs Sinclair, 'and we called him "The Prowler". We were very worried because he went around stealing stuff off our washing lines, and snooping around. In the Nissen hut, I had the top bunk and behind me was a little window. One night, I woke up absolutely petrified because something had landed on my bed. I thought it was The Prowler. It was actually a cat. It had come through the window. Oh boy, had I been scared!'

So the girls rigged up a string in the hut. 'The idea was that we could capture him if he walked in while we were sleeping. But I said, "No, we can't do that, because whoever comes in there is going to break their neck." So instead we reported him and they transferred him to somewhere else.'

There was also the occasional outbreak of theft: 'We had this girl billeted in our hut, but she wasn't in our watch, and she was on duty when we were working and vice versa,' says Mrs Sinclair. 'It was creepy – we'd come back from watches to find that our chocolate rations were disappearing. By the beds, we had little chests of drawers, and I remember hiding my bar of chocolate in between my underwear in my drawer. No normal person would have found it.' But the chocolate vanished nonetheless. 'I was completely shocked because whoever the thief was, they had found it. You know, if you left it out on the side, you could understand it being pinched. We couldn't say anything about stealing – we simply said to the petty officer, look, it's interfering with our sleeping because when we're coming off duty, she's going on, could she please be put somewhere else. So that was the end of that little episode. The thieving stopped. It couldn't have been anyone else.'

Chocolate was not the only item to disappear. There was also an interval when knickers went missing from the washing lines. Another case involving The Prowler? On this occasion, no – it was another Wren. But, as Mrs Sinclair points out, HMS *Flowerdown* accommodated a wide and interesting range of people. 'We had these two girls – I didn't even know what the word "lesbian" was,' says Mrs Sinclair, laughing. 'There was just this one couple where the girl was – well, one was all fluffy, and one was a bit butch . . . And now I realise they must have been a very close couple. But we didn't know any of that. We were just young innocent friendly girls with each other . . . What a mixed crowd!'

15 By the Sleepy Lagoon

No one could ever really be counted as fortunate in war; as we have seen, however, the conflict offered some the chance to experience the world in ways they would never have found in civilian life. Among these individuals was teenager Peter Budd. Trained in wireless telegraphy, Budd had barely before left his native Bristol; holidays had been to Weston-super-Mare and, as he says, the very idea of somewhere like Calais was as 'exotic as Timbuctoo'. Nevertheless, as the tide of the war was decisively turning, he was called upon to embark on a voyage that would offer him one of the most formative and indelible experiences imaginable; an adventure that introduced him to a world – a paradise even – that he had not seen depicted even in books. And he was to share this adventure with remarkably few others.

After months of training, he recalls, 'I went to Plymouth to wait for a ship.' Plymouth had been bombed so badly that a signals section had been set up at a holiday camp on the road to Tavistock. 'And I was there for about three weeks before we were summoned to barracks.' There was an electric thrill of anticipation in the air. 'The transport was ready for a very big convoy ready to go out to Bombay. In Plymouth, all you heard was loudspeakers all day.

Ratings on draft to Sri Lanka. Muster so and so. Ratings on draft to wherever, muster . . . The barracks were so crowded you were sleeping on the floor, there was nowhere even to sling a hammock.

'The River Tamar – you could have walked over it on the ships. There were thousands of American landing craft there, thousands of naval ships. There must have been 10,000 naval ratings in barracks waiting to be posted.'

Even before his extraordinary adventure began, Mr Budd was finding his own status within it a little anomalous. 'Those of us in the wireless group were civilians – we'd had six or seven months' training in civilian billets. But we arrived in Plymouth barracks in the late afternoon and we had to do the official "Joining Barracks" routine – we had to find our way round the barracks to know where we were going to sleep, where we were to get food. We were very much civilians rather than sailors . . . and of course we were there with matelots.'

This minor outbreak of disorientation was as nothing compared with what was to follow. 'Then on to Glasgow – and then aboard a troopship,' says Mr Budd. 'We knew we were going to the Far East. I had never been on a ship before. While we were at anchor, I was behaving like Jack the lad around a few Wrens on board who were going to Colombo and the big naval intelligence base there.

'This great fleet in the Clyde, I've never seen anything like it – aircraft carriers, battleships, great liners . . . Out we steamed off to north Africa.' Budd's ultimate destination was a great deal further than that, but before he arrived, he would have to endure a nightmare journey. 'As soon as we got out into the Atlantic, I realised that the sea which I'd loved since I was eight, didn't love me. I was so sick I wanted to die. It was terrible. I slept on deck all night, then eventually went down below – down to the bilges. Eight decks down. In the morning, everyone had to line up on the deck. We had Navy, Army, Air Force and they inspected the ship. I was sitting right down there and this admiral came in and said "What the hell are you doing down here?"

'"I'm sick," I said.

'"Sick?" he said. "The bloody ship isn't moving."

'"It is for me," I said.

'Once we were in the Med, I was fine. We stopped at Port Said, where we dropped off a lot of army and picked up a lot of American troops. Going down through the Suez Canal, it was unbelievable. We had these few Wrens . . . all the Arabs were standing along the bank, in their long white robes – and they lifted them when they saw the Wrens.'

This outbreak of coarse ungallantry aside, the voyage was mercifully calm – which was more than could be said for the weeks that followed. 'The voyage took about a month or more to get to Bombay, then there wasn't a ship available to take us to Ceylon, so we got on a train, and went for hours and hours, up into the northern desert, to an army camp named Doolallee. Heard of the phrase?' The slang term, Mr Budd says with a laugh, apparently derives from this very place. 'This area was so isolated, you'd go mad if you were stationed there for long. We had to wait there until there was a ship to take us down to Colombo.'

There was also, for an eighteen-year-old, a glimpse into deprivation which, even in the 1940s, seemed simply beyond imagination.

'We arrived in Bombay and you have never seen poverty like it. Bombay now is poor – seventy years ago, it was unbelievable. Most of the streets had a sheet of corrugated iron leaning against the wall and down over the pavement. And a family would live under there. All along the pavements would be heaps of corrugated iron – and families living there just to try and work in Bombay. Imagine the impact on a young person brought up in reasonable conditions . . . But that was nothing compared with what we saw when we came back from Doolallee to pick up a ship.'

Mr Budd may have been slowly making his way towards a sort of heaven on earth – but his journey there through a horror-film hell was not yet over. The next scene came in the form of an old ship that Joseph Conrad would have had difficulty doing justice to in his most harrowing tales.

'The SS *City of London*,' says Budd. 'She was built in 1903. And ready for scrapping in 1936. The Indian government bought her and used her for transporting Indians – very desperate prisoners – to the Adamon Islands. The Adamon Islands pre-war were like Devil's Island.

'So when we got on this ship – and there were about three hundred of us – we went below deck, turned the bulkhead lights on – and it was black. But the blackness was moving. It was a million cockroaches. The whole interior.

'There were six squat toilets and six wash basins for three hundred men. All night you'd hear the cockroaches dropping in your hammock. So the next night we all slept on deck, but we made a big mistake – we didn't keep our shoes on. Because we hadn't realised that there were also a million rats swarming – and they were nibbling our toes.

'We kept ourselves amused – we each had a piece of wood, and you'd stand by the ship's rail and see who could knock the most rats off in five minutes. Whoever did was the winner. And the food: there was a hut on deck with a big cauldron. That was curry. And that was what you ate. We had a mutiny. We all assembled on deck and asked for the senior naval officer. When he came we told him the food was unbearable. He said he'd get it improved as best he could. But of course, we were at sea. He couldn't take anything on.

'The engine broke down for three days and we drifted in the Indian Ocean,' continues Mr Budd. If the rats and the cockroaches were not sufficient sources of discomfort, there was now also the thought of what was patrolling the waters beneath them. 'Now the Germans had just sent two flotillas of U-boats into the Indian Ocean. But we eventually got to Colombo. We kissed the ground. That trip must have been ten or twelve days. But then of course you were eighteen and you didn't worry. You didn't have any work to do.'

Mr Budd's first professional task in the East was to engage with the complex Japanese encryption systems. 'We were straight into HMS *Anderson*. Intelligence, intercept and decoding. A brilliant Australian had broken the Japanese code J-25. So obviously they did some decoding there and the codes that they couldn't manage went to Bletchley Park.

'But can you imagine intercepting Japanese code? There were three codes, and all three were different. You were writing up and down the page three different codes.'

While he became more fluent in this skill, however, Mr Budd – even among the colour and tropical lushness of Colombo – soon found himself a little frustrated by his working conditions. And he had heard tell of a more remote base that appealed enormously to his youthful sense of adventure. He describes his new role as 'a story of men out on desert islands'.

'I got fed up with just being in a big control room. I'd joined up to go to sea. So I wanted to go either on a ship or somewhere else.' Somewhere else it was – somewhere excitingly far away. After Budd's application was approved, he was flown some 2000 miles out into the Indian Ocean, down to the Cocos Islands. It was to be 'the most incredible experience anyone could imagine in a life'.

On this minuscule cluster of islands in the middle of a hyp-notically jade sea was an intercept station of surprising strategic importance; a relay point between the Antipodes, India and Malaysia. Mr Budd was flown in by seaplane and sailed by dukon – a sort of local raft – to the jetty. 'Really, it was just coral sand with some overgrown parts. Only a few thistleweeds and palm trees.' But instantly he saw the romantic aspect. 'You only really read about people shipwrecked on desert islands in books. But to have been part of a little naval group there . . . And no one knew, they were very secretive about the Cocos Islands.'

Eighteen Special Wireless Operators were based on the islands; and these men were in turn looked after by the neighbouring island's native population of a couple of hundred Malays. The operators were not merely tracking and intercepting Japanese coded signals. They were also engaged in direction finding; keeping close and accurate tabs on the positions of the Japanese submarines that ploughed through the Indian Ocean, threatening Allied shipping.

One might imagine that life on this tiny cluster of islands was dazzling but basic; in fact, it was not basic at all. The men had accommodation and facilities far superior to those of their colleagues in Colombo. He and his colleagues lived very comfortably, three to a room, in specially built shacks. And thanks to the numbers – this was not like three men trapped in a lighthouse for the winter – the atmosphere was almost embarrassingly congenial.

'Imagine living there on a little island not much more than two hundred yards wide and about half a mile long,' says Mr Budd, gazing over some hauntingly evocative black and white pictures of himself and his comrades on the beach. 'It was part of an atoll. A circle of islands. The volcano died 100,000 years ago and coral started growing round the rim of the [submerged] volcano. And when the coral got within a foot of the sea, the sunlight killed it. But the coral underneath pushed it up so coral rock formed into a circle. And over the years, the waves and the wind broke it up into beautiful white coral sand – and then from the Dutch East Indies came coconuts, driftwood, palm trees. All over thousands of years. Those palm trees started to grow, birds started to land, so you had this absolutely unbelievable, natural, unspoilt group of desert islands. Sheer paradise.'

That paradise is now, some fear, at risk from the effects of climate change and rising sea levels. Nevertheless, it has become a luxury destination; the kind of place that makes travel writers salivate. On top of this, the microscopic islands and their tiny populations always seemed tougher than their intensely vulnerable appearance and geographical position would suggest. Situated midway between Ceylon and Australia, to the south of Christmas Island and west of Singapore, the Cocos (or Keeling) Islands have had a disproportionate number of visitors over the last three centuries, for as soon as the western colonising race began, the place was reckoned to have scientific, trading and – latterly – military uses.

'The Scottish East India shipmen had gone there in 1820 and cultivated palm trees for copra because that was the only oil they had – whale oil and copra,' says Peter Budd. 'And John Clunies-Ross then lived there.' In the nineteenth century, the *Beagle*, with Charles Darwin on board, swung by. 'Clunies-Ross sent to Batavia and brought back a hundred Malays and their families. And he built a little village for them on the home island and it became a British protectorate. He was the King of the Cocos and he ruled.'

By the time young Peter Budd arrived over 100 years later, hierarchies were less sharply delineated. 'There were two petty officers – and one sub-lieutenant – in charge of us.' In such a small group, discipline was scarcely an issue – each man knew exactly what work he must do, and the levels of concentration he had to maintain. In other areas, though, given the remoteness and the climate, there was a certain laxity. 'We'd gone native,' says Mr Budd. 'The lieutenant just wore his cap. He was in shorts, same as the rest of us.

'When we went over to Home Island – where the natives were – you wore a uniform then.' Otherwise, there was strategic value in keeping it casual, or so it was thought; any Japanese surveillance planes passing overhead would apparently see civilians rather than naval operatives. Furthermore, Mr Budd was still in that uneasy twilight world between civilian and military.

Amid the minute population of the island were the Malay folk, descendants of those who had come over with Clunies-Ross, and who continued to act as staff (though rather better paid and treated than in the Victorian era). 'Cable and Wireless had come here in 1903, and they built the corrugated iron huts,' says Mr Budd. 'That was when it became a relay station. The cable came from Singapore to Australia and this was exactly in the middle.'

Despite being little more than a speck in a vast turquoise ocean, the islands saw a little involvement in the First World War, with a German cruiser seeking to wreck the relay station. As the Germans prepared to destroy the transmitters, however, an SOS had been sent out and some Australian troops, on their way to Egypt, were redirected to Direction Island. The enemy was thwarted.

By the time war with Japan had been declared, Direction Island was once more fulfilling that strategic signals role, alongside the other invaluable work of Direction Finding. 'Cocos was vital – if you imagine the Indian Ocean, they had nowhere on the east,' says Mr Budd. In other words, this negligible speck in the middle of a vast ocean was of vital intelligence value – closer than most other stations for the purposes of monitoring Japanese movements and submarine positions. 'The Japanese were all down Malaya, Sumatra, all the islands,' says Mr Budd. 'So Cocos direction finding was very important.'

Even day-to-day operational movements yielded information, specifically to do with supply lines of particular importance to the Japanese forces – chiefly because they became stretched so thinly. But the Japanese were also supplying the Germans with other commodities. 'I remember the time I heard a German submarine, which at the time I heard it would have undoubtedly been a cargo one. They ran cargo submarines from Yokohama round to Brest, with rubber.'

One might imagine that the work, in such an isolated location, would lead to a sort of tropical cabin fever, where perspective would be lost and real life would seem distant. You might imagine also that given the remoteness, the intensity of the job might increase. But somehow, according to Peter Budd, it seemed that the reverse was true.

This was no place for short-sightedness, or indeed for daydreaming. One of the main concerns was to keep a sharp eye out not just for hostile craft but hostile local wildlife. 'You did twelve hours on, twelve hours off, then twenty-four hours off,' says

Mr Budd. 'The usual watch system – one on, two off. It wasn't too bad in that respect. Twelve hours duty. When you're young, you're able to cope with that sort of thing. But when you were sat in the intercept room you might, for instance, feel something crawling up your shorts. And it would be a centipede. This happened to one naval officer and he made a mistake – he knocked the centipede backwards instead of upwards and the centipede put its tail in him. The officer was paralysed from the waist down. That's how dangerous centipedes can be.' At the start of the night watches, 'you would walk out through the jungle'; in the shimmering tropical darkness, the greatest care had to be taken to avoid other poisonous fauna and flora.

'Any advice on these kinds of things, we picked up from the locals,' adds Mr Budd. Which was handy, because they had certainly received no advice before going. 'No one in Colombo knew what it was like there.

'And then you could catch dengue fever, which I did. That was mosquito-borne. It's not as bad as malaria. You're knocked out for about a week or two, and then you recover and you don't get outbreaks of it again. We had someone there with a first aid box and if you were ill, you were allowed one aspirin. If you were quite ill, two. And if you had appendicitis, you had three.'

After this came the work itself. Mr Budd recalls how, almost without thinking about it, he developed the knack for listening to two sets of signals at once, different headphones held to each ear. 'You had split headphones. So you were listening out on the U-boat frequency for the Indian Ocean, for instance, and also you were listening out to your own command, the dummy message that was being sent out from Colombo to all the DF stations in the Indian Ocean and the Atlantic. There were forty operators all over the area, listening to the various frequencies, and if a ship came up on one of them with a message, [the Colombo controller] gave a call, a special sign. You immediately started to find the frequency that he was telling you a ship was transmitting on. In your other ear, you were listening to a frequency in Japanese and writing that down.

'You'd develop the knack,' says Mr Budd. But in this, he is being rather modest, for he and his team were also wrestling with the intricacies of Japanese codes. It wasn't merely a matter of transcribing Morse – it was a case of transcribing it into Japanese. 'You wrote the symbols up and down the page,' says Mr Budd. 'You'd finish one lot of headed paper, someone would take it away, you'd finish another one, someone took that away.' So when the transmissions came, the work was frantic. But the transmissions were not constant. 'When you were listening to something like the big Japanese naval station at Saigon, they didn't transmit all the time so often you were just listening. And when it was quiet, you put American Forces Network on – you'd have that in one ear, and transmissions from Saigon in the other ear.'

To balance these stressful and repetitive duties was a prospect that Mr Budd and his comrades were daily dazzled by; their leisure hours were spent relaxing on beaches the like of which, nowadays, only the very rich can afford. 'The beautiful lagoon in my day was a marine paradise. The atoll made the water a few degrees warmer – you had to push sharks aside to get in to have a swim. Well, I am exaggerating a little. But there were sharks by the thousand in the area. There were manta rays too. We didn't know they were peaceful. We were terrified of them. And barracudas. If you went out fishing in a little boat, you were told you must bring your fishing line in within a hundred yards of the shore, in case a barracuda was following. One man didn't do it. And someone swimming had half his bottom eaten off.'

Such hazards were not off-putting (even though, in the above instance, a seaplane had to be sent from Colombo in order to pick up the unfortunate man in question). 'It was out of this world,' says Mr Budd. 'The water was much saltier being in a lagoon. And if you weren't careful, you'd get salt forming on your eardrums, which would drive you mad.' The answer? 'You had to put cotton wool in your ear after swimming.' There was also a limited amount of musical entertainment. 'We had a wind-up gramophone with about six records. You had needles in those days, one for every record, and instead of putting a new needle in, we'd sharpen the old one on a stone. And you'd hear Bing Crosby singing on that beach.'

Even the close shaves are recalled fondly. 'We were having a game of football and I was goalkeeping.' There was even a proper football pitch laid out on the island for the wireless operators. 'When we finished, it was just too hot, we all ran down the jetty to go for a swim. Someone had fixed a plank at the end, and those who were good, dived. Those who weren't, like me, jumped. I ran along, jumped, and as I was going up into the air, I looked down at the water, and there was a shark, twenty feet long, absolutely motionless in the water beneath me.'

Obviously, in mid-air, in the manner of Wile E. Coyote, there was little that Peter Budd could do about it except pray. 'I can't remember now whether I landed on its back or in the sea. All I know is that I came up from the water like a Polaris missile and grabbed the plank and was shouting "Shark! Shark!" The experience terrified me at the time – but looking back, the poor shark had been out swimming or went into the warm water to have a little doze and then something comes out of the sky and lands on his back!'

Budd's comrades were assiduous at exploiting the memory for pranks. 'Another day, I was coming in one side of the jetty, and my mate was behind me. He dived under and through my legs. I felt this smooth body – and I jumped in the air again.'

For reasons of secrecy and security, Budd's adventure was one of which his parents, loved ones and friends back home were allowed to know nothing, save that he was abroad. Letters were very strictly censored so as to prevent Mr Budd and his comrades inadvertently giving anything away. This was particularly pertinent after the fall of Singapore in 1942; following this catastrophe, the decision was taken to erase the Cocos Islands from the maps and the maritime charts, to simply pretend that they were not there at all. They were never referred to openly in communications. To all intents and purposes, Mr Budd was in a paradise that – for the purposes of the enemy – no longer existed. Even the RAF simply referred to it as 'Island Brown'.

What must his parents – who had no idea where exactly he had been posted – have been imagining at the time? 'They knew I'd gone abroad. They had no idea where I was. All they got was an occasional letter from me. You were allowed to give an address, which was HMS so-and-so, care of South East Asia command. So you could get letters. But they didn't know whether I was on a ship, on shore, or wherever. Our letters were all censored. There would be blue pencil.'

Touchingly, Mr Budd's parents attempted to send him parcels of food from home. These dispatches were rarely successful. On one occasion, he says, they 'sent some apples out to me. They were pulp when they got there.'

Happily, the system was a little more rewarding the other way around. 'I was allowed to send home tea – you could send boxes of tea from Ceylon. And I think I managed to convey that I was on an island. I used to say that I'd been out swimming.'

There are some who might have found the extreme isolation – and unvarying company – rather claustrophobic. But actually, says Peter Budd now, it fostered genuine closeness and friendship; so much so that the otherwise exhaustingly laborious work of homing in on Japanese signals seemed barely to impinge upon their lives at all. 'Every three months a destroyer would come down and offload us some supplies. So when we went down on HMS *Rocket*, we helped carry stuff along the little jetty and they said, "We'll come back in three months, we'll bring you supplies – if you're still here." You see, the Japanese were on the next island.

'We lived on fish and dehydrated potato. And whatever tinned stuff there was available.' Again, this dependence on outside supplies might have been thought to heighten the sense of threat from the enemy: that the Japanese could close in at any moment. But no: 'You would look out on the beach when you woke up to see if there was a Japanese landing craft there. Because you knew the Japanese were on Christmas Island which wasn't all that far away. Before I arrived, they had been sending aircraft over every month to see what was happening. Finally, the American submarines from Perth sank all the Japanese supply ships coming to Christmas Island, so they only had enough fuel presumably for one flight. A Japanese plane came over at 100 feet, dropped a bomb on Home Island and killed four or six of the Malays. Then it came to Direction Island. All our lads scattered into the undergrowth. The pilot dropped a bomb. And one of our lads – Challoner – was in the undergrowth and the bomb blew him out into the open and the rear gunner cut him in half. But this was before I arrived.'

The unique geographical position of the islands meant that they could offer not merely a target, but also sanctuary. 'One night we were there, we heard an aircraft circling round. Pitch dark. We went out and a Catalina was circling around. It was a Qantas mail plane. It flew regularly from Colombo to Perth. And it had engine problems.'

'Now it's nearly 2000 miles from Cocos to Colombo. The pilot found this dot of an island at night. He started signalling. We signalled back to him with the wind direction, and he came in and made a perfect landing. He stayed with us for a week until they came up with some spares.' There was a tragic postscript, though, pointing to the hazards that lay unseen in these beautiful islands. 'Just before I left, a Catalina flying boat came down with RAF technicians. It was flat calm. The pilot touched down – but somehow he got his horizon wrong. He pitched over and over. The plane caught fire. We went out into the water and brought back the survivors. Seven died. They had gone under and two died when we brought them ashore, they were so badly injured.'

Other than this, though, the days, weeks and months went by for Budd in a kaleidoscopic daze of colour. Unusually for wartime, he was able to take quite a few photographs – if he hadn't, he would scarcely have been able to believe it years later. Obviously, with supplies only coming in once every three months, one had to be careful – but Mr Budd's girlfriend back in England was the daughter of the owner of a chemist's shop. And this man had access to more camera film than most.

For various reasons, the idyll could not last. 'Our paradise was ruined when one day – it seemed – the waters around the island were suddenly full of ships. It was the RAF come down to build an airstrip on the longest of the islands. They were going to bomb the oil installations on Java. The arrival of all those thousands of troops ended the little unspoilt atoll that I knew.'

By that stage, nearer the end of the war, the islands had outlived their original strategic purpose and were instead to become a sort of forward base. Meanwhile, Peter Budd's expertise – for he had acquired a great deal of experience in those intense months – was needed elsewhere. He was later to find himself posted to Karachi, this time with a measure of authority. Like so many of his young colleagues, being flung to all corners of the earth had made him, quite without realising it, grow up very quickly.

16 Foreboding and Frustration

There were moments when all the airwaves in the world seemed alive with noise. Such a point came in the Mediterranean conflict with the fall of Mussolini on 26 July 1943. Although this appeared to indicate unstoppable Allied progress, however, the German divisions in Italy under General Kesselring were digging in. Meanwhile, on Sicily, where the Allies had landed, the Special Liaison Units were conveying Y intelligence directly to Generals Montgomery and Patton, while Enigma decrypts flashed across from Bletchley Park.

By August, the Germans had begun evacuating Sicily – and indications for the build-up of the operation were relayed, step by step, through the Bletchley codebreakers. In fact, by 11 August, both Bletchley and the Y section attached to the Eighth Army were able to confirm that the German withdrawal across the Straits of Messina was fully under way. The Bletchley official history raises the question of why – in a curious mirror image of the Dunkirk evacuation – the Allied air forces did not do more to try and halt this massive flow of enemy troops. The intelligence had been there for up to a fortnight beforehand: so why had the Allies not acted effectively upon it? Some suggest it was, in part, to do with unsuccessful Allied amphibious assaults; and partly to do with a huge amount of German firepower, concentrated in the area of the Straits of Messina, which was simply too intense for Allied pilots to get through.

Afterwards, on Sicily, there was then a lull, for which Y Service operative Harold Everett was particularly grateful:

> After the Sicilian campaign had ended, our little unit spent three idyllic weeks at Milazzo on the north coast of the island. Our leaguer was in a vineyard about twenty yards from the sea and I could reach out from my 'bivvy' and pick the abundant luscious black grapes. The weather was hot, with almost unbroken sunshine . . . we swam or lazed on the sandy beaches, 'the world forgetting, by the world forgot.'

But war could take the most surprising and unexpected tolls. In the case of Everett, it was an ulcer on his leg, which became troublesome – 'my more imaginative comrades . . . told the locals that I had been wounded fighting the Germans and that I had killed dozens of them with my tommy gun.' Soon becoming feverish and in great pain, Everett was hospitalised, and transferred from one Red Cross facility to another until a medic could finally pinpoint the exact nature of his malady: the sister 'explained . . . that I was suffering from cutaneous diphtheria, a form of the disease that had died out in the Middle Ages but which had been re-activated by the dust and the dirt of the Afro-Sicilian campaign'.[1] It is telling to imagine that a twentieth-century conflict could resurrect a medieval disease.

The Italians were surrendering; but any idea that this might hasten the downfall of the Nazis was misplaced. The determination of Kesselring's forces seemed only to be reinforced. Furthermore, certain improvements had been made to German security. 'With the development of the fighting in Italy,' wrote Hugh Skillen, 'Army Y redressed the disappointments in its [recent] performance . . . and again provided a picture of enemy activity as comprehensive as that which it had given in the Western desert and during the later stages of the Tunisian campaign.' However, 'German field security was steadily improving so that the amount of intelligence derived from (traffic) . . . greatly declined. Fortunately . . . the rediscovery in October of the enemy's VHF networks proved a turning point and restored the declining prestige of Army Y.'[2]

In other territories, the resolve of the Germans to hold on in the face of Italian capitulation was equally remarkable. For instance, Italians who had been guarding the docks and the railways in Athens were swiftly replaced by German troops. And back at home, despite a token measure of resistance from Italian troops, the German army took hold of Rome. Elsewhere, Major Phillip Worrall was parachuted into the Pindus mountain region of Greece intending to make contact with Greek partisans but instead suddenly found himself having to defend a party of Italian soldiers both from the Germans, who wanted to capture and deport them, and from the enraged locals, who wanted to exact grisly revenge for all the wrongs that had been visited upon them. Worrall's ruse was to pretend that all ninety soldiers were injured; he had them installed in a makeshift Red Cross hospital. When the German soldiers arrived, this is where they found them. Unfortunately for the Italians, the Red Cross provided no kind of protection; they were all taken out of the hospital and shot.

Despite the brutalising nature of the conflict, the Y Service operators continued to find that by listening in on enemy conversations, they could sometimes eavesdrop on unintentionally comic moments. Harold Everett wrote:

> For some reason, Italian traffic tended to produce more amusing incidents than the German. When the Italian armies were crumbling away, we listened to a long conversation . . . between two signals operators in which they spoke in gloomy terms of the Allied advance, the collapse of Italian

resistance and above all of the widespread desertions. At last one of them, after enumerating all those in his unit who had gone, said: 'Siamo . . . why don't we clear off?' His opposite number replied: 'Why not?'

As the conflict in Italy and the western Mediterranean continued to rage in the autumn of 1943, both sides almost paralysed into their positions by such factors as terrible weather, life in former war hotspots such as Cairo was, for certain social classes, regaining some of its old splendour. Hermione, Countess of Ranfurly, wrote:

Last night we went to a charity ball at the Auberge des Pyramides. The courtyard was roofed over with rugs and in the immense space below were dining tables, bars, two band-stands and dance floors . . . The scene was like a Metro Goldwyn Mayer banquet: overdressed and overfed people seething against a background of oriental carpets with great jewels and blancmanges gleaming in every direction. It seemed as if all the harems in Egypt had come – ladies of every shape and size in fabulous frocks and furs.

Yet this is not to say that those high up on the social scale were insensitive to the battles being fought, the deaths and the injuries. Back in Britain, there were those – like Bletchley Park operative the Hon. Sarah Baring – who would race off on leave to see their smart chums in Claridges; but all these women were well aware of the horrors that were taking place. Indeed, the Countess of Ranfurly, with her new grandstand view from within the office of GHQ in Cairo, was especially sensitive, not least because her husband Dan was a prisoner of war in Italy. In one entry in her diaries, she recalled watching the troop and hospital ships embarking from Alexandria and making for Sicily: 'In the lazy sunshine on this lovely day, it seemed fantastic that I was watching the launching of the invasion of Europe. "Will you come with us?" shouted the soldiers hanging over the sides. "Good luck", we shouted back. Out on the horizon in single file they went. It was thrilling, but desperately sad.'

Meanwhile, in order to bring some relief to exhausted wireless personnel, fresh blood was being drafted in. At Kafr-El-Farouk in late 1943, 'the station was asked to estimate the degree to which it could absorb British women civilians called up under the proposed extension of the "Employment of British Women – National Service Egypt Order"', according to one official memo now in the archives. And after the outbreaks of throat infections and, occasionally, typhoid, conditions were looking rather more congenial. Even the entertainments had perked up. 'The new YMCA which has been officially opened at the beginning of this month has proved a great success,' wrote the base's squadron leader. 'Several concerts have already been staged in the main hall of which undoubtedly the most outstanding and unique event was the pianoforte recital . . .' Added to this were the 'amenities' of a long-delayed swimming pool, an equally yearned-for cinema, and freshly built tennis courts at which racquets and balls would be 'lent free' to players but for which they would be 'asked to make a very small payment to ball-boys'.[3]

Morale obviously plays a crucial part in any war effort; for the listeners, such perks had the effect of making them feel human again.

Just weeks later, in January 1944, General Clark's Fifth Army landed at Anzio, on Italy's west coast some forty miles from Rome. Some within the intelligence community had an inkling that the operation was coming and were filled with a sense of foreboding, chiefly for the wellbeing of the individual soldiers who were leaving to take part in the enterprise. For Y Service operative Aileen Clayton, in Algiers with Eisenhower and Thornton Wilder, there was more than a touch of chilly premonition about the whole thing:

It was forcibly brought home to me that I, as with so many others, had mislaid my youth. One morning at a planning meeting I had seen a list of the units which were to take part in the Anzio landings. In the evening I attended a party given by one of the Army Messes, and while I was dancing quite happily with a young British officer, I casually asked him to which unit he belonged. When he told me, I recognised it as one that had been on the list I had seen that morning, and I thought: 'Oh God, you're destined for Anzio. In a fortnight you may be dead. I know this, but I cannot tell you. There is nothing I can do to warn you, to suggest, perhaps, you might write a letter to your parents which they could treasure if you should die.' I suddenly felt cold and very alone, and almost old. It was an intolerable responsibility for a young woman of 25 . . . I was to learn later that he had been killed a few days after landing.[4]

The irony was that the initial landings had taken place virtually unopposed; this was partly thanks to Admiral Canaris of the Abwehr, who informed General Kesselring with some confidence that the Allies could not possibly mount such an expedition because so many other British and American troops – who had pushing on through Italy from Naples and up the Adriatic coast – were now hopelessly tied up around Monte Cassino, engaged there in a fierce fight with German troops. But owing to American reluctance to push on until supplies had been reinforced, the Anzio beach-head landing parties – amounting even at first to 70,000 troops, and then, as the days and weeks passed, to an extraordinary 150,000 – started to look more painfully vulnerable as time went by. For General Kesselring wasted no time in summoning as many reinforcements as he could from divisions in the Balkans. The casualties that Aileen Clayton had feared began to pile up. What began as a brave invasion ended up as a near-siege that went on for several months. Allied troops were trapped within the perimeter of Anzio as the Germans fought back with startling vehemence and indeed viciousness. Some of the most savage fighting of the war took place here; on one occasion, American prisoners, held at bayonet point, were stabbed every time a German soldier was shot. The Allies appeared mired and the Germans implacable and immovable.

The Bletchley Park official history states that America's General Clark set little store by the valuable information streaming from Bletchley Park; yet he was to change his mind when the Y Service and Bletchley provided him with what the history describes as 'one of the most valuable decrypts of the whole war'. These were signals indicating General Kesselring's detailed plans for a savage attack on the Anzio beach-head.

Through wireless interception and the work of Bletchley, these plans were fed back to the Allies almost as quickly as they were being absorbed by high-ranking Germans. The Y Service expertly intercepted German High Command orders not merely to the Luftwaffe, but also relating to more diverse threats such as motor-torpedo boat attacks which aimed to cripple Allied shipping. Thanks to the instant nature of the intercepts and decrypts, the Allies were able – just – to parry an assault that might well have proved terminally damaging to their chances. Soon, with the capture of Monte Cassino, the Allies would be able to break out of the Anzio perimeter and start their move northwards through Italy, harrying the retreating German forces as they went.

Heartening progress was being made on the other side of the world. There was a busy and effective network of Y stations in New Zealand. By 1943, their numbers had been swelled with Wren volunteers, with some highly honed skills. One such was the art of 'Radio Finger-Printing', which enabled operators to identify sets and users, and was now proving extremely effective against Japanese submarines.

'Radio finger-printing . . . proved significant as it was capable of identifying not only the transmitter type but often the individual transmitter,' recalled Major T. Gray of the Royal Signals. 'It would have been even more useful had today's computer scanning of records been available for identification purposes replacing the very tedious manual search then necessary.' Manual searches would have involved identifying each craft by means of card-file indexes, which would have cross-referenced transmitters to vessels – excruciatingly dull to compile, wearying to plough through for information.

Having effectively 'tracked' the submarines by means of their radio transmissions, the Wren operators – heroically immune to tedium – alerted the Royal New Zealand Navy of positions and bearings. In the case of one particular submarine, they chose the target well: after being located and depth-bombed, the wrecked vessel was found to be carrying not merely sixty troops, but also extremely valuable coding material which, amid all the chaos and panic, the crew had been unable to destroy.

Survivors of the depth-charging made it to the shore; many escaped, at least for a time. But the code material was of greater concern to the Japanese authorities, who swiftly sent in another submarine in an attempt to completely annihilate the first vessel; not only this, but they sent in bombers too. A little too late; the Navy had managed to bring to the surface a great many codebooks.

Naturally, the advantage was only temporary. By the time the intelligence had been avidly shared out between the Americans and the British, the Japanese had taken the obvious precaution of bringing in huge changes to their coding systems. Nonetheless, the codebooks provided a logical glimmer; and hugely complex though the new system was, the Allied codebreakers knew that they would be able to burrow into it after about four weeks.

Meanwhile, in Kilindini, Mombasa, the wireless operation was seamlessly exchanging an unending source of intelligence both with Bletchley and with Melbourne and Washington DC. According to one historian, the real presiding genius of the station was

Lieutenant-Commander George Curnock. 'He was a gin-before-breakfast man,' wrote Peter Elphick. This was not Curnock's only qualification. He had spent 'three years as a language officer in pre-war Tokyo, and served with the Far East Combined Bureau in Colombo' before the Kilindini posting. Despite – or even, perhaps, because of – his aptitude for grog, 'his knowledge of the Japanese language enabled him quickly to scan the most fragmentary of texts and assign meanings to corrupt or unsolved code-groups; he seemed able to feel his way into the Japanese mind,' wrote Elphick.[5]

And for the Wrens posted there, life offered more diversion than the daily transcription and cracking of Japanese codes. 'We started watch keeping again at Alidina,' recalled Joan Dinwoodie, who was posted there after her stint in Colombo with HMS *Anderson*.

> Once again we made the best of our free time, swimming at Nyali Beach, we were shown around HMS *Revenge* and had tea with Vice Admiral Willis, visited HMS *Albatross* and HMS *Indomitable*. We also received a visit and inspection by Admiral Somerville.
>
> I had leave in September and travelled by train to Nairobi with a friend, Hetty. We flew from Nairobi to Nakuru in a Fulmar Fighter, over Lake Naivasha. I was very sick. We stayed a day in Nakuru and left by train, climbing 10,000 feet and arrived at Kisumu in the early evening . . . Whilst there, we visited Kakamega, centre of the gold mining district.

In other words, the sorts of experiences that were not normally offered up to young women from Norwich.

In the autumn of 1943, the staff of the Kilindini base were being transferred to HMS *Anderson*. One immediate setback of the workplace, recalls *Anderson* veteran Jean Valentine, was the local wildlife. 'The station was just outside Colombo. And you would get insect life. Great big flying cockroaches and things. They would hit the light – because they go for the light – and land on your paperwork.'

But there were immediate upsides too. Near the cabins where the codebreakers lived was the ocean, where, as Hugh Denham recalled wistfully, 'you could dive into the phosphorescent water when you came off watch at midnight.' The cabins themselves, he remembered, had unusual features, thanks to the pervasive, rippling heat of the island. They were partly constructed with woven palm leaves and there were 'no windows, of course, just apertures, so that during gales, the rain came in not only through the roof but horizontally through the window'.

There were disadvantages to this picturesque arrangement, and to the climate generally. As Victor Newman recalls, wearing headphones in certain conditions could be hazardous: 'Night shifts were hot and humid and you would sometimes get huge terrific electrical storms. Now when you are wearing earphones, and you get that enormous great thunderclap, it's a bit more than a crackle. It slightly deafened me and I am still like that now.' That was not all. 'It was tricky taking down signals during the monsoon rains, which would smash against the roof of the hut which was made of plaited palm leaves. It could be really difficult during the rains.'

Elsewhere, the Wireless Experimental Centre in New Delhi was also receiving a fresh influx of young recruits, gathered together at Bletchley Park. Based at a former university campus high up on what was referred to locally as 'the Hill of Happiness', this was a bustling establishment with a thousand staff, 'made up of Army, RAF, Indian and West African service personnel', wrote Peter Elphick. Codebreaker Alan Stripp was sent out there after a fruitful period working with Japanese codes at Bletchley Park:

After six months I found myself commissioned and posted to Delhi. The Mess and the long bungalows where most of us had single rooms (Majors and above had two) were at the foot of the hill . . . the Wireless Experimental Centre felt very different from Bletchley Park . . . it had little of the 'friendly informality verging on apparent anarchy' in Lord Dacre's happy phrase. There were no civilians. I do not recall any women. Although orthodox military routine did not obstruct our work, there was a sense of rigidity and hierarchy which did not help it; too often administration relied on authority rather than professionalism.[6]

He might have been referring to the commanding style of Lieutenant-Colonel Peter Marr-Johnson; in his years of working with and presiding over the Far East Combined Bureau, Marr-Johnson – fluent in Japanese – became noted for a certain aloofness that was taken for snobbery, and a predilection for secretiveness which a number of colleagues found alienating. One might argue that the very nature of the work would have justified such a bearing. But there were also occasional instances when compartmentalisation between different departments in New Delhi led to mistakes.

'I was in C section, which . . . dealt with the breaking and translating of Japanese signals; next door to us was B section which collated and evaluated signals intelligence and compiled the enemy order of battle,' wrote Stripp. 'I discovered only 45 years later that they had a map room that could have solved any number of problems for us.' One such problem: 'When the place name KA-BI-EN . . . meant nothing to us since it was not on our small maps, their large resources could have identified it as Kavieng in New Guinea near Guadalcanal, the scene of such bitter fighting. They in turn had no idea that we were stuck.'

Such disagreements aside, Colonel Marr-Johnson's Wireless Experimental Centre was not merely successful, but also demonstrably instrumental in helping the British and Indian armies led by General Slim who were holding off the Japanese 15th Army and its invasion of India. The attacks were relentless, and the Allies at Impahl and Kohima were under heavy pressure beneath the weight of such sustained ferocity. Fortunately for the Allies, the Japanese forces began to run dry of supplies; doubly fortunately, the Y Service at Delhi was burrowing deep into the Japanese air codes and were thus able to anticipate the more lethal assaults from the sky; British air superiority was, according to the official history, 'almost total'.

With the Japanese army forced to withdraw, the Allies set off to pursue them. In a book written a few years after the war, General Slim complained bitterly that in a wider sense, he had been consistently let down by signals intelligence. He was directly contradicted by Captain F.W. Winterbotham in his pioneering book on Ultra: Winterbotham wrote that not only was the general well satisfied with the quality of the information he was receiving, but Slim's certain knowledge of the growing crisis of rations in the Japanese ranks was, like so much vital information throughout the conflict, thanks to the painstaking work of the codebreakers.

17 Witnesses to Different Worlds

Although, by the first months of 1944, it was possible for the Allies to believe that the conflict was going their way, many were now more grimly determined than ever to get it finished with: from the highest military commanders down to members of the public, war-weary, and wanting simply to see the job done.

Even before the first Nazi V1 flying bombs and V2 rockets soared over the skies of Kent, that powerful sense of duty – the sense that everyone had to subsume their own wishes to ensure that the national interest was served – was totally ingrained. So much so, for instance, that when eighteen-year-old Wren Jean Valentine received official word that she was to be sent on a perilous voyage to Ceylon to help break the Japanese codes, her father – from whom permission had to be sought – granted that permission immediately.

Jean Valentine was an only child who had never left her native Scotland before the outbreak of war; after volunteering for the Wrens, and handsomely passing an intelligence and aptitude test, she was whisked down to Buckinghamshire to operate codebreaking bombe machines at Bletchley and Adstock, a Bletchley out-station. This in itself was quite a culture shock. What was to follow, however, was to shape the rest of her life in every conceivable way.

Jean was born in Perth, a pleasant and staid town with streets of grey stone and people of strict middle-class respectability. In those days, there was no such designation as 'young people'; from a child you became an adult, and if you were a woman, you were expected to marry and make a home. Outside the big cities, notions as eccentric as careers for women were rare. Had war not broken out, this is conceivably the future that Jean, an extremely bright girl, would have faced. It is more than possible that she would never have left the sobre streets of Perth.

As it was, when she was old enough, she volunteered to do her bit. And when, finally, she arrived on the other side of the globe in the tropics of Ceylon, it quickly became apparent that she would not easily be able to return to small-town Scotland. She swiftly acquired a taste for the colour and the splendour and quite understandably found that she could not give it up.

'I did a course at Adstock to prepare me for going overseas,' says Jean. 'A sign went up on the wall saying "the following are required to go overseas. Those with an asterisk. Get your parents' permission".

'If my father had refused, then they would not have been able to send me. And I secretly rather hoped that he would refuse, because there were a lot of U-boats and things out there. It wasn't the best time to go sailing the seven seas.'

Her father, a successful Perth businessman, was, it seems, remarkably unyielding over the issue. 'When I went home to him,' says Jean, 'and told him that I had been required to go overseas – I wasn't allowed to tell him where, even though I needed his permission – he said: "You joined up to do your bit wherever they need you to go. You go. Permission granted."

'He knew that the posting would clearly be some distance away. Europe, obviously, was overrun. But in general, there was a different ethos then. The country was in a bad state and I think that anything anybody could do was considered acceptable.

'For the first time in my life,' Jean adds, 'my father didn't ask my mother. Usually, he always asked my mother permission over anything. But on this occasion, I can't imagine him saying "well, we'll have to see what Mum says about that". His reasoning was: if I could do anything to help, then I had to go and do it.'

Jean's parents would have to spend the next few weeks speculating where exactly in the world their only child was being sent. Jean was forbidden to tell them until she had reached her destination. She wasn't even allowed to let them know where she and her fellow Wrens stopped off along the way. Like so many before her, Jean Valentine found that the voyage into this new world was itself fraught, full of adventure and hazard; also like so many before her, she coped with it with a sort of amused insouciance.

As soon as she arrived at HMS *Anderson*, the Bletchley out-station in Ceylon, Jean was put to work on a branch of cryptology; she and her colleagues were there to drill their way into the Japanese meteorological codes. There was scarcely even time to absorb the strangeness of her new palm-leaved surrounds, the noise of the Colombo streets, the unfamiliar food, the flickering pervasive heat which – as a native Scots girl – she had never experienced before. She was hurled straight into her new job.

'Before we went, there was a short course, only about two or three weeks, to familiarise ourselves with the structure of the Japanese language,' she says. 'And we had to learn Japanese Morse, which is like international Morse, but different – each letter is much longer. The reason for that was, if you were trying to break something and it didn't make sense, then you could say perhaps it wasn't that letter at all, it could have been something else that hadn't been heard properly.' There was also 'a little bit of Japanese history and geography, just to get us in the right mind, I suppose'.

Life in and around the out-station was touched with the kind of romance that she would have been hard pushed to find in her native Scotland. 'My job was very different to the bombe operating I had been doing back at Adstock.' There, her role had involved engaging with vast, complex machinery, masses of drums and wires, ensuring that the code-crunching functions of the bombes kept running smoothly. Her new work presented a more tranquil prospect. 'I quite simply had a paper and pencil. Wireless operators would bring in the signals to us – sailors would come round every so often with a batch of papers – and you would log them, and then examine them, because there was the chance you could break into the first two or three groups. We had a lot of captured documents. Code books.'

On top of this, the nature of the messages themselves gave key clues to unravelling the codes. 'A lot of the coded communications started with the time of the message, so the wireless operator would have written on it the time that it was received, and the time it was received was the time it was sent – obviously. This would then be followed by the written call sign for that particular wavelength. So you'd get information like this and then you would apply it to the encrypted messages and see what matched.' In other words, the established routine of messages enabled the codebreakers to crowbar a way in. 'We would then carefully take down the relevant books and quietly go through them,' says Jean. 'Once you'd found two or three code groups together, you could read the rest off. So really, as long as you had got the first few groups sorted out, it was just patience. Equally, though, it was satisfying when you had done it.'

When her part was done, Jean would hand over her workings to another Wren. Then they would be sent off via teleprinter to places such as Melbourne.

'We worked eight-hour shifts – that included night shifts, in rotation,' says Jean. 'And of course night shifts were lonely. You were there all by yourself, eight hours, and the only person you saw was the sailor who came in every hour, every couple of hours, with a batch of new signals for you to sort out.' And after all this – the silence of the work disrupted only by the high-pitched exclamations of young women attempting to fight off huge tropical flying insects – it was back on the bus to be returned to their accommodation in Colombo itself.

Jean Valentine was not a timid girl; and when it came to questions of the local fauna, she was able to keep a steady head in what would have been trying circumstances for anyone with a phobia. Accommodation, for instance, involved 'palm leaf roofs and walls that went up so far and the space in between for the air to go through. I went to the loo one day and there was a very big spider there and I did go "Waaah!!"' she says with a laugh. 'I can't remember what I did with the spider. But we weren't too bothered with that really. There were snakes too.'

Jean recalls that she had no difficulty adjusting to the local cuisine, even after the notably stolid diet offered in Scotland. This had been made easier, she remembers, because of the terrible food on the voyage out to Ceylon; having spent weeks picking weevils out of bread, she was ready to throw herself with gusto into the fresh, delicious food.

After long spells of intense hard work, proper breaks were allotted. And these gave Jean and her young female colleagues a chance to explore a world they would never otherwise have seen. 'Every three months or so, we got a week's leave, and we went up into the hills. Some people went to a rest camp. I was fortunate to have made a friend who happened to be a tea planter – and I and my friends would spend a week up there on his plantation.

'It was a different life. This man lived by himself. I don't know much about his history – he certainly had a daughter who was married to a tea planter. I never heard about a wife, so I don't know what happened to her. But this planter would sit at the table, and when people put down their forks and knives, the servants would miraculously appear. The planter had a bell, and he'd just touch it and they'd appear. It was a different life. And of course the food was beautiful.'

Jean was in fact witnessing the last efflorescence of a colonial world, one in which a wealthy white British tea planter could summon servants to his table with the discreet ring of his bell. At the time, though, few could have been consciously aware that such a set-up already had an antique patina.

'And the surroundings were lovely,' she says. 'There was a local club where the tea planters all foregathered. It was really a very pleasant climate. None of the blistering hot days that you got elsewhere in the tropics.

'When we first got to the plantation, tea was brought in to us every morning. They drank tea barely coloured . . . it was very pale. Very flavoursome, but very pale. That was first thing in the morning – early morning tea and a banana. The servant arrived with it.

'And then we'd spend the day lounging around, lying in the garden. Or our host would take us out for a run in the car, in the countryside . . . If you've been working hard, it's quite nice . . .'

Even back in Colombo, the intense concentration of the work was broken up with a lively nightlife. 'We had a wonderful social life because we were somewhat outnumbered by the male population. We were never short of people to take us to dinners or dances. I remember going to the cinema only about once because that's not what you did. Instead, you were invited out to the Goreface hotel to a dinner dance – or to the Grand Oriental, the GOH as it was called.'

Even so, the etiquette for such occasions remained relatively rigid. 'We had to go in civilian clothes because we were normally with officers and the officers couldn't be seen with other ranks,' says Jean, her eyebrows raised. 'We got so many plain clothes passes a week [i.e. permission to go out in plain clothes] – two passes a week, I think. But nobody checked you going out, so you were OK to go out in plain clothes . . . We would go out in plain clothes, taking our uniform in bags, and then change into them when the night was out. The first time I did it, I went out with this bloke and I said, "Excuse me, I've got to change now." And I changed into my uniform in the back of the taxi. So when we walked in through the gate of HMS *Anderson* again, we were in uniform.

'Anyway, we had a pretty good life,' she adds. 'We really did. Because we could always trot down to the sea and have a swim . . . and there was a swimming club where we could go . . . it was really very nice.'

Like Victor Newman, she fondly recalls one place in particular: 'We would go to a place called Mount Lavinia. There was only a hotel and a few little huts. There was a very nice beach – you could lounge around on that and have a bit of a swim . . .' Nor did money seem much of a worry to young Jean. Although Wrens' pay was far from spectacular, things changed when she was dispatched abroad. 'I got a little extra, so in terms of wages, we're talking about £1.50 a week.' That modest sum would go quite a long way: 'Dancing and social life? Men were only too happy to pay for all that if you went out with them. And I bought the occasional garment. I think my mother sent me the occasional bit of money.

'There was no special intensity,' she concludes. 'But then I don't think I was a very emotional sort of person, I just sort of went along. Took what was coming. Probably quite grateful to have had the experience. But it was just part of life's rich tapestry. You didn't feel special or anything, and maybe you were quite glad to have got away from the miseries of the blackout. We were just enjoying a new experience. Doing the sort of things that people do now for a holiday.'

For Victor Newman, the work in Ceylon was hard, but it was also in some respects curiously congenial. 'We were watch-keeping for the first couple of months,' he says. 'Then we were asked by the authorities if anyone could use a typewriter. Well, I could because before I was called up, I used to work in a little office attached to a corn-grinding mill.'

In his first few days, Weybridge lad Mr Newman had met an old friend of his from the town who had been posted to HMS *Anderson* a little beforehand without either of them knowing. His new duties brought another coincidental reunion: 'I was given a short course on touch-typing, and it was around then that I met another person from Weybridge: Edna Frost, a Wren.' This left the Weybridge interest disproportionately represented in Ceylon.

'So there were eight of us who made up the various watches. The Wrens lived separately, away from the base, and they were transported up every day to work. It was around this time that we opened up the high speed link with Australia.' This was a new automated Morse-sending mechanism: 'A hundred and twenty words per minute of Morse, on a machine that looked a little like a seismograph, with the needles going up and down. There was also a high speed link with England.' The work was faster but, thanks to the new technology, a shade less repetitive and grinding. And even if it was still quite a slog, those long shifts were smoothed out by the promise of a turquoise sea and rich sunshine.

For codebreaking clerk, or 'cipherine', Barbara Skelton, the opening up of the Mediterranean by 1944 led her into a way of life that, although harrowing, was yet many times more attractive than the frowsy, depressing London she had left behind. It was announced, she wrote, that 'once the Germans had retreated over the Greek border, the Embassy in Athens would open up, and [her friend] Mary Foreman and I had been chosen as the new cipher team. Soon after, to the envy of the other cipherines, we were driven to Alexandria to board a crowded troop-ship bound for Italy.'

Skelton was apparently in high good humour, a superior remarked to her as she negotiated her way on to the packed ship past countless troops. Yet arrival on the Italian coast was more sombre:

Mary and I disembarked at Salerno, where we spent the night. It was raining and sad as practically the whole of the town had been wiped out. We were then driven to the Palace of Caserta . . . Lions leered down from the tops of stairways. The grounds were laid out with terraces and fountains with water cascading over marble statues of the hunting goddess Diana, with her leaping hounds. The cobbled courtyard abounded in jeeps.

A little later on, she recalled snatches of scenes – a 'picnic in a forest of cork oaks where most of our lunch was given to a troupe of ragged barefoot children gathering acorns, then a wartime coffee substitute'.[1]

Miss Skelton was soon transferred back to Greece for her 'cipher' duties and remembered wryly the booklet that was issued to soldiers on the voyage there. It contained admonitions and advice; reminders that the soldiers were lucky to be going to Greece, and that the Greeks were worthy allies. There were warnings, including one not to admire babies – their mothers might interpret this as 'the evil eye'. They were also counselled against boasting that they had won the war. By this stage, they hadn't.

Levity was also discouraged for the very good reason that a number of evacuated Greek families were slowly starting to drift home; given the atrocities, alongside the wholescale extortion that the Nazis had visited upon the Greeks, it was clear that they would be coming back to an impoverished, broken land. The country would be riven with internal tensions, and a pervasive sense of suppressed rage and violence would soon find other ways of erupting. Greece had been utterly violated, and a vast amount of its wealth had simply been stolen.

For someone like Barbara Skelton, moving within exclusive British diplomatic circles, there would be a degree of shelter from the aftershocks of conquest. Athens had not been completely flattened, and the people had not been crushed – not, that is, in the obvious sense. 'Unlike the sallow Italians, the Greeks had fresh brown complexions,' wrote Skelton. 'There was a smell of pine everywhere, which is not the case now [today], alas, the pine trees having been replaced with shoddy buildings . . . From my room, I had a view of a tiny Byzantine church surrounded by cypresses.'

She and her friend Mary attended to their wireless duties within the grounds of the British Embassy. For the most part, life was lived at a fairly basic level – the wartime diet even there consisted largely of Spam and bully beef. Barbara and Mary would sneak out of the embassy during breaks and surreptitiously rush down to the meagre local markets, where they managed to supplement all that processed meat with the odd cabbage. She noted that, despite the conditions, the Athenians had lost none of their taste for very sweet cakes, and that the city still seemed to abound with small patisseries.

At the more exalted end of the social scale, there was something almost comically enduring – with a tinge of bathos too – about the way the whirl of parties reasserted itself. 'We were taken to a round of parties given by the Greek aristocracy,' wrote Skelton, adding that on some occasions, 'in the evenings, we would drive into the country to stop at some wayside taverna. In exchange for tins of bully beef we would be given a delicious dinner of pigeons roasted over a pinewood fire.'

That was a brief period of calm; soon there would be further thunderclaps over Greece, in the form of civil war.

The consequences of brutal invasion were also reflected in Algiers, as the Countess of Ranfurly found:

> The French, Poles, Greeks and other nationalities I have met in the Mediterranean theatre are nearly always cheerful. We meet them at work and at dinner parties but rarely discover the tragedies behind their facades. Nearly every week people manage to reach Algiers from Occupied France . . . No escapees talk of their adventures or their grim journey – it is

kept quiet for fear of jeopardising the chances of thousands
of others who are trying to get out . . . the French have taught
me that behind the gayest faces lie the deepest tragedies.

Yet a place like Algiers itself had the power to wipe clean memory
and overwhelm European senses. 'Green lizards basked on the
edge of the paths. The trees are at their best now; the acacias are
frilly white and there are wild flowers everywhere.'

For Wren Rosemary Morton, Algiers was a little less romantic; it
was, she recalled, a miasma of flies and smell. And in work terms,
even the retreat and surrender of the Italians seemed to bring no
immediate let-up in the frenetic and gruelling pace:

> When Italy capitulated to the Allies, it was decided to move
> the Wrennery down to a villa on the coast which had been
> occupied by some very brave naval commandos. They had
> been sailing across on dark nights to unidentified craft to
> raid enemy positions, bringing back any secret documents
> they thought might be of value to the Allies. There was a
> wild idea, as [these commandos] were not linguists, that they
> should take along a Special Duties Wren who would be able to
> identify which documents would be best to steal.[2]

Given the chilly reception that young women like Aileen Clayton
had received simply by arriving in north Africa, it seemed unlikely
that that idea would be taken up.

However, signals watching did slow down, at least in that part of
the world. And this gave Rosemary Morton more time to absorb
her extraordinary situation. Apart from anything else, she and
her Y Service colleagues were now living at close quarters with
captured Italian soldiers. There was a welcome bonus: the gift of
fresh tagliatelle made by the men (also enjoyed by fellow Wren
Beatrice Bochman). But that was not all they brought to the party:

The kitchen in the Villa la Vie was in the basement, dark and frequently filled with smoke from the old range on which the Italian prisoners of war cooked for us. But this didn't deter them from singing – they had beautiful voices and despite being semi-literate, they all seemed to know their Italian operas . . . they concocted their own midday meal and all ate it from one big dish . . . One day I looked in the oven to see how our lunch was progressing and found Santo's wet sandals in there – he was hurt and mystified by my reprimand as it was quite clear that they needed to be dried.

In the Cocos Islands, young Peter Budd's idyll had drawn to a close, as it had for the two dozen or so other listeners on Direction Island. After an eighteen-month stint, he was informed that he was to be shipped out to take his direction finding skills to a quite different location: Karachi.

Even the journey there had something of an epic quality – first, the 2000-odd miles back to the mainland, then 2600 miles by rail from Colombo to Karachi – and it was during this vivid sensory journey that Mr Budd found himself standing face to face with one of the most totemic figures of the twentieth century.

'At Madras, we changed on to a troop train,' says Mr Budd who was accompanied on his new posting by two fellow naval operatives. Anything you might read about Indian railways now was surpassed by the nature of their journey. 'An Indian troop train was a goods wagon with benches. No windows, no toilets. We'd been on it for about twelve hours and it was shunted into a siding. It stayed there for three days, south of Hyderabad, thousands of miles from anywhere. Now all we'd been issued with was a docket saying we were allowed to have a meal on a restaurant car or railway station. We had nothing for three days and if the Army hadn't shared their rations with us . . . you'd go out to the driver in the morning with an army tin mug and he'd give you a mug of hot water, which you could use for tea, shaving or washing.'

Eventually they arrived in Delhi. 'A lot of Indians lived on the station,' continues Mr Budd, 'under cover. We were sitting there waiting for the Bombay train to come in. Suddenly about a thousand Indians poured in. I was pushed right up to the edge of the rails.' And when the train arrived, an extraordinarily distinctive figure disembarked almost nose-to-nose with Budd. 'Closer to me than you are was Gandhi. And next to him was Nehru. They'd just been let out of prison to go to Stafford Cripps's first talks on Indian peace. And silly to say it – but he looked just like Gandhi.'

For the next leg of the journey, Mr Budd and his comrades were in the relative luxury of second class. But the final stage, in which they crossed the desert, was an ordeal. Instead of glass windows, their carriage merely had shutters. 'So you either got sand-lashed or suffocated.

'But we eventually got to Karachi and the three who were being relieved were waiting for us. The one in charge said "Who's taking over from me?" I looked on the documents and apparently it was me. So I was put in charge of the direction finding operation there.'

It might not have been a remote desert island but Mr Budd swiftly found some spectacular consolations in Karachi. The direction finding station itself was a tiny place out in the wastes and the wilds – but they didn't have to live there. In fact, their quarters, by comparison to most, were highly desirable.

'This is where a life of luxury began – we were taken to the European YMCA. So, being in charge, I had my own room, with a bed, and sheets, mosquito net,' says Mr Budd. 'We got fed in the YMCA. We had a motorbike which we all had to learn to ride – to go out in the desert, where the direction finding station was. So there were four operators and myself.' Like the Cocos Islands, there was a formidable remoteness about the place. They were in contact with HMS *Anderson* at Colombo, thousands of miles away.

Other than that, says Mr Budd, 'No one knew anything about it, we were right up in the north-west of India. Bombay was the nearest big place and that was a hell of a long way away.'

The lack of obvious supervision had other unexpected effects. Being so far from the centre of operations, for instance, the bureaucracy was a little hazy; which, for five young men carrying out their duties but otherwise left to their own devices, carried immediate benefits. 'In the Royal Navy you get a paybook,' explains Mr Budd. 'And if you are moved to a ship (or establishment, like Karachi) where they haven't got your documents, they'll pay you as long as you're a month in arrears. Well, we went to this Indian Navy pay place and because we were European, the Indian clerk there thought we were naval officers. We wore civvies up there.

'As a result of this, we were allowed to draw whatever we liked. And you know, when that sort of thing starts, you soon get enmeshed. We were soon overdrawn, months and months in advance! We lived the life of Riley. We had tailor-made suits from our own tailors, ate out in restaurants . . .'

As if this was not quite enough during wartime, there were technical perks too. 'One of the HROs broke down and the authorities must have thought we were reasonably important because they flew a civilian technician up from Colombo. He brought a new HRO with him. He managed to repair the other one and he said to me, "Have you got a radio in your room?"

'I said no, so he said "You have this HRO, we'll put the new one in."

'So, a while later, when the war finished, we closed down and I had this HRO. So I went down to the pay clerk, who I was very friendly with and gave me advances whenever I wanted them, and said: "I've got this and I want to get it back to the UK."

'"Oh, no problem, sab, no problem." They were going to send it back via a system called officers' personal belongings. Next morning, a half-ton truck turned up with six Indian ratings. They put the HRO in, screwed it down, addressed it to Mr Budd and off it went. I thought, well, I shall never see that again . . .'

In the meantime, back in England in the late spring of 1944, there were those like wireless interceptor Betty White, based near the south coast, who could see the massive build-up of troop numbers, and who knew, despite all the secrecy, what was coming. In the days and weeks prior to June 1944, in fact, there were a remarkable number of people who simply put two and two together. For Betty, located at that time in a small village in Hampshire, it was reasonably obvious because 'you couldn't walk down the road without having to jump on to the pavement to let a tank pass.' Not far away was a stretch of railway; the local girls heard the rumours that Winston Churchill had used a train on the Meon Valley line to meet up with Eisenhower and de Gaulle to discuss the forthcoming landing operation, and that on this very train, Churchill had requested that the British join in with the proposed landings.

Betty also knew – although they were strictly not supposed to talk about it – that her soldier brother was in the area, and every day she would run to the top of a local hill in the distant hope of catching a glimpse of him before he left. Both she and he knew that D-Day was looming.

18 D-Day and After

Among the tense preparations for the D-Day landings, those in the mobile Y Service found themselves receiving some very specific training. In the course of an intensive three-day exercise spent in full battle dress, the wireless operators not only had to deal with such hindrances as gas masks, but the even more significant hindrance of 'constant interruptions from very senior officers', as Major Hugh Skillen recalled.

The idea of the exercise was to replicate as closely as possible the demands that would be placed upon the operators' focus and concentration as the invasion of the Normandy beaches unfolded. As part of the exercise, the operators were given a slew of messages; according to Skillen these were old communications to do with north Africa, for of course, the very idea of Operation Overlord had to remain completely secret.

Nonetheless, Wren Margery Medlock – based in Scarborough – vividly recalls how in the weeks beforehand, the volume of signals reached a frenzied level. 'For some months prior to D-Day, all leave was cancelled,' she recalls, 'and the piles of wireless transmission red forms reached astronomic proportions.' These were the transcribed messages, to be sent on for decoding. 'We did our very best to reduce these before the next watch took over. At the end of a watch we were exhausted, especially after the starboard watch, from 10 p.m. to 6 a.m.'

In April 1944, further arrangements were made for Scarborough: twenty new receivers, stated a secret memo at the time, 'whenever required for new tasks resulting from OVERLORD. These receivers would be made available by discontinuing watch on unprofitable groups, either Med. or perhaps one or two Home Waters exercise groups.'

Other contemporary memos now in the National Archives illustrate vividly how meticulous the Y Service preparations were. At Bletchley Park, the logistics within Hut 18, which covered Intelligence, were calculated to the last aerial. There is a pleasing politeness and calmness about the memos, such as this note to senior Bletchley codebreaker Harry Hinsley: 'Mr Treadgold arrived yesterday a.m. and tested receiving conditions . . . [he] found that reception was very good . . . By the time the emergency period comes along, we should be in an excellent position to make the greatest possible use of this small "Y" unit, which we are all convinced is going to be most beneficial.'

Careful contingency plans were made. Should there have been an air attack on the Scarborough listening station, for instance, HMS *Flowerdown* would deal with 'traffic priorities' in sending material back to Bletchley. And at the Park itself, details as fine as the rationing system for extra Wrens and WAAFs during the 'emergency period' were taken into account; just days before the landings began, officers were ensuring that there were sufficient supplies of chocolate, soap and cigarettes ('Following rates are for your guidance: Woodbines: 20 for 1/1. Kensitas: 24 for 1/6'). Even on 5 June, the needs of the female telegraphists drafted into Bletchley Park were – rather touchingly – being ministered to. One memo sent to Lieutenant-Commander Bloodworth from Lieutenant Dugmore states: 'You were good enough to promise to try to get anything they [the telegraphists] wanted in the way of stores and I wondered whether it would be possible for you to supply them with an electric iron. At the moment, they have no facilities in this respect and consequently collars and flannels are rather rumpled.'[1]

But if such concerns seem frivolous, it ought to be borne in mind that all these women and men were continuing to work extraordinarily hard, through all hours and with a heightened degree of dedication and focus; amid the buzz and the excitement, efforts were being redoubled. Indeed, a note sent a few days later from Bletchley's Head of Naval Section, Frank Birch, to Lieutenant Dugmore and the Wrens on X Watch illustrates what a crucial role they played at this time:

> I have been much impressed by the zeal shown by the Wren Assistants carrying intercepts from Hut 18. They are astonishingly quick off the mark and you know this has made a great difference to the time at which Admiralty and Allied Naval Command Expeditionary Force receive information from us, which in its turn must have considerable effect on operations. Would you please congratulate them and thank them from me.[2]

And, just two days before D-Day – a brilliant operation to deceive Field Marshal Kesselring having paid off – came the propaganda coup of the Allies' entry into Rome. The German army's subsequent retreat was harried and hindered by Army Y Service units picking up and translating their communications. Indeed, the Y Service, according to the Bletchley official history, was 'performing as well as it had ever done in Africa, with two of the German divisions transmitting the highest volume of traffic ever intercepted'. The men sitting in those cramped trucks, hunched over their small desks and clutter of radio equipment, were doing an invaluable job.

Then came 6 June. And as the Normandy landings were launched, Rommel (who had been in France for some months

beforehand in preparation for such an incursion) was, thanks to
more deception from British intelligence, anticipating that the
bulk of the Allied forces would materialise in the Pas de Calais.
Amid the courage and the carnage – the grim sea crossing for
the troops, the lethal German fire that turned the beaches into
bloody death-traps for so many men – the small Y Service units
were there, and a little later, were able to provide forewarning of
imminent attacks from Panzer divisions. This ability to raise the
alarm repeatedly proved acute over the coming weeks, as the Y
units dug themselves into Normandy, intercepting and decoding
German strategies for counter-attacks. Although in a wider sense,
progress at first seemed dispiritingly slow, with tension between
the American and British hierarchies rising, by August the Allied
forces were firmly on the move throughout France.

Then of course there were the straightforward espionage
operations behind enemy lines. SOE operative David Pearson
recalled the days of peril immediately after the D-Day landings.
For this mission, he was given both a fake identity and a Y Service
operative:

> Eventually at the end of July 1944, I was dropped with a radio
> operator into . . . Eastern France. Having made contact with
> reliable resistance elements . . . I moved around the Lorraine
> countryside contacting the various resistance groups, most of
> which were quite well organised but desperately short of arms,
> ammunition, explosives, money, food and clothing . . . with
> the help of my radio operator, London was made aware of
> this situation and began some big parachute operations.

Capture would have meant torture, even death. And the hazardous nature of the mission increased in intensity the longer the
two men spent among the resistance groups. Other tiny cells were
dropped in across the country – specially trained agents, together
with professional wireless operators. But the enemy had an idea

of what was going on. 'The operations of the wireless operators became very risky,' remembered Pearson, 'as the messages became longer and more frequent and the Gestapo stepped up its radio detection operations with mobile RDF (Radio direction-finding) vans.' But the missions were fruitful:

As well as our close work with a number of maquis in the region, 'Bruno' – the code-name of my operator – and I (the two of us constituted Mission Pedagogue) – had excellent contacts with various networks of information gatherers . . . when Patton's troops began moving forward again, our people had been feeding the Americans information as to German troop withdrawals.[3]

And back in England, it was thanks to the work of Hugh Trevor-Roper – now promoted to major – and his department in analysing the communications of the Abwehr, that such special commando units (always effective in sabotage operations) were able to target transmitters and teleprinters with ever more lethal accuracy, forcing the Germans to fall back on more cumbersome means of sending messages.

Meanwhile, Y operatives in the field – who had been specially trained to decode the German army's sub-Enigma code, Double Playfair – found that the Germans were now using an even more complex system. By the time it took to un-knot the code, therefore, any immediate front-line information to be gleaned would be outdated. There was, however, an unlikely plus side: the code was fearsomely difficult to *use* in the field. It involved 5 x 5 letter grids and a daily change of stencils (used for a further layer of letter transposition), and mistakes were regularly made in messages as a result of this complexity. While the mistakes alone were of no use to the cryptanalysts, they could make good use of the fact that messages then had to be repeated in order to compensate for the errors.

Even in those nerve-strung days, when a combination of high morale and hope were balanced against the often fanatical fightbacks of the German army, moments of levity were provided by Y Service operatives. One particular message, intercepted from deep in Ukraine, gave a pleasing insight into the thoughts of German operators. Bletchley's deputy director, Nigel de Grey, gave it wider circulation among his colleagues: 'On the 28th August, one of the operators from the German Army Group, South Ukraine, while working Supreme Army Command broke into violent remarks about Hitler, using the peculiarly foul language in which the Germans delight. The operator at Supreme Army Command tried to shut him up in equally filthy language.'

For many at Bletchley and out in the Y Service stations at around this time, priorities were being recalibrated, and increasing numbers of women and men were trained in the Japanese codes. For Wrens Pat Sinclair and Marjorie Gerken, this meant being temporarily removed from their happy base at HMS *Flowerdown*. They were also to be instructed in the fine arts of direction finding. The experience – especially at that point in the war – was one that they found unnecessarily irksome.

They were first sent to Bedfordshire for a short, sharp course in Japanese. 'Marjorie and I were singled out,' says Mrs Sinclair. 'I took to that Japanese stuff, I loved it.' But then came the DF training with a formidably eccentric tutor out in a village in the countryside. 'Marjorie and I were on night duty. We were in this little hut in a field. And the man teaching us was a civilian – to us he would seem middle-aged, because we were young, but he wasn't actually that old. He would probably have been in his fifties, and probably would have been in the Navy between the wars. Marjorie told me that this man had a caravan, and his poor wife was stuck there.

'Anyway, when we first met, he came to pick us up at the station on a motorbike and sidecar. I was in the sidecar with our luggage, and Marjorie had to sit on the pillion. We didn't have helmets in those days. And he was driving like a madman.' Furthermore, says Mrs Sinclair, 'he tried to flirt with us but we weren't having any, we didn't like him on sight. Apparently he had had a go at the previous Wrens, with his poor wife stuck there in that caravan. He didn't cut any ice with us at all.'

Soundly rebuffed, the tutor's campaign took a sinister if comical turn while Marjorie and Pat were on night duty, direction finding in the little hut. Without them knowing, 'he came along and chucked this huge piece of concrete on the corrugated roof in the middle of the night. We nearly jumped out of our skins. His explanation was: "I was just testing how you would react if I was a German parachutist landing on the roof."'

Though often meeting with ferocious and sometimes almost irrational German resistance, the Allies pushed steadily through Europe. Hugh Skillen quoted Harold Everett's recollections of the day that Brussels was liberated. Entering the city unannounced, the Allied armoured divisions were apparently met first with sullen indifference by a populace that thought that they were simply more German soldiers, rolling through the streets in German tanks. Eventually a few citizens realised; and then word spread with lightning speed. The result, for Everett and his comrades, was a never-to-be-forgotten exhilaration:

At 11 a.m., one of our operators picked up a news flash on the BBC: 'British troops are entering Brussels' and suddenly all the population of Brussels was round us! There were literally thousands and thousands of people milling around, cheering, shouting, waving Union Jacks and Belgian flags and throwing flowers into our van. Some stood silently weeping but the deliriously happy majority struggled and jostled each other in rapturous good humour, just to get near us and to touch us.

The van containing Everett and his fellow radio operators was invaded by men and women, crowding forward to hug and kiss them. One young woman got into the van and sat with 'her skirt hitched high' and 'kicking her legs in the air' until another woman of a certain age warned her that this might be giving quite the wrong impression. Perhaps it was giving exactly the right impression. Nonetheless, said Everett, the noise and the ecstasy and the knowledge that the British were 'the cause of this great outburst of joy' gave him an intense pride and pleasure and left him feeling 'emotionally super-charged'.

Despite the clear turning of the tide, the German war machine, far from slowing down, escalated new tactics, such as the launching of the lethal V1 missiles across the channel. Voluntary Interceptor Ray Fautley recalled their arrival: 'Then there were the buzz bombs – the number of times I dropped flat on my face in the middle of the road. And you saw businessmen, all smartly dressed up, doing the same, when we heard the engine cut out. That's when it was going to come down and wherever you were, you went flat down.

'The nearest one went off to me was about 100 yards away. They were big bombs. And you could feel them. If you were standing, they would knock you flying. That's why you had to get down. Everyone went down. There were old ladies pushing little kids down.'

Wireless Group Intelligence officers stationed outside Brussels picked up distinctive signals – long dashes – just at the point when these rockets were taking off overhead. But the signals, puzzlingly, could not be unlocked; they seem to lack significance. It subsequently turned out that they were dummy signals sent out to confuse potential codebreakers and misdirect attention.

The bravely fought disaster of September 1944 that was Operation Market Garden – in which General Montgomery and the Americans sought to seize the bridges at Eindhoven, Zon, Vegehl and Arnhem (the last being the responsibility of the British) – was not a failure of intelligence, or down to a lack of data provided by the Y Service. Days before the attack, intelligence had been supplied concerning the possible presence – 'elements' of four Panzer divisions that were in the region for 'rest' and 're-fit'. Montgomery chose to interpret this as meaning that they were effectively out of action, or at least not in a position to be brought into action. And so the bridges were captured – but the bridge at Arnhem was famously one bridge too far. And those German tanks were now roused into deadly action in the town, against British paratroops with negligible anti-tank weaponry. The houses they fought in were pulverised, and troops were forced back not merely by artillery but by phosphorous smoke from the shells. Nearly 1500 men from the parachute division were killed; about 6500 were taken prisoner. Even now, Y Service veteran Betty White recalls with horror how her brother was caught up in the carnage and, even though he escaped, was badly hurt, losing 'half a hand' and sustaining a serious abdominal wound. In another sense, though, he was fortunate; they managed to get him back to England where he ended up spending six months in hospital. He went on to live until the age of eighty-six.

But in broader terms, despite this grim episode – and despite the surprise Ardennes offensive a few weeks later, when Allied forces in that deeply forested region of Belgium were thrown into disarray by a vast and vicious German attack, after which Bletchley Park found itself blamed for not giving enough forewarning – it was widely known that the question now was when, not if. No matter what the Germans threw back at the Allies, their power was being whittled away.

19 The End and the Beginning

It was too soon for elation. In the Far East, the Japanese forces were proving utterly intractable. Elsewhere, life in bases such as HMS *Anderson* continued to offer consolation for the wearying slog of the shift system – daubs of colour and brilliance from luminous nocturnal insects to lizards on the football pitches.

Back in England, such everyday escapism was harder to find; and for the expert wireless operators at Beaumanor, the frictions of enforced communal life occasionally broke out into open hostility over minor irritations. 'Tolerance and thoughtfulness are two good virtues but very hard to acquire,' wrote Privates Peggy Doherty, Peggie Moran, Peggy Evans, Alice Cooke and Lynda Courtnage in an indignant letter to the staff magazine. 'In little things, however, tolerance should be easy to exercise. Sad to say, some people who frequent the canteen are lacking in it.' The root of the ladies' complaint? A battle over the new sound of popular culture.

'A short time ago, a swing programme was being appreciated by several ATS who, being young and vital, enjoy these lively tunes,' wrote the women collectively. 'In the middle of our favourite, a gentleman – ??? [*sic*] – rushed to the radio and without further ado, switched off. I don't blame this personage for disliking such "music",' the letter went on, a little disingenuously. 'His taste probably lies somewhere in the higher regions but if he is an admirer of Grieg, it still doesn't give him the priority for use of the wireless set.'

It is all too easy to envisage this standoff between a band of high-spirited girls and a crusty older man. In the Powell and Pressburger film *A Matter of Life and Death*, American swing music is played at the Heavenly Court to terrific comic effect, causing various angelic hosts to wince. Such music, though, was a foretaste of the more Americanised world to come.

So indeed were some of the romantic arrangements at Beaumanor. Just after D-Day in 1944, the staff magazine had a happy announcement to make:

> To Sgt Betty Coombs, 'A' Watch, no 1 Wing, whose wedding is to take place in Surrey on July 24th. The bridegroom is a Private Quick of the U.S. Army, and judging by the comparatively short time that the Yanks have been in the district, it seems that he is appropriately named. Good luck, Betty: may you never have any leisure.

Betty Coombs was not a lone case. Also receiving congratulations in the same issue was 'Private Helen Brown of "B" Watch, no 1 Wing, who is to marry Sgt Mulligan of the U.S. Army towards the end of September.'

The advent of the Americans was not, however, a source of universal jubilation. An anonymous contributor to Beaumanor's scandal sheet recounted the day when 'the Yanks came to our village.' The young women were advised to stay indoors and keep away from them. The young women did no such thing. Meanwhile, some of the older male villagers in the area were furiously resentful of the invasion, and of the way that local women viewed the exotic newcomers. One such man, Steve, was so disgruntled to hear of his daughters attending American dances that, one evening, he 'flung' himself off to the pub and didn't return for some time. When he did, extremely well refreshed, he was in the company of a couple of US servicemen and a 'huge tin of preserved chicken' – unimaginable luxury in those days of rationing.

Transferred from Egypt to Sardinia, young Special Operator Bob Hughes was taking the war with a certain insouciance, even though it had brought adventures a very long way from his former life working for the Post Office. 'Sardinia was quite an experience, in a way,' he says with a chuckle. 'Very rugged country, bandit country. We got there and the first thing we did was get into the regulating office. The sergeant there immediately said: "Any of you lads play football?" So we thought, well, he's pretty good . . .

'We were there for some time, well after D-Day. We were there for straightforward direction finding. When we had to do this in Alexandria, it was easier because three-quarters of the area range was land. On an island, you had to cover 360 degrees of water. That was difficult but you obviously did your best. You'd get a very narrow window.'

Every day in Sardinia, Mr Hughes says, 'We were driven out to our little unit, built out of packing cases. Couldn't swing a cat in there, it was so narrow.' But beyond work, the possibilities of the island were rather more varied than those he had found in Alexandria. 'We got in with the transport people, and when we were off, we'd drift round and say, "You going out anywhere today?" That's how we got round the island, bunging lifts.'

In Sardinia he found the local people perfectly affable. But there was one serious – and occasionally terrifying – hazard that he and his fellows had to face on lonely night shifts in tiny listening stations up in the hills. For the small cabins in which the radio equipment was installed were not as secure as they might be.

'Of all the experiences I had during the war – and this includes all the bombing of London,' says Mr Hughes, 'the nearest I got to death was in Sardinia. They used to drive us out for our shifts from the airfield, about three or four miles, and there were little farmhouses dotted about. I call them farmhouses. Apparently the people were so poor there they paid one lira a year as rent just to say they weren't slaves. They produced food for the government. The farmhouses always had a dog chained up and these dogs used to run in semi-circles. And sometimes the dogs got loose.'

So it was that Mr Hughes was taken to the cabin for his night shift. 'The authorities used to give us a tin of sardines or something.' This was intended as a snack to keep the operator going. 'But this particular night they gave me a bone with meat on it – probably lamb. I can remember now starting the shift in this very tiny hut. It was very hot. And because Sardinia was a nasty place for malaria, you had to wear battle dress right up to the neck.

'It was so hot, I left the door open. Occasionally, you know, you would nod off in the small hours with the heat.' Mr Hughes did so. And when he awoke, he gradually realised he was not alone. 'There was this huge bloody German shepherd dog and it had its feet planted on the entrance to the door, just standing there looking. He was obviously aware of the meat in the corner – which I didn't want anyway. We had a Sten gun, which was on the wall opposite, and I couldn't – I wouldn't have shot the dog anyway. He's looking at me and I'm looking at him. And I jumped up and screamed and threw my hands in the air and he ran. Now if he'd jumped at me, I would have been gone. But it was pure instinct. And did I shut that door fast.'

In the midst of the sweltering Sardinian climate, Mr Hughes's passion for football led him and his fellow Y Service colleagues into a couple of unpredictable matches with Sardinia's finest. 'On one occasion, we raised a football match with the local people. So we played a few games and obviously settled in with them. Now, we played one particular game against the local football team, which actually had a big stadium. We played this first match and we were winning one-nil. Nothing happened much – just a bit of kicking here and there.

'But with ten minutes to go, the ball got kicked into the crowd, and suddenly it was thrown back and someone had put a knife in it. So that was that. Game over.

'There was another match,' adds Mr Hughes, laughing. 'The stadium was bursting with local people – they didn't have any entertainment otherwise so it was a big event. It started off and immediately the referee began to give fouls to the local team. And then he gave a penalty which wasn't a penalty. Then there were a few fists raised, and it got a bit heated – and then on strode the sergeant from the carabinieri with the leather boots, the red stripes and everything.'

There was a moment or two of freezing tension, before the sergeant 'got hold of the referee, took his whistle from him and ordered him off. The sergeant took over the match. And we won that match and when we were coming away, the crowds were gathering round and I was the only one on the back of the Bedford van wearing my matelots – white. Because I stood out, they shouted "Marine, marine, you cheated, you're cheating!" and chased us as we drove off.'

After the surrender of Italy, the focus of the war had shifted away from the Mediterranean. There were fewer enemy transmissions to listen for, and the listening stations began to be wound down. With less to concentrate on, Mr Hughes had time to admire how the entire operation had been carried out. 'The logistics were amazing. There was the American air force there, a small Free French unit – anti-shipping wing – and the RAF. There were all these aircraft – they told us there was an underground reservoir filled with aircraft oil.'

There were also signs that a semblance of normal life was returning. 'In the local town, suddenly the bus company started to operate again. A proper, regular bus service. We investigated. It turned out they were running the bus on aircraft high-octane.'

And what of the listeners, who were finding that suddenly the signals that they had been intercepting were no longer being sent?

'We didn't do a lot. One time, we were in Sassari and we went to get our ride back and there was a surrendered Italian officer there. The driver at that time happened to be a man we called Smithy. Smithy had been through the desert with the Eighth Army and,' adds Mr Hughes, chuckling, 'he used to sip aircraft octane.

'An officer asked if Smithy would take this Italian officer back. He said "I'm not taking no so-and-so-and-so Italian. Tell him to p*** off."

'It all got a bit heated. But the officer said, "No, you've got to take him."

'My friend Eric and I got into the back – you couldn't be with the driver, the vehicle was divided. Anyway, we'd had quite a few drinks, and there was this Italian officer there with us in the back. And at the front, Smithy did it purposely.' That is, he drove like an utter maniac on the hazardously narrow mountain roads. 'How Smithy took those bends I don't know. But the Italian officer was literally screaming. He was shouting, "Stop, stop." Eric and I were completely oblivious, laughing at him. But we could all have gone over the side of the mountain anytime. However, we got to Alghero safely, after all these miles of very dusty roads, and the officer got out. He brushed himself and there were clouds of dust. We stood and laughed and laughed. I'll bet he'll remember that day too.'

Because of the way that we mark significant dates, there is still a subconscious general assumption that, for everyone involved, the war ended in August 1945. Certainly hostilities ceased; but for many thousands of young people, the everyday life – the uniform, the drill, the duties – continued until the vast and logistically complex operation of bringing all the soldiers home, and filtering them back into the lives from which they had been taken, could be completed. Servicemen in the Far East – particularly those who had been prisoners of war in the unimaginably barbaric camps – were among the top priorities. Even before VJ Day, there was an ever-mounting sense of impatience to have it all done, especially among the families back home wanting to see their children return. Jean Valentine recalls that her mother wrote to her in Ceylon from Scotland in May 1945, just after VE Day, wanting to know when precisely her daughter would be home. Jean had to patiently reply that just because the war was over in Europe, that didn't mean it was over everywhere else.

Nonetheless, some would affectionately recall that VE Day brought at least a foretaste of freedom. At Forest Moor near Harrogate, for instance, the news of the German capitulation, though hardly unexpected, instantly changed the atmosphere of the place. 'The wireless station on the moor was surrounded by a high wire fence, and when the night shifts were exchanged all was in darkness,' Y Service operative Cynthia Humble recalled:

Came the day in May 1945, we had been on the midnight to 7 a.m. shift, and the sets had been very quiet, with very little Morse, and some messages in German language coming through. Wearily we rode back to our huts to sleep. It was a lovely day and sleep deserted us for we knew something important was to be announced. We sat outside the hut on the grass, in our blue and white pyjamas, and eventually we heard – THE WAR WAS OVER! Half the shift, me included, had to go on the 7 p.m. to midnight shift. We sat twiddling the knobs on our sets with nothing coming through, and those five hours passed slowly, but enlivened with soup plates of raisins (luxury) put by our wireless receivers to nibble the boredom away!

Come midnight, and we were relieved by the incoming laughing and happy shift, telling us we would need dark glasses. Puzzled, we went through the open doors to find the whole station ablaze with light. The blackout was over! In the grounds was a large static water tank to be used in case of fire. The whole watch spontaneously made a circle around it,

joining hands and singing 'There'll always be an England',
and the Scottish girls adding 'As long as Scotland's there'![1]

Across the world, however, for the thousands of wireless operators
and interceptors who had spent years hunched over headsets, the
signals did not simply come to an end. In fact, it is just as well in
some cases that they didn't. For a number of codebreakers and
wireless operators, the glimpse that they had been afforded of a
new, colourful, exotic world brought about philosophical as well
as practical changes.

For Jean Valentine, it was a case of not being in a particular rush
to get back to Britain, despite her mother's anxieties. The war had
opened up wide vistas that the young woman had never before
considered. In Colombo, she had met the man she was going to
marry. And their immediate post-war lives would be spent a great
distance from the miseries of rationing, scarce fuel and housing
shortages that marked the landscape of late 1940s Britain.

'When I got back to Britain, I was demobbed right away,' says
Jean. 'And my husband was still in the Navy, so I joined him. He
was at an airfield down in Somerset. We had digs – or a couple of
rooms in a house – down there. And eventually he was demobbed,
some months later. Then he applied to join [airline] BOAC, and
while he was waiting to get a job, he took a job in the City as a
clerk with a shipping company and I went to work in Selfridges.
I think we both earned something like £5 a week each. But it was
enough to pay the rent and we had a car – somehow we managed.'
But the drabness of British life suited neither of them. 'Then his
appointment to BOAC came through, so that's what we did – his
first posting was to Rangoon in Burma.'

In other words, war work had given the couple a tremendous
advantage; these young people were already citizens of the world,
enthusiastic about moving into unfamiliar, exotic territory. Even
if that exotic element had the odd moment of pure fright. 'I
remember going into my bedroom one evening and between the

bathroom and the dressing room, there was a snake coiled up,' says Jean. 'So I yelled for the boy to come and deal with it – which he did – and then when I went off to bed, I found its mate coiled up in the dressing room.'

'We went from there to Karachi in 1947,' says Jean. They were there in time to witness an extraordinary moment. 'Partition actually happened when we were between Calcutta and Karachi.'

They stayed in Karachi for a while: 'After this, we went to Bombay, and we were there for about a year.' Here, they lived a life that would have been quite inconceivable back in England – to say nothing of Jean's native Perth.

'We had four or five servants,' she says brightly. 'I had had my eldest daughter, Stephanie, by then.' Little Stephanie had a nanny. Meanwhile, there was 'a bloke who called himself a butler – which was polishing his ego a bit. He was the number one boy, and then there was his assistant, and the cook, and the driver. Five servants in Bombay. In a flat.'

For Robert Hughes, who had been moved from Sardinia to direction finding in Malta, the process was protracted – not least because of some unexpected health issues. 'In Malta at that time, bubonic plague broke out,' he says, shaking his head at the memory. (Malta was not alone in this; there had been similar cases in the Middle East.) 'That obviously was very serious, and we were all scared in case we had to have the injection, which we were told – whether this rumour was true or not – put you out for forty-eight hours.

'And it was just at this time that I was getting ready to come home. Anyway, I boarded the ship [out] and the first morning I got up to wash, I went bang, straight out, fainted. I came round – thought, bloody hell – walked a few paces – and then bang! – went out again. It happened four times. Someone took me round to the sick bay. There were quite a few laid out there, picking up troops along the way. I had a very high temperature. But by the time we got to Marseilles, I had more or less recovered.

'So I didn't know until I got home. It was malaria. Now, my father [a ship's stoker] had also got malaria, when he was in Freetown. For him, the malaria only ever got repeated at Christmas, when he drank. There was some reason why the alcohol stirred it up. Anyway, the same thing happened to me. I was never a drinker, but when I had a drink with the lads, I got ill.'

Eventually Mr Hughes's malaria petered out; tropical diseases aside, he recalls the moment in August 1945 when the news of Japan's capitulation came through. It was during his voyage home, between fainting bouts: 'It came over the ship's tannoy that Japan had surrendered. You can imagine the cheer that went up. Because at that point, all of us on board simply expected to have six weeks' leave and then out again. That was the rumour that had been going round.'

His military duties, however, were not quite over – there was a short and claustrophobic spell yet to come at Chatham docks on the austere north Kent coast – rather a comedown from the glamour of Sardinia and Malta.

'There was a big drafting office in one of the old Chatham tunnels – it was a honeycomb,' Mr Hughes says. 'It was a big area where they had thirty Wrens, and they decided that this had to be manned twenty-four hours. So we got bunged down this drafting office and had to take it in turns to sleep down there.' During the year of heavy night-time bombardment, those old tunnels in the Kent cliffs must, to some, have been a comfort; in the aftermath of VJ Day, however, the dark passages took on a more oppressive aspect. Not that young Mr Hughes was as worried as some of his comrades. Indeed, as his friends fretted about sinister old legends, Mr Hughes was beset by quite another apprehension. 'You took your hammock down. And what used to worry me was that I was a very heavy sleeper. Imagine sleeping in total darkness in these tunnels. You'd get in your hammock, and I used to dread being still there, sleeping, when all these Wrens came to work in the morning.

'One weekend, this chap who was with us was petrified. He said he'd seen a white ghost. We said "Aahh, get out of it." But he was serious, really frightened. I never saw anything – I slept too soundly. But funnily enough, some time later, there were stories from other people saying they'd seen the ghosts of French prisoners dressed in Napoleonic costumes.'

When his demobilisation came through, Mr Hughes was approached to see if he might be interested in doing work for the nascent GCHQ. Mr Hughes gave the matter careful thought. But immediately after leaving the Army, he had got married; the GCHQ job would have involved, as he says, a lot of 'embassies' and the requirement to be out of the country for at least five years. He had had enough of voyages for the time being; so he returned to his former employer, the Post Office, staying there for the rest of his career.

For young Chris Barnes, who had been drafted into Beaumanor as a civilian wireless operator, the end of the war ironically brought his introduction to life in the Army. 'On VE Day, I think there was a 24-hour party in the Beaumanor canteen, running continually.' A few weeks later, when the atomic bombs were dropped on Japan, 'I was due to be drafted for India in the Army.' The end of the war brought about a change of destination, though Mr Barnes still got his chance to serve in uniform. 'I was posted – among other places – to Harrogate – now the training college, that was Forest Moor.' This was followed by the chance to go abroad. 'Then I went to Cyprus, so I did the better part of two and a half years in the Army. But not when there was any fighting going on.'

For some, even though the transition back to the sorts of lives they had led before was reasonably easy, they still hankered for the freedoms they had enjoyed. Having been a wireless telegraphist in Colombo after working in a Weybridge mill as a lad, was Victor Newman disorientated by the return? 'When we came back to England, some of us were sent on to HMS *Flowerdown* – and we finally got demobbed in September 1946.' So his military career had continued for a year after the end of the war. 'I never did that kind of work again, never worked with telegraph or wireless. Instead I went into agricultural work, and worked on farms. I worked on the farm for the rest of my life. But the knowledge of Morse – you never forget it. It's absolutely in there, still. I might not be quite as quick at it as I was, but it is like riding a bike, it's something you never lose once you pick it up.

'The thing I missed most about Colombo was the swimming in the sea. Obviously you missed your mates after demob, and also, after years in the services, you had to start thinking for yourself. With the forces came regulations. Afterwards . . .'

And what of Peter Budd, who had spent eighteen months amid the dazzling beauty of the Cocos Islands, and then an exhilarating spell in Karachi? What would his native Bristol have looked like after all of that? As it happened, he was able to take a slightly longer voyage home; his duties were not yet over, but nor was his capacity for amusing adventures. The process of demobilisation was a sort of extended tour and indeed an extended education for a very young and – in some ways – naive man.

'If you can imagine the most beautiful French provincial town you have ever seen, this was Algiers,' says Mr Budd, almost with a nostalgic sigh, thinking back to the early autumn of 1945. 'At that particular time, there were more Europeans there than natives. And so we would wander round all afternoon buying bottles of wine, hanks of bananas . . . And you've always got an old sailor in a group – I mean, someone thirty-five or so. One day, this old sailor said, "You've got to go to the Blue Moon. It's up the Casbah."

'Now, the Casbah had been out of bounds to the thousands of troops in the place throughout the war, but now you could go. So one afternoon, we went through these narrow little streets, and there was the Blue Moon. We went in – it had the longest bar I had ever seen. We were all sitting up there. Suddenly a door opened at the other end and about twelve ladies came out, in dressing gowns, and I thought, that's funny, it's only four o'clock. Very innocent. Never having talked to a woman for two years.'

Indeed, it is almost impossible to grasp now exactly how much of a culture shock this must have been to young Peter Budd. As he recalls, many young people back then were younger in a sense than their equivalents today.

'One of these twelve ladies came up to me,' he says, chuckling at the memory. 'She said, "Hullo, cherie, you buy me a drink."

'I said "Maybe." Well, of course, I did. And I had a great shock because her dressing gown was undone and that was the first naked woman I'd ever seen in my life. I was nineteen and a half years old.

'Anyway, at the far end of the bar, the other men began to peel off one by one with these ladies and as they did, they would pass all their bottles of wine and hanks of bananas down the line – and of course I was right on the end.

'The petty officer next to me said, "Budd, I'm sorry to do this but you've got to stay here and look after this lot." And I sat there with this stuff. What a night.' In one crucial sense, though, Budd had had a narrow escape, even if romance had eluded him. Only the next morning, thanks to their excessive consumption of drink, did his comrades' suffering really begin.

Even before that, getting back to his ship had been complicated by grog rations. 'Before the evening had started, everyone had felt so sorry for the duty motorboat crew (the designated drivers, as it were) that they'd all given them drinks, half bottles of wine et cetera. So when we got back from the Casbah to the dock, the motorboat crew was so roaring drunk they couldn't actually find the ship that we were berthed on. It was the only one anchored in the bay, all lit up. Half the crew weren't there.

'And as it happened, I didn't really mind having had to sit at the end of the bar because next morning, on board the ship, there was a long queue outside the sick bay of people who got so drunk, they hadn't taken the precautions they should.'

*

Back in Britain, even for Wrens the winding-down process was pro-tracted. At HMS *Flowerdown*, for instance, Marjorie Gerken and Pat Sinclair found that they were required to stay quite a few weeks after the end of hostilities. Obviously the airwaves were by then relatively quiet, so there was the question of how to keep all the youngsters occupied. 'All that time after VJ Day, they kept us busy and gave us little courses,' says Mrs Gerken. 'And we still had enter-tainment. But although we were happy, we did want to get home.'

When she got back to London and returned to her administration job in the civil service, a curious silence fell on the subject of the last three or four years of her life. Because of the Official Secrets Act, she was forbidden to discuss her work. But there is also a sense among many veterans that even if they could have done, the subject never seemed to be raised; there was a feeling that people simply did not want to talk about the war. And so those years were quickly consigned to a hazy twilight. 'After a few weeks, I went back to the office,' says Mrs Gerken. 'No one had any idea of what we had been doing in the war. My parents never knew. My husband Norman's oldest brother was in the regular air force, Fleet Air Arm – and Norman never told him what *he* did.'

'After VE Day, we just carried on,' says Pat Sinclair. 'May 1945, we were all hooray, hooray, down into Winchester, dancing. Then, in August 1945, we were all up to Leicester Square, dancing. But I was stationed at HMS *Flowerdown* until March 1946. They must have kept us occupied. We still had the routine, of going on shifts, of going to the canteen.'

Her husband Peter was based at the time in Laindon, Essex, and he recalls the complex procedure of trying to telephone his sweetheart from a public call box and enlisting the sympathy of the operator when he did not have enough change. 'It took so long to be demobbed because they did it according to date of birth, length of service, whether you were married, had children,' he says. On top of this, 'they had to give out civilian clothes and it took some time before all that was available.'

His wife laughs proudly. 'I wasn't given civilian clothing. I was a Leading Wren at the end.'

For Peter Budd, after years abroad, with his closest family having no idea where he had been, settling back in was a long process: the Y Service had not quite finished with him yet. After the experience of living in paradise, this was perhaps for the best: a period of decompression before emerging into the pervasive grey and pinched poverty of post-war England. 'We sailed back, we came to Portsmouth and we were home,' says Mr Budd. 'And then I was sent to HMS *Flowerdown*, and found myself working on intercepting Russian naval communications. I knew Scarborough was the big intercept station but I didn't know about *Flowerdown*. And that was the end of my naval career.

'I was at *Flowerdown* for a matter of months and then I was demobbed. In our branch, they didn't ask us to carry on because no one knew what anyone was going to do when the war was over. They were only just starting to think about Russia as a Cold War enemy rather than an ally. The barrack to Devonport had "Joe for King!" written on the door.' Joe was Stalin. 'It was very much that way during the war . . .'

There were unexpected bonuses, one of which was the prized American HRO radio set that Mr Budd had had sent on from Karachi. In a tribute to an apparently indefatigable postal service, the machine finally materialised; Mr Budd turned the van driver around and had the thing sent on to a prospective buyer who had shown great interest. 'A fortnight later, I got a cheque for £25 – and that cheque paid for my engagement ring two years later.'

There was one other financial matter hanging over Budd's head: the money advanced to him while he was working in Karachi. Mr Budd was sure that the debt would at last be noticed by someone in authority. 'When I was in Plymouth barracks waiting to be demobbed,' he says, 'an announcement went out over the tannoy – such things could terrify you – "Budd report to the Pay Office at the double!" I thought, my God, they've found out about all my money.

'When I got there, there was a very young lieutenant paymaster. He said: "I notice from the records that you haven't been paid for a year."' This was not the twist that Mr Budd had been expecting. 'Well of course, this was the money for when I had been on the Cocos Islands,' says Mr Budd. 'The paymaster said, "I can let you have half of it now and the rest next month – will that be all right?" What could I say? To this day, when the doorbell rings, I expect to see two naval policemen come to arrest me.'

Then the grind of post-war life set in. 'I worked for British Overseas Airways. I joined them just before the war. And then to get a promotion – which meant my wage increased from five pounds a week to five pounds two shillings – I went to work in London at their headquarters, occasionally going down to Heathrow.' The airport was not at that time quite the endless megapolis it is now: 'At Heathrow then, there were two tents: arrivals and departures. A third of the tent was curtained off and there were three armchairs, and that was the VIP lounge. And there were duckboards going out to the concrete runway.'

Yet even with the prospect of marriage and good, interesting work, it was impossible for Mr Budd not to think back to his extraordinary wartime experiences. 'Life was very different in England in the immediate years after the war. Shortages were terrible. Food rationing was worse than during the war. The winter of 1947 was unbelievable. Obviously the poverty, the desolation in Europe was terrible, in Italy it was bad as well. But it was bad here too . . . I had lodgings in south Ealing, full board. I lived in a house with a widow and her daughter. There were shortages of everything, especially consumer goods. Purchase tax was ninety per cent on luxury goods. Having said that, everyone was so relieved the war was over. People went to Butlins and thought it was wonderful . . .

'I wouldn't think about the Cocos Islands when I was up to my eyes in business and young children but that was an experience that has been with me all through life and I can never forget – it was a life-changing experience. To find yourself swimming in a sea full of marine life and worrying about whether you're going to have your leg bitten off by a shark . . . to go to this little island . . . was amazing. What an experience for someone of that age, never been abroad, or mixed, never been to the tropics, never been cast away on a desert island.'

For Geoffrey Pidgeon, who was now nineteen, away from the secret workshops of Whaddon Hall and in uniform with the Royal Corps of Signals out in India, news of the end of the war did not cause exultation. 'On our arrival in Calcutta, we were given the first news of the bomb dropped on Hiroshima,' he recalled, 'without comprehending the meaning of "atomic" or the devastation it had caused . . . VJ Day was celebrated thankfully, rather than wildly, since we were uncertain as to what the atom bomb was and sobered by the sheer number of casualties.'

There was a lot of winding down to be done. The Y Service in India was gradually dismantled and Mr Pidgeon was among those transferred to Singapore for a few more months. Here he was reunited with the Y Service operative, Wilf Lilburn, who had got him into the whole thing a few years back. Again, was this a life that Pidgeon wanted to pursue into a new, chillier era of espionage? The answer was no: like many, Mr Pidgeon had been proud to play his part, from assembling secret wireless sets for agents at Whaddon Hall to manoeuvres in the Solent and the voyage out to the Far East. But real life was back at home; his mother had inherited a bathroom business, and she was keen for her eldest son to come and work in it so that he might take the reins. Nonetheless, he now looks back at his war with needle-sharp clarity. And in common with many Y Service veterans, his lively intelligence and wit give Geoffrey Pidgeon the appearance of someone fifteen years younger. Were these veterans perhaps fortunate enough to retain that 'flexibility of the brain' that, according to Bob Hughes, they all needed?

20 The Legacy of the Listeners

'Some people did get earache and ear problems in later years,' says Marjorie Gerken. 'Recently I went to have my ears tested and told them that I had worked with headphones throughout the war. But they told me that my hearing condition was more down to age!'

Nevertheless, all those years of listening with furious concentration to faint signals against an all-pervasive background hiss must have had some effect. 'We had heavy headphones, but they were soft against the ears,' says Mrs Gerken. 'Sometimes when signals were good, you could wear the headphones pulled forward a little on your head, a little in front of my ears, so that they would not just be resting in one place. In some ways, you became automated yourself.'

According to Betty White, however, the after-effects of those years of work could be more insidious and unexpected: 'After the war, a few of us had what you might call a relapse. One day, I was at the shops with my mother and I just passed out. The doctor I saw put it down to what he termed nervous debility. It was to do with the body getting used to normal rhythms and sleep patterns again.' Of course, the doctor in question had to diagnose her without knowing what sort of work she had been doing. 'Lots of us had something in the way of complaints,' she says.

There was another source of post-war discontent: frustration. Even though he enjoyed his work, one aspect of it slightly annoys Bob Hughes to this day: 'Of all the years we were out there, in the Mediterranean, we Special Operators never got any feedback about our work. Of all the work we did, we never knew what the results were. We only knew when these books started coming out in the 1970s. Other than that: nothing. The officers may have got told something but it was never relayed back to us.'

But those years had a profound impact in wider senses too. Not in the obvious ways, like career paths – as we have seen, following demobilisation, a great many Y Service operators returned to their old interests and jobs, from farming to the civil service to the Post Office – but in subtler ways. Peter Budd, for example, had not merely lived through a terrific adventure: without realising it, he had developed a capacity for self-reliance. This helped him enormously as, some years after the war, he went into business for himself. This capacity was also apparent in an extraordinary motorbike trip that he and a couple of other friends undertook around shattered post-war Europe.

The same might be said for Jean Valentine. The experience of being transported across the oceans into a wholly unknown world had given her a taste of splendour; both she and her husband later found the pinched greyness of austerity London too cruel a contrast, and they spent a great many years abroad thereafter, from Burma to continental Europe. At a time when foreign travel was a rarity for the majority, Jean and her husband were extraordinarily cosmopolitan. Of course, Jean had been a forthright soul since her Scottish girlhood; but as with Peter Budd, the nature of her experience taught her to open her eyes to the wider world.

Hugh Trevor-Roper's endless quarrels and tussles both with his intelligence bosses and with the Bletchley Park authorities culminated in exquisite vindication at the end of the war; it was upon his shoulders, and not those of the colleagues for whom he had so little time, that a terrific opportunity fell. Just weeks after VE Day, Trevor-Roper was posted to Germany to interrogate Nazi prisoners. Also working there was one of his friends in MI6, Dick White. The two met in an abandoned *Schloss*. The shattered continent, with the Soviets poised to brutally acquire so much of it, was febrile with rumours. Many of these concerned Hitler; he had not died in the bunker at all, it was said, but had been spirited out and had escaped to the west. It was decided that Trevor-Roper would be the man to lay this ghost once and for all. He visited Hitler's bunker and interviewed those who were close to events at the fall of Berlin. To the helpless rage of Trevor-Roper's enemies, he then turned this mission into a book, *The Last Days of Hitler*, which was published in 1947 and became an instant bestseller. His academic colleagues continued to fizz with resentment for decades afterwards – not least because Trevor-Roper was so venomous about the work of others. So, in 1983, when he committed the blunder of authenticating the so-called 'Hitler Diaries' for the *Sunday Times*, the exultation when the documents proved to be fake made for a gruesome spectacle.

That one ghastly mistake aside, we see in Trevor-Roper's wartime work the seeds of what would become the keynotes of his lively academic career: both a ferocious talent for interpretation (either of Abwehr codes or of seventeenth-century economics) combined with a gleefully waspish attitude towards those who might have been considered his elders and betters.

Elsewhere, as Bletchley Park was gradually wound down after the end of the war – its functions transferring first to Eastcote in Middlesex, then to the new GCHQ, which was taking shape in Cheltenham – so the Y Services were consolidated into a new form to face the fresh challenges posed by the Cold War. In Beaumanor, the group of ATS girls and civilians may have been gradually disbanded, but a dedicated rump were to stay on. In the late 1940s, the establishment, now known as War Office Radio Services, began recruiting again. One man who ended up there had been actively seeking wireless operating work since the end of the war – in the interim, he had taken a welding job – and Beaumanor's new life was a source of delight. The only setback was that the numbers of women had dropped dramatically. The job – that of receiving Morse, never sending it – made him feel in one sense 'half an operator'; nonetheless, it was a very specialised skill that brought its own satisfactions. And the work was exactly the same as those during the war had been doing, with one notable difference: 'The only thing that had altered was the target.'

There was another element of continuity: discontent over low pay. Military signals operators knew that they were being paid substantially less than the civilians working alongside them, who were on civil service grades. In spite of that, the place fostered an atmosphere of camaraderie and the listeners' target was to remain the same for a number of years until, finally, Beaumanor came to the end of its natural life. Now, it fulfils the role of a luxury conference centre.

An establishment not too far away that remains firmly clandestine to this day is Hanslope Park. Alan Turing spent some time there in the months after the war working on his voice-encryption idea, 'Delilah'. And in the aftermath of VJ Day, it was decided that a certain amount of Y Service work would be consolidated there in the form of the Diplomatic Wire Service. This branch was to be at the centre of a web of communications between British embassies around the world, as well as transmitting key BBC World Service programmes. A number of its other functions remain classified even now.

Hanslope Park's most recent public mention was as the establishment that harboured secret documents to do with Kenya in the years before Britain's withdrawal. The association immediately reawakened old images of the British establishment's fetish for secrecy, and of mysterious requisitioned properties surrounded by barbed wire in which the darker arts of intelligence gathering were practised.

As the history of GCHQ makes abundantly clear, both the importance and the secrecy of the listeners remained an unchanging factor in the new geopolitical landscape, where NATO's central aim was to prevent Soviet Russia from overrunning western Europe. There was some continuity in terms of personnel; after his stewardship of Bletchley Park, Commander Edward Travis was promoted to a wider role in the new organisation. Later directors of GCHQ who had served at Bletchley (and at RAF Chicksands) included Eric Jones and Arthur Bonsall, who back in 1940 had watched the work of the 'human computors'.

In the early post-war years, Britain had plenty to offer as an ally to America; not least all those out-stations across the world in British colonies and dominions. The British had reach where the Americans had none. Come the 1950s and 1960s, this was to change; but even as it did, so did the technology of the listeners. We were moving from a radio age to a computer age; encrypted communications in Morse were becoming as outdated as the telegraph itself. Now satellites in space floated around the earth, beaming messages back and forth. The art of interception had to keep pace with the technology of transmission.

But all this helps to bring into focus the remarkable achievements of the war years, and the dedication of all those thousands of young men and women. In the digital era, it is very difficult to imagine sitting down with pencil, paper, a clunky radio set, and listening to the monotony of Morse signals for six or even eight hours at a stretch. Imagine the time it takes to travel from London to Scotland by train, and then imagine sitting in one position for the same length of time – very often in the middle of the night – concentrating ceaselessly on the fuzzy noise coming through the ether. At the very least, to do so requires exemplary self-discipline, to say nothing of a certain mental hardiness and lightness of humour.

For some Y Service veterans, the music of Morse can still be heard occasionally today; chiefly in old black and white films. Whenever a scene in one of those films involves Morse, veterans may find themselves automatically clicking back into it; without any effort, they can make out all the different letters, even after seventy years. It is also a source of amusement when the old films, as they quite frequently did, got the Morse wrong.

The old skill is worn with pride, and with good reason: not everyone was able to deal with Morse, particularly at the speeds demanded by the Y Service. For all the young women at *Flowerdown* who relished their work, quite a few were forced to drop out: candidates who were highly intelligent yet not quite nimble enough, and unsuited to the intense pressure.

There is another dimension too: that of class; many of the young women enrolled into the WAAF and the Wrens and the ATS came from working-class backgrounds. As such, before the war, their opportunities had been very limited. The war changed this: many female Y Service veterans recall not merely the pride of their achievements, but also how their expertise saved them from menial duties such as cooking or driving. Of course, everyone had their role to play, and no disrespect is intended to the fine women and men who undertook the less glamorous duties with energy and good humour; but for the Y Service veterans, there was the knowledge, which like the codebreakers they had to keep secret for decades afterwards, that they had made an active and vital contribution.

Then there were those in the service who were quite simply way ahead of their time. Think of Aileen Clayton and her extraordinary war: a young woman in her early twenties moving from Egypt to Malta to Algiers. Straightforward courage in the face of danger is one thing: the straightforward gumption to also face the ingrained hostility of men who believed that women had no place in the theatre of war was another. Much as it is assumed that the 1960s and 1970s ushered in a revolutionary period of feminist emancipation, the truth is that women like Aileen Clayton were some distance in front; and the challenge they issued was borne out of the simple burning desire to do their duty.

For the men, too, there was an element of escape from what might otherwise have been a life cramped by lack of opportunity. To be a Special Wireless Operator was viewed by many as a genuine privilege. After so many of them passed through the initial social comedy of the training camp at Butlins in Skegness, with the partitioned beds to prevent them 'getting at one another', there was the voyage out into that wider world. Many Y Service veterans acknowledge that they were among the lucky ones: they were spared the horrors of capture in the East, the carnage of the Normandy landings. And as they sailed down the Suez Canal, or travelled on terrifying clifftop railways through India, or suffocated in the heat of Aden, or froze on the steel-grey waves of the Arctic, they had a grandstand view of history. From Baghdad to Palestine, from north Africa to Sicily, they were active witnesses, faithfully recording and reporting the countless signals that accompanied the ebbs and flows of the conflict.

And though not many of them would pursue wireless work in their later lives, the Y Service also left many with a deep residual love for the medium. Voluntary Interceptor Ray Fautley, who had carried out his duties from his parents' front room as a young lad, now has a study filled not just with wireless equipment, but other wonderful memorabilia from the height of the radio age.

Some old habits, even if they had to remain secret, were stubborn. My grandfather never lost his interest in radio, and indeed in translating Morse; on quiet evenings, he would plug his headphones into his radio set and start jotting in a meticulous hand. My grandmother would always make the same observation as he sat there: 'This is your captain speaking.' Now Morse is a dying art, superseded by the digital age; a language that came and went within the space of a century. No one will ever again acquire that fast-fingered, fast-thinking skill that the Y Service veterans mastered. Yet to hear Morse now – in those excerpts from old films

– one is struck by how hypnotically musical it is; the high-pitched dots and dashes representing every state from calm to panic and desperation.

Like that of Bletchley Park, recognition of the vital work of the Y Service was a long time coming, and for many, a great deal too late. In 2009, veterans received a commemorative medal, together with a letter from Prime Minister Gordon Brown ('a friend of mine got hers and was furious,' says Pat Sinclair. This was on the grounds of political disapproval and dislike of Brown. Mrs Sinclair, on the other hand, was thrilled to have received her citation from a Labour Prime Minister).

While the story of Bletchley Park is one of extraordinary ingenuity in the face of implacable mathematical conundrums, the story of the Y Service is more about furious dedication, great technical skill, brilliant accuracy and above all, patience and endurance. As one veteran has remarked, their work could only start when the enemy himself started work: and then they were required to perform at dazzling speeds with minds concentrated like laser beams. And as other veterans have pointed out, this was not a job for older people; even those in their mid-thirties were liable to burn out swiftly under the weight of the pressure. But for eager teenagers and young people in their twenties, the brain was supple enough to cope; and after their arduous shifts, they were equally good at seeking out the fun and the laughter that would shake all of that weight off.

Theirs is not quite the story of the course of the war being changed by one single factor. But were it not for the amazing technical efforts – the Special Liaison Units, the stations, all those encoded messages relayed with such care – then the codebreakers of Bletchley Park would have had very little to go on. All the boffins, all the brave young Wrens sailing out into dangerous oceans, the intrepid agents out in the field, hurrying from border to border in an effort to stay ahead of the enemy . . . and this is to say nothing of those thousands of preternaturally focused young women, permanently damaging their hearing for the sake of doing their duty – it was their combined efforts that made the revolutionary leaps of Bletchley Park possible.

More than this, they dutifully kept the secret as closely as any of the Bletchley codebreakers. But even as the secrets of Bletchley were unveiled in the 1980s, a great many Y Service operatives modestly kept their counsel, sticking to the Official Secrets Act they had signed. Happily, though, unlike the more compartmentalised denizens of Bletchley, the various branches of the Y Service were adept at keeping each other in touch and ensuring that their own memories continued to burn bright; they might not have revealed to their nearest and dearest exactly what it was that they did, but among old comrades, they could keep those unique recollections fresh. Ray Fautley is just one of many veterans to be in constant communication with his colleagues; Many Y Service veterans still telephone each other on an almost daily basis, and though the old Morse skills are still there, other veterans are also hooked up via email and the internet.

Possibly due to their numbers – and because of the extraordinary adventures that so many of them had – the various branches of the Y Service seem to have been better at organising reunions over the years, giving a sense of community and remembrance denied to many who had worked at the more secretive Bletchley Park. And when reunions were not possible, there were lively newsletters, filled with cartoons and poems and memories and all the latest news on members. Even if no one else knew, they did; and they knew that they had good reason to be very proud.

So there are a great many reasons why this great unsung multitude of Y Service veterans deserve – finally – to step out from the larger shadows of Station X. The melancholy truth, of course, is that there are now not so many of these brilliant people left. But they should be commemorated properly, as having played their parts in one of the greatest achievements of the twentieth century.

Notes

1 Tuning in to the Enemy

1   Maurice de la Bertauche's memoirs of his time in the Y Service can be found in the Imperial War Museum's collections

2 Reporting for Special Duties

1   de la Bertauche, Imperial War Museum
2   Peggy West, address given to the 2003 Australian War Memorial history conference 'Air War Europe'
3   Vivienne Alford in Gwendoline Page, ed., *They Listened in Secret*, George R. Reeve Ltd 2003
4   Geoffrey Pidgeon, *The Secret Wireless War*, UPSO 2003
5   Elizabeth Mashall in Page, *They Listened in Secret*

3 The Human Computors

1   Peter Gray Lucas in F.H. Hinsley and Alan Stripp eds, *Codebreakers*, Oxford University Press 1993
2   West, address to 2003 Australian War Memorial history conference 'Air War Europe'
3   Pidgeon, *The Secret Wireless War*
4   Pidgeon, *The Secret Wireless War*

5   Shirley Cannicott in Page, *They Listened in Secret*

6   Sybil Welch in Page, *They Listened in Secret*

4 The Listeners at Large

1   Lucas, *Codebreakers*

2   Lisa Ison in Page, *They Listened in Secret*

3   Daphne Baker in Page, *They Listened in Secret*

4   Imogen Ryan and Elizabeth Agar in Page, *They Listened in Secret*

5   Daphne Baker in Page, *They Listened in Secret*

6   Aileen Clayton, *The Enemy is Listening*, Hutchinson 1980

7   Ronald Lewin, *Ultra Goes to War: The Secret Story*, Hutchinson 1978

8   Frederick Winterbotham, *ihe Ultra Secret*, Purnell 1974

9   Ralph Bennett in Hinsley and Stripp, *Codebreakers*

10 Hugh Skillen, *Knowledge Strengthens the Arm*, Hugh Skillen 1990

11 Skillen, *Knowledge Strengthens the Arm*

12 Memo in the National Archives, HW14 series

13 Memo in the National Archives, HW14 series

14 Hugh Skillen, *Spies of the Airwaves*, Hugh Skillen 1989

15 de la Bertauche, Imperial War Museum

16 Joan Nicholls, *England Needs You: The Story of Beaumanor Y Station*, Joan Nicholls 2000

17 Skillen, *Knowledge Strengthens the Arm*

5 The Blitz and the Ghost Voices

1   Clayton, *The Enemy is Listening*

2   Imogen Ryan in Page, *They Listened in Secret*

3   Jean Campden in Page, *They Listened in Secret*

4   Memo in the National Archives, HW14 series

5   Skillen, *Knowledge Strengthens the Arm*

6   Memo in the National Archives, HW14 series

7   Skillen, *Spies of the Airwaves*

8   Harold Everett in Skillen, *Spies of the Airwaves*

6 Heat, Sand and Ashes

1   Henry Dryden in Hinsley and Stripp, *Codebreakers*

2   Hermione, Countess of Ranfurly, *To War with Whitaker*, Mandarin 1994

3   Clayton, *The Enemy is Listening*

4   Barbara Skelton, *Tears Before Bedtime*, Hamish Hamilton 1987

5   Skillen, *Spies of the Airwaves*

6   Clayton, *The Enemy is Listening*

7   G.A. Harries quoted in Skillen, *Spies of the Airwaves*

7 A World Wide Web of Intelligence

1   Ron Charters, writing for the Tel (s) (Telegraph Signals Association) newsletter, 1994

2   Pidgeon, *The Secret Wireless War*

3   Pidgeon, *The Secret Wireless War*

4   Harold Everett in Skillen, *Knowledge Strengthens the Arm*

5   Joan Dinwoodie in Page, *They Listened in Secret*

8 Feuds, Farce and Panic

1   Elizabeth Mashall in Page, *They Listened in Secret*

2   Harold Everett in Skillen, *Spies of the Airwaves*

3   Memos in the National Archives, HW14 series

4   Harold Everett in Skillen, *Spies of the Airwaves*

5   Report in the National Archives, HW14 series

6   Communication in the National Archives, HW42 series

7   Hugh Trevor-Roper, *The Wartime Journals*, I.B. Tauris 2012

9 Wilder Shores and Secret Missions

1   Hugh Denham in Hinsley and Stripp, *Codebreakers*

2   Peter Elphick, *Far Eastern File: The Intelligence War in the Far East*, Hodder and Stoughton 1997

3   John Boylan in Skillen, *Knowledge Strengthens the Arm*

4   Clayton, *The Enemy is Listening*

10 This is No Holiday Camp

1   Cynthia Grossman, interviewed by the BBC in 2003

2   Dafydd Williams, interviewed for Bedford Museum

3   Miggs Ackroyd in Page, *They Listened in Secret*

4   Vivienne Alford in Page, *They Listened in Secret*

11 Storms in the Desert

1   Rosemary Norton in Page, *They Listened in Secret*

2   Clayton, *The Enemy is Listening*

3   Countess of Ranfurly, *To War with Whitaker*

4   Clayton, *The Enemy is Listening*

5   Memo in the National Archives, AIR29 series

6   Harold Everett in Skillen, *Spies of the Airwaves*

7   Dryden in Hinsley and Stripp, *Codebreakers*

8   Countess of Ranfurly, *To War with Whitaker*

12 Rommel and the Art of Dirty Tricks

1   Skillen, *Knowledge Strengthens the Arm*

2   Clayton, *The Enemy is Listening*

3   Patrick Wilkinson in Hinsley and Stripp, *Codebreakers*

4   Dafydd Williams, interviewed for Bedford Museum

5   Pidgeon, *The Secret Wireless War*

13 Not So Quiet on the Domestic Front

1   Margaret Smee, interviewed by the BBC in 2003

2   Sybil Welch and Joy Hale in Page, *They Listened in Secret*

3   Vi Mitchell, contributing to Caithness.org 'Women At War' project

4   Wilma Hall, contributing to Caithness.org 'Women At War' project

5   Memo in the National Archives, HW42 series

6   Hugh Trevor-Roper's reports in the National Archives, HW19 series

7   Trevor-Roper, *The Wartime Journals*

8   Reports in the National Archives, HW19 series

9   Clayton, *The Enemy is Listening*

14 **Life-long Friendships Were Forged**

1   Tom Goff, writing in the Tel (s) newsletter, 1997

16 **Foreboding and Frustration**

1   Harold Everett in Skillen, *Knowledge Strengthens the Arm*

2   Skillen, *Knowledge Strengthens the Arm*

3   Memo in the National Archives, AIR29 series

4   Clayton, *The Enemy is Listening*

5   Elphick, *Far Eastern File: The Intelligence War in the Far East*

6   Alan Stripp in Hinsley and Stripp, *Codebreakers*

17 **Witnesses to Different Worlds**

1   Skelton, *Tears Before Bedtime*

2   Rosemary Morton in Page, *They Listened in Secret*

18 **D-Day and After**

1   Memo in the National Archives, HW8 series

2   Memo in the National Archives, HW8 series

3   David Pearson in Skillen, *Spies of the Airwaves*

19 **The End and the Beginning**

1   Cynthia Humble, contributing to the Bletchley Park website

Acknowledgements

With huge thanks to Kelsey Griffin and Sue Litchfield of the Bletchley Park Museum for putting the word out, and for introducing me to so many brilliant veterans. Among these, and their families too, special thanks and huge appreciation to Geoffrey Pidgeon, Majorie Gerken, Pat Sinclair, Ray Fautley, Peter Budd, Robert Hughes, Peter Sinclair, Betty White, Jay McDonald, Victor Newman, Cherrie Ballantine, Iris Sugg, Mimi Galilee, Jean Valentine, Alison Trelfa, Ted Mitchell, Chris Barnes, plus members of the Tel(s) Associations around the country. Many thanks also to Graham Coster at Aurum, and to editor Steve Gove for his enduring patience. Thanks also to readers of *The Secret Life of Bletchley Park* who wrote with their own stories and family memories. Thanks also to everyone else at the Bletchley Park Museum: an invaluable institution that just gets better year after year.

On top of this, there are some terrific books to be recommended; vivid memoirs and collections of memories. For its sheer eye-opening quality, there is Aileen Clayton's *The Enemy is Listening* (Hutchinson, 1980), a personal account of her war. For technical expertise – especially in terms of the work of Whaddon Hall and its operatives – there is Geoffrey Pidgeon's *The Secret Wireless War* (UPSO, 2003). Mr Pidgeon also put together *Edgar Harrison: Soldier and Ultra Wireless Operator* (Arundel Books, 2008). The fascinating stories of a great many Wrens were collected by Margaret Ackroyd and edited by Gwendoline Page for *They Listened in Secret* (George R. Reeve, 2003). Hugh Skillen covered the subject – and the story of his own war – in hypnotic depth across several volumes, the most gripping of which is *Knowledge Strengthens the Arm* (1990).

Slightly more laterally, Barbara Skelton's memoirs *Tears Before Bedtime* (Hamish Hamilton, 1987) are often howlingly funny; and the Countess of Ranfurley's *To War with Whitaker* (Mandarin, 1994) is social history at its colourful best. Many Y veterans enjoyed Joan Nicholls' account of her time at Beaumanor in *England Needs You: The Beaumanor Y Station* (2000). For an absorbing insight into the lively, poetic and often waspish intellect of RSS operative Hugh Trevor-Roper, his recently published *Wartime Journals*, edited by Rupert Davenport-Hines (IB Tauris, 2012) are now available.

Meanwhile, collected essays and memories of key Bletchley personnel, describing the intricacies of the work, can be found in *Codebreakers*, edited by Harry Hinsley and Alan Stripp (OUP, 1993). Added to this, the account by Frederick Winterbotham in his pioneering book *The Ultra Secret* (Weidenfeld and Nicolson, 1974) still makes for a fascinating read. Many interesting titles are available at Bletchley Park's brilliant shop.

Index